THE CULTURAL HERITAGE AND CONTEMPORARY CHANGE
SERIES IVA, EASTERN AND CENTRAL EUROPE, VOLUME 12
General Editor
George F. McLean

CREATING DEMOCRATIC SOCIETIES:
Values and Norms

BULGARIAN PHILOSOPHICAL STUDIES, II

Edited by
Plamen Makariev
Andrew M. Blasko
Asen Davidov

FORDHAM
UNIVERSITY
LIBRARIES

WITHDRAWN
FROM
COLLECTION

THE COUNCIL FOR RESEARCH IN VALUES AND PHILOSOPHY

Copyright © 1999 by
The Council for Research in Values and Philosophy

Box 261
Cardinal Station
Washington, D.C. 20064

All rights reserved

Printed in the United States of America

Library of Congress Cataloging-in-Publication

Creating democratic societies : values and norms / edited by Plamen Makariev, Andrew M. Blasko, Asen Davidov.
 p. cm. — (Cultural heritage and contemporary change. Series III, Eastern and Central Europe ; vol. 12) (Bulgarian philosophical studies; 2)
 Includes bibliographical references and index.
 1. Democratization. 2. Post-communism. 3. Democratization-Bulgaria. 4. Post-communism-Bulgaria. I. Makariev, Plamen. II. Blasko, Andrew M. III. Davidov, Asen. IV. Series. V. Series: Bulgarian philosophical studies ; 2 .

JC421. C75 1999
320.9171'7'09049—dc21

99-37509
CIP

ISBN 1-56518-131-X (paper).

CONTENTS

INTRODUCTION   1
FOREWORD   9

PART I. TOTALITARIANISM AS POINT OF DEPARTURE

Chapter I. Communism and Its Implosion   27
    in Eastern Europe
    Serghei Stoilov Gerdzhikov

Chapter II. The Power of Perception: 41
    the Case of Soviet-style Aesthetics
    Andrew M. Blasko

PART II. THE COMPLEX TRANSITION

Chapter III. Democracy and Human Rights   67
    in the Aftermath of the Totalitarian Challenge
    Miloslav Bednář

Chapter IV. Liberalism and Liberal Democracy: 85
    Paradox and Puzzles
    Joseph Margolis

Chapter V. Values, Norms, Individuals: Modern   105
    and/or Post-modern (Twenty Theses on
    Post-totalitarian Individualism)
    Asen Davidov

Chapter VI. Identity as Openness to Others   117
    George F. McLean

Chapter VII. Social Values in a Time of Change: 139
    An Hegelian Approach
    Tom Rockmore

PART III. FEATURES OF DEMOCRATIZATION

Chapter VIII. Beyond Modernity   155
    Vessela Misheva

Chapter IX. Bulgarian Cultural Identity   205
    Anna Krasteva

Chapter X. Christian Values and Modern Bulgarian Culture   229
    Georgi Kapriev

Chapter XI. Promoting Inter-ethnic Dialogue in Bulgaria   239
    Plamen Makariev

INDEX   257

ACKNOWLEDGEMENTS

Gratitude is owed first of all to the authors who worked hard and long to produce this excellent volume. Its combination of depth of insight and devotion to a people, along with a wise sensibility to national and international currents, makes it one of the most outstanding volumes in this series and a most valuable contribution to the search of the peoples of the Balkans for their road into the future. Upon their success the peace of many peoples will depend.

The project was undertaken by a team of Bulgarian philosophers led by Asen Davidov and Plamen Makariev. It was strongly support by the editorial assistance of Andrew Blasko for whom Bulgaria is in a sense an adopted home.

The Univeresity of Sofia provided a context for this work.

The manuscript was copy-edited by Nancy Graham and brought into final form by Hu Yeping.

To all is owed a debt of deep gratitude by all who will draw upon this volume in their own search for a progressive identity at this turn of the millennia.

INTRODUCTION

BEYOND IDEOLOGY
Creating Democratic Societies: Values and Rights

It would be an exaggeration to claim that philosophy has contributed much to the transition from the totalitarian to a basically democratic order in the countries of Central and Eastern Europe. Its role has been different in the various cases, of course, but especially in Bulgaria the events do not seem to have followed a rational design at all — though surely there have been certain "calculations" behind the actions of the people who started the process. What the philosophers can do now is to help rationalize this social movement. Almost ten years after its start, there is still much confusion and disorientation in the intentions and activities of its agents. There is still considerable risk that the changes which ought to establish harmonious social relations and an efficient economy, might bring instead corruption, moral decay and political violence. Philosophy can do much to clarify the relations between means and ends among actions in the economy and politics, and also provide for the moral regulation of world views. In a word, philosophy can contribute to greater self-consistency in the undertakings needed to bridge the gap between post-communist reality and democratic ideals.

This volume has the combined efforts of philosophers from Bulgaria, the Czech Republic and the USA to find new reference points which could provide better opportunities for orienting the efforts toward building a democratic society. Certain notions from the early stages of the changes have already proven to be too simplistic or utopian. Some have turned out to be mere "mirror images" of well-known conceptual "instruments" from the arsenal of totalitarianism. There is, however, a unanimous rejection of the paradigm of ideological confrontation.

A common feature of the papers in the present volume is an approach to philosophically relevant social issues which is centered around an pluralistic notion of culture and pays tribute to the multi-dimensional depth of human existence. It is to be hoped that this

change of fundamental theoretical dispositions is not merely a next philosophical "fashion", or a conformist turn in accord with the new social constellation — i.e., a servile *post factum* justification of the political victory of some. We
believe the text offered in this publication to exemplify a serious philosophical reflection on human rights, social values and norms, religion, cultural identity, intercultural relations, etc.

What do we mean here by a philosophically enlightened, pluralistic attitude towards culture as an alternative to ideology? Can it be asserted that there is a paradigmatic difference between ideology and
culture? Is not ideology itself a kind of culture, and can not culture in its turn be an ideology (to borrow a formulation from Z. Baumann's "Intimations of Post-modernity")?

First of all, "ideology" here is meant in the narrow sense - as a means of representing a private interest as universal. This has been the general practice in Marxist social science. The interests of the proletariat were considered to coincide, in the long run, with the interests of humanity. The working class can emancipate itself only by constructing, in the final account, a perfect social order to the benefit of everybody. The realization of this holistic project presupposes a profound knowledge of the social relationships on behalf of Marxist theory. It justifies any manipulation of groups and individuals, which is indispensable for the achievement of the final goal. Human beings are treated as theoretically transparent, predictable entities, which are to be arranged in an optimal way by the competent "hand" of a party, acting in accordance with the social pattern.

On the contrary, the philosophical reflection on culture typical for the papers in this volume takes into account the complexity of the human reality, and the autonomy and creativity of the individual. The behaviour of the Other can never be ultimately explained. However, this careful attitude towards the human being does not exclude social activity. This is not in the form of moving people around, but rather as interaction between equal partners, respecting mutually each other's interests.

Part I studies the "starting point" of the transition from totalitarianism to democracy. It is important to study the inconsistencies within the intellectual sources of the former social system in order to avoid repeating mistakes. According to S. Gerdzhikov in Chapter I, "Communism and Its Explosion in the European Life-world," one of the main fallacies of communism was the assumption that the social world can be constructed and reconstructed like a machine. The author regards communism as a "grand experiment of Western reason". It was based on the rationalistic notion that the same logos rules both human thoughts and social regularities. Gerdzhikov applies phenomenological methods to substantiate his thesis that the order of human reality is rather of the type of the "logic" of life. The human life-world should not be treated as an artefact, lest the outcome would be quite different from that planned by the "demiurge".

The paper of A. Blasko in Chapter II, "The Power of Perception: the Case of Soviet-style Aesthetics," deals with the ideological function of Soviet-style art and aesthetics. The research is guided by the belief of the author that an examination of the aesthetic dimension of social life may reveal those values and principles which organize the perception of social life. These relations of power appear as implicit, taken for granted, and generally unquestioned elements of daily life. Consequently, aesthetics may be used as a social science in order to uncover the ways in which non-cognitive types of knowledge serve to ascribe a desired meaning to the social processes. An especially interesting mechanism of ideological influence through art, discussed by the author, is the manipulation of the relationship between subject and Otherness. Controlling this relation, the "supreme agent" can project his or her intentional organization upon the behavior of a mass of human subjects much more efficiently than by means of direct, vulgar propaganda.

Part II of the study is devoted to the complexities of the transition to democracy. The authors are aware of the risk that old stereotypes, especially ideological attitudes, relapse under the appearance of well meant undertakings. For one reason or another even some of the classical requisites of Western social order may turn out to be inappropriate to the political and economic systems taking shape in the "new democracies". What can be done on behalf of philosophy in this situation is to work for the clarification of the categorical dimensions of the recent events.

M. Bednář in Chapter III, "Democracy and Human Rights in the Aftermath of the Totalitarian Challenge," for instance, points out substantial differences within modem liberalism which are relevant to the political choices that must be made in the former socialist countries. On the one hand, we have the tradition of natural law and natural rights, represented typically by the philosophy of John Locke. Bednář underscores especially the religious-ethical grounding of the natural law as the basis of human rights in this tradition. On the other hand, there is the secularist interpretation of liberalism by Hobbes, Rousseau and their followers. The contractarian approach towards social norms has nourished a religiously and ethically indifferent liberalism. Historically it proved to be too weak before the totalitarian tendencies in European political life. Nowadays its inability to provide a plausible ultimate ground for liberal policies is opening more and more space for communitarian theories.

J. Margolis in Chapter IV, "Liberalism and Liberal Democracy: Paradox and Puzzles," goes even further with his critical analysis of liberalism. He sees a danger that liberalism may become just another ideology by pretending to become an absolute world order. We should not forget that liberalism, in all of its modifications, is rooted in a historical tradition, just as are its alternative political models. Whatever arguments may be presented to legitimize liberalism's influence, they do not suffice to justify the direct imposition of Western standards on other cultures.

The universal value of democracy as such can be argued more successfully. The latter has different historical sources and forms. It is not committed to individualism or collectivism - e.g. apart from liberal democracies there exist also "Confucian" ones. Without professing some kind of communitarianism or post-modernism, Margolis recommends greater sensitivity towards the *"sittlich"* (in the Hegelian meaning) element in political life, especially as far as the reforms in the "new democracies" are concerned.

A. Davidov in Chapter V, "Values, Norms, Individuals: Modern and/or Post-modern (Twenty Theses on Post-totalitarian Individualism)," is concerned mainly with the possibility that the transition from totalitarian collectivism to the apparently democratic individualism might "run aground" the traditional difficulties of the latter and thus revive ideological attitudes. The author demonstrates that neither post-modernist methodological innovations nor the communicative ethics of Apel and Habermas can be of particular help in this situation. What is needed is more spirituality in the form of philosophical and religious insight.

G. McLean in Chapter VI, "Identity as Openness to Others," reinforces this view by studying the notion of identity on the basis of freedom to see if this is a process of the self assertion of one against the other or rather a matter of the transcendence which characterizes the human person. In the later case, love rather than hate or even competition should characterize the relation between peoples. It is a lesson experienced in family and neighborhood, but so surprisingly difficult for social theory and practice that philosophers must share responsibility for the present problems and correspondingly are needed in working out future paths.

T. Rockmore in Chapter VII, in "Social Values in a Time of Change: An Hegelian Approach," raises the issue of the dynamics of social values in times of change. On the one hand, the "stability" of values is an important condition for their legitimacy. On the other, each significant social change is a transition towards an unprecedented state of affairs, i.e. it involves considerable novelty. Can static, traditional values regulate such processes? Rockmore argues in favor of a pluralistic and consensual approach to values.

Part III outlines some specific features of the democratization processes in Bulgaria. This manifests the cultural sensitivity, characteristic of the philosophical approach to social change, and expressed by the authors in this collection.

Quite typical here is the interpretation by V. Misheva, in Chapter VIII, "Beyond Modernity," of the marginal position of Balkan societies with respect to European culture. What is generally assessed to be a shortcoming — isolation from mainstream cultural tendencies, lack of clear collective identity, etc. — is represented by the author as a potential advantage. It is argued that living at the intersection of two civilizations gives unique capacities to contribute to the process of self-reflection within each of them. What Misheva calls the "in-side — out-side position" is a necessary condition to distance oneself from one's own culture, without ceasing to belong to it. It is impossible to exercise self-reflection from within. In this respect the Bulgarian viewpoint is superior that of any of the "great powers" in European cultural life.

A. Krasteva in Chapter IX, "Bulgarian Cultural Identity," analyzes the intellectual discourse on Bulgarian cultural identity. She reflects on a wide range of texts: from the first decades of our century to our day; from poetry to school textbooks. It emerges that several themes predominate and thus exhibit their importance for Bulgarian culture: the Bulgarian tongue, Eastern Orthodoxy, the Balkan Range, the people as a family, the communal man. All these themes are characterized by Krasteva as referring to "the own" as a basic constituent of cultural identity. Another such component (according to the author) is "the alien". The concrete themes which represent it in the texts are: the "own" as "alien" (i.e. texts which deal with the alienation within the Bulgarian people, e.g. of the intelligentsia and of the political class); the deconstructed "own" (post-modernist deconstructions of national identity and of national pride); the "alien" as Crown (the interiorization of influences from world culture); the "alien" as other (as model or as antipode). Krasteva concludes that what cultural identity needs most of all is a dialogical relationship between "the own" and "the alien".

A more concrete approach towards Bulgarian culture is that of G. Kapriev in Chapter X, "Christian Values and Modern Bulgarian Culture," whose paper deals with Eastern Orthodoxy in Bulgaria. Kapriev points out some culturally important features of this form of Christianity. One of them is the greater autonomy and responsibility of the human being. This explains why there is no centralized Orthodox church. The head of the Church is considered to be Christ himself and no earthly person can substitute for Him. Hence, there are several autonomous Orthodox churches, among which there is no hierarchy. For the same reason the ecclesiastical hierarchy has only a liturgical role. The characteristics of the persons who belong to it are not substantial for the quality of the Church as such. Also in this vein it is possible to understand the incommensurability between the activities of the Orthodox Church and political life. It is contrary to the spirit of Orthodoxy to compete for political influence. And (ideally) this Church should not allow interference into its affairs by the political powers.

The last chapter, Chapter XI, by P. Makariev, "Promoting Inter-ethnic Dialogue in Bulgaria," examines the potential of several political theories to serve as conceptual bases for resolving the ethnocultural contradictions in Bulgaria. The ethnic issue is represented as a competition between cultural communities, each striving to preserve and consolidate its identity. The paper tests the applicability of liberalism, communitarianism and discourse ethics to this competition of cultures. Special attention is paid to the unique features of the Balkan social and cultural "constellation". The conclusion of the author is that the ethical theory of Habermas and Apel offers a synthesis of Right and Good (which is conceptually impossible within either liberalism and communitarianism), but it cannot be directly implemented in the relations between cultures. Even if we ignore the generally utopian nature of discourse ethics, we should take into account the discrepancy between its rationalism and the traditional traits in cultural identities (especially in the Balkans). However, the author has tried to trace possible ways of modifying the methods of discourse ethics so that they become more relevant to this task.

It has been the endeavor of the authors of this collection to escape the convenient groove of simplistic ideological interpretations, and to direct their research to the whole complexity of the democratization process. It is to be hoped that this will not sound a discouraging message to the reader for it is much more difficult to interact with human beings in the rich context of their cultural "environment", than with objectified abstractions. However, the actual events have shown that there is no alternative to engaging the concrete culturally specified life. Philosophy can be of real help by contributing to the rationalization of these interactions, rather than by offering miraculous solutions.

Plamen Makariev
Philosophy Faculty
University of Sofia, Bulgaria

FOREWORD

It is difficult to think of anything approaching the extraordinarily rapid political collapse of the important series of countries constituting the so-called Soviet bloc. . . . The dimensions of this political collapse are evident when it is realized that these countries comprise roughly half the population of the entire world. Although history records many examples of countries that disintegrated under intense pressure in time of war, there is apparently no real precedent for the series of events that has befallen official Marxism in less than a decade, in a time of peace and without so much is a single shot being fired.

In these words Tom Rockmore describes graphically the dimensions of the challenge of creating democratic societies in our days. This work is a superb response to that challenge. This "foreword" reflects critically upon the chapters in a somewhat different order then they appear in the volume in order to draw out new insight. A first group of chapters studies the impact of totalitarianism. Miloslav Bednář see this not as a thing of the past, but as a continuing presence, now in new liberal forms but coming from the same deep roots in modernity. Andrew Blasko studies the aesthetics of the way in which this became not only the effect of a few controlling persons, but the joint work of a broad populace. Serghei Gerdzhikov replays this theme in the cacophonic tonalities of post modernism.

A second group undertakes the constructive process with a brilliant study by Anna Krasteva of the root dynamic of the self and the other, "the own" and "the alien". She analyses the components of each separately and in terms of Bulgarian culture and then suggests the ambiguous dynamics to be dealt with in creating democratic societies in the face of disintegrative forces. Pleman Makariev looks in greater detail into the crucial problems of interethnic peace in a Balkan context and relates to this contemporary discussions in the West developed, on the one hand, on the basis of the primacy of the individual and the nature of rights and, on the other, the basis of the primacy of the community and the common good. Tom Rockmore urges incisively the need for any such discussions to proceed not *a priori*, but in terms of concrete engagement with the socio-cultural dynamics of the peoples involved.

A third group treats a remaining, but most fundamental challenge. There is an emergent consensus with Habermas, reflected in Rockmore and Makariev, that the reconstructive process must be carried out through dialogue. But there remains the issue of whether this is going to go beyond simply a consensus between peoples built upon a shared bad faith — conceivably, a past upon evil made among thieves — or whether this is going to be an unveiling of at least some part of the real good to which we feel obliged in our various cultures and in which we find ourselves on convergent paths. This is the argument developed through the exclusion of alternatives by Asen Davidov, related to the situation of Orthodox religion in Bulgaria by George Kapriev, and elaborated through analyses of freedom and culture by George F. McLean.

Let us look more in detail into the work of these studies, the insights they suggest, and the problems they raise for further investigation.

Miloslav Bednář in "Democracy and Human Rights in the Aftermath of the Totalitarian Challenge" quickly dispenses with one of the great illusions of our times. This is the liberal interpretation of the events of the last decade and indeed of the last century as the realization of a great campaign against totalitarianism. The supposition is that of Cold War rhetoric, namely, "the free world" against the slave, totalitarian states. In this view, with the defeat of fascism in World War II and communism in the Cold War, the task has been accomplished and there remains now only the easy task of implementing the competitive freedoms of people in order to constitute the liberal utopia.

For Bednář this view is naive for it fails to realize the origins of modern totalitarianism, and hence of the way in which it radically pervaded not just one, but both sides of the Cold War. For this view he focuses on the difference between Locke and Rousseau with regard to natural law. For the former this was given by the creator as love or goodness itself, and written as the inner nature of humankind and of our world as the good way to live. Human freedom is the ability to follow this good way of living. This entails the identification of right with good, and this within the framework of human participation in the eternal by means of the law of nature. Human rights emerge naturally then along with the recognition of the human person as a free or self-determining being and hence as a center of responsibility.

Bednář contrasts this to Hobbes, Rousseau and Grotius who dispense with this grounding in the divine. Instead they base the body politic in a hypothetical state of nature in order to be able to begin abstractively with the human will in the act of constituting a social contract. Grotius and Rawls similarly would dispense with any grounding in the divine (Grotius) or any other "comprehensive vision" (Rawls) in order to be able to work out the contents of a theory of justice on the sole basis of the operation of human reason. Rawls would later come to recognize that this would seem reasonable only to one who already shared liberal principles and convictions.

If this be based on experience that this is the good way to live then we seem to be heading rather into the natural law position about the way (nature) to live (of being) reflected rather in Locke then in Rouseau. If, however, one insists on founding social ethics in human reason precisely as affirmed by the will then social order can result only from the primacy of some wills over others, on our will over all — which is the essence of totalitarianism.

This indeed becomes the great challenge of our times. For if we recognize a plurality of cultures and hence of world visions and of the values these entail, then the search for a universal ethics becomes in fact the effort to affirm one culture and enslave all others. This is the totalitarian writ large. (See D. Pavicevic, "Democracy and Stability," in *Models of Identity in Post-Communist Societies* [Washington: The Council for Research in Values and Philosophy, 1999]).

Andrew Blasko in "The Power of Perception: The Case of Soviet-style Aesthetics" provides amazing insight into the manipulation of the mind in a totalitarian context. He does so by moving beyond the level of science, at least if this be taken to be concerned with the conceptualization of reality. In the totalitarian context that would leave one at the level of ideology, or even the opposing ideologies of the Cold War. Blasko's interest is rather how such an ideology becomes interiorized and especially how it becomes the basis for action schemas and their actuation in ways so frightful as to surpass all comprehension from the outside. This issue is important not only to understand the concentration camp executioner, but the indispensable acquiescence or at least positive accommodation to the system on the part of the general populace.

Central to Blasko's position is the embodied condition of human consciousness whereby the situation in all its social complexity becomes a constitutive element in the work of the aesthetic imagination. I suspect that more needs to be done on this in order to preserve the realm of freedom and responsibility, but he elegantly describes how the self can turn into a virtual "other" along lines delineated by a superior or absolute social power. Here, what is "taken-for-granted" becomes the formative force, while precisely as "taken-for-granted" it is not engaged or questioned.

This insight is especially important today. For, if we have become aware of the destructive effects of technical reason in this century, we are much less aware of how the focus upon such reason constitutes the process by which we are blinded to the effects of its manipulative powers and hence how we become effective accomplices in the dehumanization of society. Blasko's chapter points out how this works and thereby constitutes an implicit call for the development of an aesthetic consciousness in terms of which effective self-liberation of the contemporary consciousness becomes possible. This will be essential if we are to respond positively to the newly emerging sensibilities which bear the legitimate hopes for the new millennia.

Asen Davidov in "Values, Norms, Individuals: Modern and/or Post-modern: Twenty Theses on Post-totalitarian Individualism" provides a series of meditative insights regarding the struggle to proceed beyond totalitarianism to reestablish the place of the human person, without falling into a typically modern individualism. This requires that he move beyond the modern paradigm but without dissolving the person as would the "post-modern" perspective. The effect is to move him via a phenomenology of values to a deeper level, an ontology of values. It is fascinating to see him work inversely in terms of participation to the essential character of community and beyond this to the divine and hence the religious community as the living sign of unity in diversity. In this light the situation of the Church as object of past external oppression by totalitarian powers and of present internal conflict takes on special significance as the people try to evolve its stance for the future. In this light his reference to the Polish Church is of special philosophical interest if it be noted that K.Wojtyla, its leader in the 1970 (and now Pope John Paul II), was working on this precise synthesis which Davidov suggests between the traditional metaphysical (Thomistic) and phenomenological existential (R. Ingarden) types of anthropology.

Serghei Stoilov Gerdzhilov in "Communism and Its Explosion in the European Life-world" takes the reader on a happy, but ultimately disastrous journey. It begins by pointing to a phenomenological path which takes one beyond the usual more surface level of analysis in terms of the measurable factors of space and time, the clear and distinct factors, to the life world. This is familiar territory; it is the place where I was born and lived my childhood, where I meet friends and relatives; it is a world brimming with meaning — at times with personal crises, but also with life's achievements and celebrations. One awaits its unveiling, articulation and fruition as the source of new life for society. But not yet.

First it is important to review the realm of *logos* as clear rational structure and Communism's attempt to build in its terms a modern utopia. One is happy to note with Prof. Gerdzhikov that human life is not an artifact and cannot be made artificially, and hence that any attempt to do so will be humanly catastrophic.

At this point one looks for a better way ahead, one that will improve upon the unthematized life world and for the work of *logos* to play a positive role within a richer whole. But there awaits only "explosion and storm". Even the Marxism which as *logos* was too simple and clear becomes suddenly in its consequences unclear and unfathomable. The minimal liberal project built upon open space for the exercise of freedom is trashed. In the place of all the above is substituted a mindless physical model of blind states of equilibria blindly and violently sought.

Thinking back from this elegant journey into darkness one concludes either that there was never any real value in my life world nor any reality to the long philosophical and scientific tradition of work in terms of logos, or that the paper ends when it is still at the beginning. Typical of post-modern thought it establishes a critique of the modern which should open the way to the rich development of a new era. But that would require a new way of thinking. For lack of this it remains in modern thought, but only in its negative, critical mode. Convinced rightly of the terrors it has generated and anxious to stop them at all costs it proceeds to destroy all truth and value, meaning and hope after the death of Communism. It carries out intentionally the destruction which the false utopia may have entailed, but could never foresee nor ever would choose. Seldom has the experience of post modernism been so seductively and vividly expressed as in this chapter of Professor Gerdzhikov, which deserves long to be included in philosophical readers.

But not all is so negative. If the forest has burnt down, it has released new seeds, new hopes, new dynamisms and new values which previously were trampled on the forest floor. There is a new agenda (culture, women, minorities) and new means (phenomenology and the aesthetic) and these have the genius of recuperating and integrating what was known (*logos*) with what was ignored and suppressed (personal freedom). Life has not exploded forever, for the work of creation goes on and philosophies should feel called upon to play an important role.

George Kapriev in "Christian Values and Modern Bulgarian Culture" provides a focused, but too brief, overview of the character of the Orthodox spiritual culture in general and its role in the history of Bulgaria, with a view to identifying its present state and future prospects for that nation. The context of its struggle to be independent from Rome without being absorbed by the political regime has both necessitated and encouraged the development of its exhalted spirituality. This treasure of the Christian heritage bears much that is particularly needed in the context of this post-Communist and hence post-atheist period.

At the same time, the history of the Church in Bulgaria has been so intimately tied to the national identity of its people that the establishment of its distinctive identity and hence its ability to make its proper contribution is variously compromised and rendered particularly difficult. This has happened in ways so distinctively proper to this people that no general formula could serve to help.

Kapriev sees hope in the development of interest in Orthodox theology by some among the intelligentsia, but fears that their position as well as the content of the theology renders improbable a concrete contribution from these quarters to shaping the social process of the nation. On the other hand, one might see something providential in this. For if there is an intellectual task to be carried out in order to draw out this meaning and articulate it for the present and future then this work must be done precisely not by the churchmen, but by the intelligentsia with their varied literary arts and social sciences. The task is to find or develop the instrumentalities which can bring their human resources together in an effective and productive manner.

On the other hand, Professor Kapriev recognizes that the Orthodox identity has been strongly affirmed by the more mass public movements, but seems resigned to its being manipulated to less worthy ends by a nationalism in terms of "blood and soil". A more optimistic reading might hold that while the Orthodox identity and vision remain part of that mix the game is not over. It is really a question of what will prevail, the higher or the lower motivation. Since any desirable outcome must wisely integrate both in order for the nation to be inspired and for the faith to be at work in the projects of the people, there is much work to do for both church and nation and in this the clergy should find a worthy challenge.

In the late 1970s, during a colloquium with the Bulgarian Philosophical Society, an audience was arranged with the Patriarch. When he finished his discourse on peace, it was asked what had been the role of religion in the history of the Bulgarian people. At that he lighted up considerably, took a deep breadth, exclaimed "Now that is a noble question!" and launched enthusiastically into a 45 minute response. The question is even more vital today!

Anna Krasteva's "Bulgarian Cultural Identity" is a veritable *tour de force*. She distinguishes the notion of self-identity into its twofold dynamic. On the one hand, the constitution of the people's sense of their own identity and of being one therein, and, on the other hand, the role of the other as helping to delineate the "own" and keep it from so embracing the self as to annihilate it.

To each of these, the chapter devotes a study sufficiently detailed to constitute a work in its own right. By setting them in dialectical relation to one another it is able to protect both from excesses and point the way to positive future development.

From this complex whose richness consists above all in the weaving together and integration of its many themes, it is difficult to sort out special elements. But because of the special light this sheds it is difficult not to point up the following which are of special importance to the work of this volume.

1. The modern social sciences have proceeded rather univocally to campaign against any ascriptive identities from family to nation. The near unanimity in this campaign against what the people hold to be most dear and sacred, and in the face of the most obvious objective fact that life is carried on in just these terms and that it manifests general progress, points to a factor of the subjective order controlling the methodology of these sciences. This is the analytic supposition of an atomic individual as that real and the relegation of all else to being interpreted as either a support and hence good, or an impediment and hence bad, with regard to the individual so conceived. This calculation that paints all ascriptive identities as detrimental to the individual as an atomic center of free choice corresponds, not incidentally, to the notion of the consumer in the economic order. The result has been a process of social disintegration and personal *anomie* in which the social sciences have been willing accomplices if not the major proponents.

Professor Krasteva points rather to the counter-fact that it is in relation to others and to the community of family, freedom and people that Bulgarians find their identity. "It is notable that the primacy of the communal is not seen as the totalizing homogenization and subordination of the individual, but rather as the interaction in which the individual attains a higher personal meaning through harmony with the community and unity with others." Community is not set against the person in a zero sum game: rather the two are related positively so that the community is the context within which individuals emerge and flourish. This is obvious to most parts of the world and to most dimensions of Western society as well, but it still needs to be taken into account by the analytical methodology of the social sciences.

2. Correspondingly the chapter points up the significance of considering the other/the alien for the process of freeing the person from the embrace of the community in order to make possible the

criticism and creativity upon which change and progress depend. This could be left simply as an additional and countervailing force; Professor Kristeva proceeds instead to integrate the two in her notion of "assimilated objectivity": "It is objective as the framework of a guaranteed world, but it is also assimilated in the relationship."

She brings the two elements of self and other: "own" and "alien" together within the "us relation". This she sees in Levinas's sense: not of a shoulder-to-shoulder relation that submerges both in a collective, but an eye-to-eye relation that unites proximity and distance and prevents one's difference from dissolving in the collective.

3. A third dimension of the chapter of Professor Kristeva too rich to pass over is her sense of the basic ontology of the Bulgarian people. There is an almost mystical sense of identification with the land, not only as a generic source of fruitfulness as with the Andean *Pacha Mama*, but specifically with their land, the Balkan Range: "The highlander is not a regional, but a spiritual identity designating one who is lofty in the Bulgarian spirit, not one who merely lives on high ground."

But this extends to the nation as well, which is idealized and sacralized. This is true not only in older times, but even more today and to such a degree that Professor Kristeva wonders whether religion is being merged into nation. It is a question raised in the paper of Professor Kapriev as well and brings us to a crucial — perhaps the crucial — issue in the life of any person or people, namely, the basis of their meaning, their destiny and their hope.

On the one hand, it is possible to so identify the religious and the national spirit that the absolute character of the divine in transferred to the nation, whose political power then takes on an absolute character to which all is sacrificed. This is idolatry: perhaps more common and certainly more destructive in this last century than in the time of Moses. Both authors are rightly concerned.

4. On the other hand it is possible that religion at least in some areas so emphasized the transcendent character of God at the expense of His immanence that He became distant and lost His meaning in the life of the people. This it would seem is presently — and perhaps always — in the process of readjustment. Indeed it may be that the continual search for equilibrium in this matter is the driving force for human progress. This can be important for a number

of presently needed projects, such as the dignity and hence the rights of the human person and of civil society vis-à-vis the overpowering human state, and the inherent sanctity of the life of persons and peoples as a basis for absolute commitment to family and patriotic service to the nation.

It would be wrong, however, to consider this to be a zero sum game so that what is recognized for one is taken away from the other; Professor Kristeva found that it was in community that the person truly emerged and that this required Levinas's sense of an "eye-to-eye" relation of proximity and distance. This, of course, points back to the perennial discussions of transcendence and immanence, and of participation. Indeed, Whitehead considered all of Western philosophy to be a series of footnotes to Plato for whom participation was the central notion. In this light the life of society becomes once again too important to be left to the sociologists, and the metaphysical and religious issues come to the fore.

Plamen Makariev in "Promoting Inter-ethnic Dialogue in Bulgaria" approaches this issue through the prism of Western political theory. This is its strength and, it would seem, its weakness.

Among its many strengths is that it approaches the issue from within the Balkan social and psycho-social reality. Hence it is sensitive to the particular socio-cultural commitments of the people of the region, their ethnic origins and mixtures, their level of sophistication in industrial centers vs. mountainous regions and the history of their attempts to live together.

It is remarkable how in a few sentences he could summarize exactly the arguments for assimilation (and insensitivity) used by my own majority Irish culture vis-à-vis the French speaking minority in Lowell, Massachusetts, over 50 years ago, and now of groups vis-à-vis the new Spanish and Cambodian minorities when they want to begin their own charter school today. But I do not hear so clearly the humiliation and frustration which accented the words of my grandparents as they describe their efforts as minorities almost a century ago to establish their own families, nor the fears which drove the mass exodus of Turks at the proposal of a rebirth process in the 1980s. This gap of feeling between people of different cultures — whether majority or minority — is the seed of tensions that can descend into terror and which can be healed only by a countervailing love. It points to Aristotle's recognition of the need for *sunesis*, the ability to, it were, live the experience of the other.

Another strength of this chapter is the precision and force of its analysis of the Western liberal position. Dr. Makariev follows incisively its development, the challenges it received and its response. But ultimately he points to its ever increasing formalism and sedulous abstraction as it attempts to establish a universal position around the rights of the individual at the explicit cost of the concerns of the community and questions of the good. But in this he may not pursue his argument far enough, for what kind of freedom is being provided by a theory which precinds precisely from the good involved. Is not freedom a characteristic of the will and is not the business of the will the pursuit of the good? Freedom that is not an engagement in the good must be superficial and/or forensic. Theories which set rights over against the good and provide for the former while precinding from the latter can be no real friends of freedom, or if these be its friends then surely it needs no enemies. This adds a third step to Makariev's analysis of the cultural mismatch and the problems of the inner logic of liberalism for use in the Balkans. "Liberalism recognizes only individual rights, not collective rights, and eroding a community's cultural identity is not regarded as damaging the rights of the individuals who comprise it. It is only natural that this approach is not taken seriously in the Balkans."

The chapter then turns to the communitarian perspective. But these seemed better asserted in the above critique of liberalism. Here they are not developed, but only problematized on the way to the concluding section of the chapter: "The Way to Dialogue". There Habermas's discourse ethics is brought to the fore as the only way for diverse cultural groups to work out ways of living together which are mutually complementary rather than contradictory.

Professor Makariev seems to encounter here two main problems. First, that the discourse ethics of Habermas which could regulate the interchange is purely formal in character and hence too sophisticated for the peoples involved, and second that the cultures of the two or more parties are supposed to be different and conflicting. The first leaves Makariev with more of a challenge than a solution: the questions are difficult but not impossible and the introduction of the paradigm of discourse would enable the formulation of problems in a new way. Here I would make a suggestion, namely, that dialogue is important when people speak of what they have deeply experienced for generations and what stands at the center of their own efforts to build family and community. Then their words carry passionate insight, truths which are savored, and in the realization of which they have already engaged their entire lives. Paulo Freire, in his *Pedagogy of the Oppressed*, points out the riches that this brings to a discussion and the ingenuity of the supposedly unsophisticated in its fruition.

But the greater potentiality would seem to lie in the other problem, namely, the supposition of the difference and contradictory character of the cultures involved. In the face of it this seems amazing, for if peoples are fully and successfully engaged in the same task of raising their families and of earning a living in order to do so, whence the supposition of the contrariety rather than complementarity of their cultures? It may well be that it is a supposition of the Western context within which the discussion is set, particularly the rationalist paradigm admitting only the clear and the distinct and smashing the idols (Bacon) that bore the traditions which were considered unworthy of the newly Enlightened age. In another chapter I will attempt to explore the nature of cultures to see if it cannot offer hope to Professor Makariev on his path of dialogue.

Tom Rockmore in "Social Values in a Time of Change: An Hegelian Approach" carries the discussion significantly further by breaking out of the closed circuit of liberal individualism to look rather at the values which move a people and orient their action. His question is whether there is any *a priori* set of such values which can be justified and which can be applied universally. The challenging context which he sets for this question is the uniquely radical character of the change in social life in Eastern Europe during the last decade. His answer, simply put, is: no.

The main thrust of his argument is against the Kantian project of deducing an *a priori* deontological ethics from the character of practical reason itself. His critique is that this leaves the ethics formal and empty, which of course seems to be what Kant intended. He wanted to say something essential about all moral acts, namely, that in which their essential morality lies; and he did so.

Rockmore wants more content for ethics, as do we all. He

follows Hegel's lead in pointing to the need to engage concrete social reality. Even Hegel knew that history cannot come from essence alone, so this chapter points to the need to engage the socio-cultural context and "to arrive at values that can be accepted by thinking through concrete problems in order to arrive at the widest possible consensus."

Yet his conclusion does not seem fully to live up to his original challenge, namely, "to show that they are more than the expression of what a particular group or subset of the population happens to think at a given time and in a given place." This part of the challenge seems at first not to have been taken up. But on reflection this may not be entirely so. For he does refer to Plato's sense of a transcendent level where, by definition, things must be different. And he does see all changing reality as participating in, and hence being normed by, this transcendent reality.

Unfortunately, he discards this too quickly as static when upon further investigation Aristotle would find it to be a living process of reflection, a *noesis noeseos*, which should be the envy of those engaged in "thinking through concrete problems," especially if they are in search of points of convergence with other participants.

The other area in which Professor Rockmore was engaged in showing that social values are more than "the expression of what a particular group . . . happens to think at a given time" was what he sees as the original religious form of which Kant would develop a more secular form. But a number of things seem to go wrong here and keep Rockmore from mining the rich religious vein which he has struck: (a) He sees creator and revelation as prior sources of subsequent conclusions requiring that freedom and history be eliminated; but freedom is precisely what creation and revelation are about. (b) It cannot be fair to the Rabbi or Imam struggling long over the implications of their revealed sources to reduce their work to *a priori* deduction, rather than to the arduous and delicate work of unfolding the meaning of their sources through history. (c) The Catholic Church had spoken almost 40 years ago and most solemnly in Vatican II of the many valid ways to God; its recent encyclical "*Fides et ratio*" describes at length the autonomy of reason and of philosophy and the need of such for universal principles for human interchange and effective principles for unfolding the meaning of the scriptures.

All this suggests that Rockmore was onto something crucial for his project of finding more than a passing consensus when he took up this reference to Plato and to religious meaning. His project calls, with Kant, for an element of authority in ethics, but will not allow that to be solely a self-justifying deduction either by or from reason. With Hegel, his project calls for engagement in the socio-cultural context, but in a way that is grounded not essentially, but existentially.

Studied absolutely or out of time and culture this would be a task for classical metaphysics and theology. But both of these sciences have moved with Professor Rockmore into the age of subjectivity and hence of relating this work to the process of culture. Thus, the chapter by G.F. McLean entitled "Identity as Openness to Others" studies the way in which cultures and cultural traditions are generated and how they evolve with time, how they gain their authority through their cumulative insight into the reality of life, how this authority is grounded not only in what people agree upon, but in what they come corporately to know and acknowledge, and how the multiple traditions when adequately understood converge rather than contradict each other.

This chapter argues that the approach to the issue of peoples living together generally is approached on the basis of a deficient ontology which sees identities as conflictual rather than as communicative and complementary. This is due to beginning from sense perception and its presentation of things in physical terms. Instead the reality of being in its source and goal is one, and things which participate therein are essentially related and complementary. In this light one's identity consists most fundamentally in the way one participates in being and thereby is related to other persons and peoples.

Vessela Micheva in "Beyond Modernity" makes a particularly rich contribution to the overall study by analyzing in great depth the character of a small nation on the border of civilizations and closely attached to its land and traditions. Here the usual attitudes of self-affirmation are inverted. The people's identity is rather a non-identity, similar to that of the chorus in a Greek drama, but its vision is lofty and essential to the workings of the world. She carries Masaryk's study of the life of a small nation to a much deeper level, employing the full range of contemporary competencies from anthropology, to political science, to literary theory. The chapter is a *tour de force*, essential to anyone who would wish to understand not only Bulgaria but their own position in this complex world.

Joseph Margolis in "Liberalism and Liberal Democracy: Paradoxes and Puzzles" is concerned with the effort of liberalism to claim universality and thus wittingly or unwittingly to impose itself upon all parts of the world. In this it fails to recognize its own historical situatedness. Indeed for epistemological reasons the creature of enlightenment rationalism is incapable of taking account of the concrete nature of the human person and their second nature as born and raised in a language community. This directs it toward form and procedure which are empty and insensitive to content and hence to the historical and cultural commitments of peoples.

The prospects are for a re-emergence of these values of history, culture and community, but the means of doing so which will retain the gains of liberalism with regard to the recognition of the sacredness of the human person have yet to be developed.

George F. McLean

PART I

TOTALITARIANISM AS POINT OF DEPARTURE

CHAPTER I

COMMUNISM AND ITS IMPLOSION IN EASTERN EUROPE

SERGHEI STOILOV GERDZHIKOV

INTRODUCTION

This paper aims to utilize elements of the phenomenological method, particularly the notion of the life-world (*Lebenswelt*), in order to begin an examination of communism and its explosive demise. Edmund Husserl introduced the notion of the life-world into phenomenological philosophy in *The Crisis of European Sciences and Transcendental Phenomenology*, defining it as the world of everyday life prior to any scientific knowledge of unquestionably clear things, i.e., as a world of "pre-predicative evidences" (Husserl 1977). Even though this world has a fully anonymous status, it is not immediately recognizable, and we are normally unaware that it exists as a particular world which has been defined and explained within a sociocultural context. For us, it is simply "the world".

Communism and the post-communist situation are not discussed here in terms of psychological, economic or politological description and explanation. Rather, an investigation is begun into how people have been living in the European countries of "real socialism," including the Soviet Union, Romania, Bulgaria, Yugoslavia, Poland, Czechoslovakia and Hungary.

A PHENOMENOLOGICAL APPROACH

The life-world is not some suspended network of meanings. Rather, it has its own space, time, logic and basic meanings, all of which are interconnected. Furthermore, it is extended through time, involving genesis, expansion and decline. These characteristics held true for the phenomenon of communism as well which, in its developed form, created a life-world of its own.

Communism developed in both European and non-European countries, and it was "immersed" deeply within the context of contemporary civilisation. However, the fact that it was highly isolated from the rest of the world is one of its intrinsic characteristics. In any case, the communist attitude, the communist idea and the communist phenomena of conscience and action constructed a separate social life-world having their own specific mentality, space and time. "Real socialism" was not simply the domination of one party, a planned economy and a totalitarian system, but was primarily an ethos, a mentality, a phenomenon. It did not disappear after having been rejected by its own institutions, but was then merely transformed into something else insofar as its power, like the power of all energy forms, can only be transformed and not destroyed. The basic meanings and notions that made communism a living reality still exist side by side along with the slowly advancing reform.

The attempt to comprehend communism constitutes a hope for orientation and control in the post-communist period. It is painful and perhaps impossible to change the former system upon the abstract basis of what a "normal" society and what its institutions should be when there is no understanding of the life-world. This problem is compounded when the result is that new institutions are merely transplanted, and thereby weakened, into the still living communist and socialist mentality. Without an understanding of the roots and the life forces that nurtured it, it is not possible to exit communism wisely.

But even if exiting from communism remains a spontaneous process not governed by wisdom, a comprehension of the phenomenon of communism will surely be useful in the face of any other projects that strive to engineer the human life-world. Today these include cloning, genetic control, artificial intelligence, biorobotics and various other tendencies to "rationally organize" life on the planet as a whole.

The phenomenology (more precisely, phenomenological sociology) of communism involves a clarification (Husserl's *Erklärung*, Ideation) of meanings, something which cannot be done from an outsider's position. In *The Crisis*, Husserl presents phenomenology as a philosophy that, contrary to both pre-scientific and scientific objectivism, goes back to knowing subjectivity as the location where all objective meanings and meaningful validities are formed. Its program is to undertake the task of understanding the world of existence as a mental formation of valid meanings (Husserl

1977). The most adequate paradigm for an "understanding" of the theory of communism is the phenomenological paradigm of the social as a living network of meanings that are intended and discovered by people. This way of comprehending communism (and post-communism) is acquired by people who have lived or still live in such a society. Phenomenological social knowledge is not speculation but rather experience as it has been thematized by means of phenomenological notions that describe the constitution of a great variety of events: life-world, phenomenon, meaning, significance, idea, attitude, vision, mentality, mental form and dynamics.

This type of social knowledge gives rise to a dynamic clarification of the phenomenon of communism in its development as a living entity of meanings and significances which does not rely upon exclusively causal explanations. While such clarification may be expressed through interpretations of texts and teleologically explained events and "rational actions" (Max Weber), it originates from the idea of the phenomenon as a living and full possession of the object of the intention (Husserl). Communism is precisely such an intended living entity and not an "objective fact" (communism as a non-implemented project remained only a vision within the main meaning). The scientific character of the phenomenological approach has today become widely recognized in the international scholarly community, one result being the development of new areas of research in phenomenological sociology and, in a broader sense, social knowledge as a whole. Prominent examples include the works of Alfred Schütz (constitutive phenomenology of the natural disposition), the ethnomethodology of Harold Garfinkle and the research of the contemporary phenomenologist Richard Gratchoff. Instead of working with "objective notions," this sociology rather utilizes "types" similar to the "Ideal Types" of Max Weber (Weber 1960).

People recognize, understand, and act towards things and events in the life-world with ready norms of significance, and they do not have unique requirements for every fact or event. For the people living in the world of "real socialism," things such as "money," "power" and "dignity" and events like "revolution," "queue" or "shady deal" meant something familiar and specific that was nevertheless unknown to people outside the system. These names contained codes for understanding and action that were valid only for real socialist life, comprising a set of meanings that existed only in a common intersubjective life-world (Husserl 1977; Schütz 1981).

In addition, life is not only a quality but also a form of the life-world and its phenomena. Through its form, life is an organic unity of components and processes that reproduces itself in conditions of spontaneous disintegration and chaos. Life is the reproduction and expansion of order in chaos; it is always a motion towards life, an order and escape from non-life, from chaos. That which is alive is born, grows against entropy and finally dies, disintegrating into chaos. Moreover, every form of life, every biological species or social formation, has its own unique identity that it projects in a unique form (order) of its life-world. Human space, time and logic are specifically human, different from the space, time and logic of the other forms of life.

Communism is a human social form, i.e., it is a concretization of human form in its sociality. The human world in this particular social form is a characteristically human intersubjective world.

LIFE PROJECT AND WORLD PROJECT

What meaning is to be ascribed to the "phenomenon of communism"? This is ultimately the broadest set of mental forms that have given life to the texts, actions and events concerned with the argumentation, planning and realization of communism. This set is both varied and homogeneous, much in the same way as Wittgenstein's multitude of "family resemblance" forms. I will endeavor to consider those which are most strongly represented and can be idealized as "pure types."

Communism is understandable as a phenomenon of Western civilization that is alien to the mentality and practices of the Middle and the Far East. In addition, certain writers, primarily such Russian historians and philosophers as Geller-Nekritch or Nikolai Berdiaev, have been tempted to describe communism, Bolshevism in particular, as a Russian phenomenon. But while Bolshevism is an historic fact, it does not necessarily carry an understanding of the mental form of communism as a project. In any case, there should be no mixing of the rationalistic phenomena of Western engineering with traditional Eastern societies (Weber), among which Russia is included to some significant degree.

The present investigation into the phenomenon of communism begins with a genetic statement, namely, communism is rooted in the archetype of *logos*. The vision of the world as a *logos*, i.e, an objective order that can be presented in words and figures, also contains the vision of the world as an object of technology. The latter involves the demiurgic vision of a "better world" different from ours that can be created by human beings through the use of the world's laws, its *logos*.

But communism reached a deadlock and collapsed before it fulfilled its declared design. Furthermore, the effort to realize the communist project brought about huge destruction. Why did communism not succeed? Would it be possible for another such project to survive? Against the background of such questions, the major supporting thesis of the present discussion is that this type of project is doomed to failure because the demiurgic vision of "world creation" is false. The world (the human life-world) cannot be exhaustively grasped and expressed as *logos* and it is not the object of technology. Realities such as "freedom," "man" and "justice" that are compatible with the human life-world are not technological in nature. Life is not an artifact.

Plato's state was moral, perfect and ideal, representing a sensible projection of the idea of justice that exists in a better world, the world of ideas (Plato 1984). Society was to be organized in a *holon* where each person and action would find its own functional place. Charles Fourier proclaimed that the "human breeding" that was to take place there would be in harmony with the idea of justice, thanks to the radical acquirement of human reason and the discovery of the "four phases of history" (Fourier 1953). Now, for Karl Marx as well, the world must not simply be explained, it must be changed (Marx 1978b). Moreover, communism was to be a "real human history" that would replace the current "pre-history" (Marx 1953a) in that people would come to create their own history in compliance with the laws of history. In doing so, they were to make the "jump from the kingdom of necessity to the kingdom of freedom" (Marx 1953b).

Communist ideology, rather radically expressed in *Manifesto of the Communist Party*, envisioned a total revolution in which basic values of Western civilization were rejected as class-determined" values and new ones approved, including a new status for the "person" after the "bourgeois person" had been eliminated. The *Manifesto* puts forward the project of a communist revolution that is to be implemented by means of the expropriation of property and the replacement of the parliamentary order with dictatorship. Revolutionaries in Lenin's party as well as communists in the rest of the world implemented precisely that project when they carried out their designs for a "new world," a "new life" and a "new man."

Communism was a grand experiment of Western reason that was born from the ancient understanding of the world as *"logos"* and "idea." According to this view, the world is ordered in a certain manner (*logos*) and is permeated with laws that are knowable and expressible in words and figures (*logos*). Furthermore, reality can be changed on the basis of this notion (*techné*). Consequently, the world is grasped not as a boundless and undefined reality, but rather as a transparent and technological sphere. In the West, only that which is initially logical and profoundly transparent is taken to be reality. To this is added the Western belief, inherited from the Renaissance although somewhat weakened today, that reason is able to construct our world.

However, this view eliminates the difference between a living creature and a non-living artifact. It also renders invisible the human form standing at the basis of the creation of artifacts that would seem to indicate the limit of technology. *Logos* does not recognize the boundary between the world and man. When *logos* is made the universal principle of order, all differences and oppositions are eliminated between knowledge and the hidden, the knowable and the unknowable, the attainable and the unattainable. If the Universe is ordered by means of *logos*, then it is entirely achievable in and through *logos*, i.e., in and through speech, science and action. Consequently, the world can be designed, or at least reconstructed and changed. This is the general mental form of "demiurgic intention."

When the world apparently escapes explanation and control, a demiurgic adjustment that endeavors to design a world project is solicited. Life is not just; people are not equal. The recognition of this reality gave rise to a grandiose, demiurgic attempt by Western man to take control of life and the world in concordance with the *logos* archetype. Such is the general mental form of the Utopian project in Western civilization. The term "rationalistic Utopia" is widespread, and where else if not in the West is rationalism the quality of an entire civilization? Now, Max Weber differentiates between, on the one hand, Western rationalistic society and "rationalistic control," and, on the other, Eastern and pre-modern "traditional" and "charismatic" society and control (Weber 1970). A demiurgic project is impossible in the East, where the world as definable in words is empty and unstable, and the unborn and the undisappearing absolute is beyond logic and inaccessible to language, outside of *logos* (Suzuki). Such a world cannot be subject to technology, at least not in the Western sense.

The ancient Western world prior to the emergence of the *logos* archetype was not demiurgic, nor is the modern Western world that has been developed by means of contemporary liberal democracy. Neither of them is the fruit of some global plan for world restructuring. On the contrary, both have been based upon the recognition of the inalienable human rights of life, freedom, dignity and property within an accepted world (Locke 1965). Parliaments, separation of powers, private property and its legal guarantees, ship transport and science itself — all of these have emerged through an accumulation of human ideas, practices and attainments within the context of acknowledging human reality as being in itself a value in the Christian spirit. All of these achievements have appeared without a general scheme, like an unfocused net of local projects and spontaneous creative acts (Hayek 1952).

In contrast to this spontaneous order, which August Hayek called an extended order, communism has sought to produce a planned and thoroughly controlled order in accordance with an all-encompassing theory and scenario of epochal proportions. This has been the case in all the countries where communism became dominant without exception. This type of order corresponds to the vision that Marx and Engels outlined in such works as "Theses on Feuerbach", *The German Ideology*, the *Manifesto*, "Critique of the Gotha Program," "The Development of Socialism from Utopia to Science," *Feuerbach and the End of German Classic Philosophy* and *Anti-Düring*. The Lenin doctrine on revolution and proletarian dictatorship as presented in *State and Revolution* comprises a power monopoly project that is consistent with this view in all important respects.

But what shall we say about "capitalism"? Is it too not a *logos* project? Does it not design a world? Although Western capitalism is rational as a state and as an economic process (Weber), this rationality concerns only institutions and not control over social life (Hayek). Capitalism and liberal democracy comprise techonolgies for controlling non-living structures, such as state institutions, laws and market rules, not technologies for controlling life. No one within the tradition of liberal democracy has yet intended to construct some grand vision of a social system of life through utilizing the forces of society as a whole. What has instead been done is to establish a legal order that rests upon the idea of human rights.

Western scholars of totalitarianism have drawn, albeit not very clearly, this important distinction between liberal democracy and communism. For them, totalitarianism is a form of utopian engineering that differs from more gradual types of social engineering only by its restriction of criticism and its scale, not by its attitude to life (Popper 1962; Fukuyama 1992). The communist project may thus be regarded entirely rationally and critically, just as may be done with any other human project. It is, although borderline, a mental and active experiment that aims at radically changing the world. If it would succeed in creating a new world, a new human life and, moreover, a new human form at a higher level of life ("happiness, welfare, freedom"), then it would be false to maintain that the world and the human forms which correlate with it are unattainable. If, on the other hand, it would lead to the destruction of a human or world form, then it would be false, weak and lifeless. In the latter case, chaos would conquer a new space within peoples' life.

Any rational project orients and fixes the spontaneous movements of life towards wholeness and expansion. But if it is possible to create cities and states, cannons and machines, theories and poems, philosophy and religion, then why should it be impossible to create a whole new world for human beings? What is impermissible here?

It is one thing to build cities or write poems, but it is an entirely different thing to breathe, laugh and feel pain and enjoyment, i.e., to live spontaneously. Can we design our life the way we design artifacts? Since each creation is a definition in itself, it is a distinction within a living context that itself remains undefined. If and when we seek to define the "world as a whole," does this mean that we are capable of rationally enveloping and controlling it?

No. The latter effort would comprise both an intention and a practice that are inconsistent with the form of life itself. When people intend to create a new society and a new human being, they set themselves a task that cannot be completed because it "transcends" the limits of human form and thereby falls into absolute impossibility. Such an effort wrongfully renders life as an object of technology and design, and mistakenly identifies life as an artifact.

The fundamental distinction from the perspective of the present examination between a "world project" and ordinary human actions is that the linguistic structure of the former is ontologically inconsistent. Life is a forward movement of living form against chaos and towards re-synthesis; life "emerges" from the ocean of chaos by means of its own activity. The world is precisely this and nothing more. (This situation is analogous to the structure against entropy of open systems in physics). Life is a movement of the preservation and expansion of life, and it possesses a teleological form (the form of *entelechia*). Life is vigorous only so long as it succeeds in compensating for its spontaneous disintegration and in creating a redefined form for itself.

Human beings neither choose nor deliberately design human form, nor do they design the life-world in the way they design their machines. Neither human form nor the life-world is subject to technology. On the contrary, the life-world is discovered by the human being who has been born into the world, who has already become shaped into a human and cultural form. A human being first preserves the world s/he has found, then expands it, and finally loses it in death. Human consciousness is one moment of human life, and it moves in the same direction as that life, continually re-synthesizing itself against its own loss. A human being cannot make human form subject to one or another distant realization and objectivation. If one were to do this, one would somehow have to step outside of human form, come to know it and then exercise one's influence upon it. But this would mean to step out of the only world that belongs to a human being as such, namely, the human life-world. The human life-world thus permits all human actions, but none of these actions, insofar as they possess a human form, refer to some "transcendent" intention and practice whereby human form as such could be deliberately altered. When human beings design machines, write poems and create science and religion, they do not change human form, but rather only project it and expand the horizons of the life-world.

EXPLOSION AND STORM

Not only is building a world a project that is ontologically problematic, it is a type of nonsense similar to that of trying to create a *perpetuum mobile*. The world has a human form insofar as it is a projection of human form. This transcendental perspective shows us that every attempt to create a life-world can actually be reduced to the creation of something within this world that does not change the form of the latter. Moreover, such an attempt is in fact destructive because of its disintegrative affect upon certain basic structures of our living social body. We can never create the world, just as we can never create the human form. Every act of creation is rather a dynamic within this form.

The outcome of communism in Eastern Europe and its deep crisis outside of Europe (except in China, where a communist economy no longer exists) together comprise the implosion of a world that human beings sought to build according to a demiurgic plan. There has hardly been a more drastic change in Western history than the change to post-communism, and even today no one knows how it will turn out. None of the post-communist countries has reached a state of equilibrium that can be compared with the equilibrium of Western democracies, nor is it clear whether any future equilibrium might correspond to the criteria of modern society. Indeed, it might very well be the case that post-communism is a type of chronic disease that will never lead to equilibrium. The best possible scenario is that any future equilibrium that may emerge will bear deep traces of communism.

The post-communist storm has resulted from the powerful gradients for imbalance that existed within communism. An unsound system was destroyed because of the destructive tensions within it. But precisely what tensions did the catastrophic end of communist release? What forces has the catastrophe set free, what kind of genie has been let out of the bottle? Perhaps more importantly, what tensions have been created by the subsequent partial stabilization? Any attempt to predict what might happen demands a deep insight into communism, but only time is capable of giving us answers. The fact is that economic, political and cultural meanings and texts are now rapidly changing. However, any false stability that may be attained can be forcibly maintained only for so long before it will implode, unleashing more violent forces. Such a dynamic state is so uncertain that it can only be defined as a shock.

What will the consequences be of this shock? Will a normal market economy, normal democracy and a sound mind emerge in the foreseeable future? The deformations into which communist forms have been transformed comprise the cost of any future equilibrium, but it is still not yet clear precisely what they are. And if this equilibrium will itself be fraught with anomalies and the sources of new disequilibrium, what will these be?

The "ship of democracy" is sailing in the storm of post-communism. Reform is carried out as a series of actions by state power in order to create a system of market economy and democracy. What chances does the ship stand? How do the existing "unhealthy" tensions effect the attainment of the goals of reform? Perhaps the waves of the storm displace forces and meanings in a way that is essentially independent of the goals of government and essentially anomalous in a "normal" state. Unfortunately, such anomalies may be chronic in the absence of forces capable of neutralizing them in the foreseeable future.

Post-communism thus appears to be a period of intensive recovery complicated with vestiges of communist anomalies and forces for destabilzation, the effects of which are unique and unprecedented in history. Post-communism is indeed unique. Never before has there been such a phenomenon and there is no theory that adequately describes it. No one knows where post-communist transitions are leading, just as no one knows what the effects of a series of earthquakes will be. In this regard, our understanding of post-communism is in phase with its movement.

Post-communism is essentially chaotic and undefined. It is analogous to the "dissipative" structures and processes that lead to "metastable states" in Prigogine's sense. Such a dissipative process is one effect of an explosion B, the explosion of highly tensioned communist totalitarian society. The result is some future metastable state B at some unknown distance from thermodynamic equilibrium, from absolute chaos. There are forces and flows in this dynamic — forces of wealth, power and mentality, and flows of money, political actions and social thinking. In this non-equilibrium, the positive forces of the reform, i.e., the actions of the government, are in contraphase with the negative forces of free fall, illegal money making, unhealthy and inadequate policy, and the conservative mentality of a closed society. In such a period, certain new forms of mentality, power and wealth arise that can be understood only as a network of rational actions (Weber).

Philosophy Faculty
Sofia University

REFERENCES

Filmer, P., M. Filipson, P. Silverman, and D. Walsh (1978) *New Directions in Sociological Theory*. Moscow: Progress (in Russian).

Fourier, Ch. (1953) "The New World." In Ch. Fourier, *Textes Choisis*. Paris: Editions Sociales.

Fukuyama, F. (1992) *The End of History and the Last Man*. New York: Penguin Books.

Hayek, F. (1952) A. *Der Weg zum Knechtschaft*. Erlenbach-Zurich: Eugen Rentsch Verlag.

Husserl, E. (1977) *Die Krisis der europäishen Wissenschaften und die transcendentale Phänomenologie (Eine Einleitung in die phänomenologische Philosophie)*. Felix-Meiner-Verlag: Hamburg.

Locke, J. (1965) *Second Treatise on Government*. In John Locke, *Two Treatises on Government*. New York: New American Library.

Marx, K. (1953a) *1844 Manuscripts*. In *Die deutsche Ideologie*. Berlin: Dietz.

____. (1953b) *The German Ideology*. In *Die deutsche Ideologie*. Berlin: Dietz.

____. (1978a) *Manifesto of the Communist Party*. In R. C. Tucker (ed.), *Marx-Engels Reader*. New York: Norton.

____. (1978b) "Theses on Feuerbach." In R. C. Tucker (ed.), *Marx-Engels Reader*. New York: Norton.

Plato (1984) *Republic*. In *Plato's Republic*. Indianapolis: Hackett.

Popper, K. (1962) *The Open Society and Its Enemies. Vol. I. Plato*. London: Routledge and Kegan Paul.

Schütz, A. (1981) *Theorie der Lebensformen (Fruhe Manuscripte aus der Bergson-Periode)*. Frankfurt/Main: Suhrkamp.

Weber, M. (1960) "Idealtypus, Handlungsstruktur und Verhaltensinterpretation." In *Methodologische Schriften*. Tübingen: J. K. Mohr (Paul Sieblek).

———. (1970) *Sociology of Control*. In *From Max Weber: Essays in Sociology*. London: Routledge and Kegan Paul.

CHAPTER II

THE POWER OF PERCEPTION: THE CASE OF SOVIET-STYLE AESTHETICS

ANDREW M. BLASKO

The Larger Historical Picture

Terms such as "Post-modernism," "Post-totalitarianism," or "Post-communism" are often used today to describe the most characteristic features of our societies. "Post-Cold-War" is perhaps a better term to use to gain an understanding of the situation in which we now find ourselves after the way intellectual and cultural life developed over at least the last 40 to 50 years.

The Cold War was an "internal war." The very visible face-off of military forces during the Cold War period was itself only a sign of a deeper division between the two opposing camps. The two hostile parties were so divided on basic social and cultural issues that they were concerned to do everything in their power to create a world which was "different" from that of the enemy. They were driven specifically not to integrate with each other, to resist the influence of the "enemy" other in every way possible, and especially to root out the "enemy influence" as it was perceived to exist "within."

This is particularly true in respect to philosophy, one of the principal combatants in the Cold War by virtue of its mission to secure the "front line" in the area of "ideological struggle."

Because of such divisions, neither society (in both camps of the Cold War), nor intellectual life as a whole, (and philosophy especially in Soviet-style society) developed primarily from their "internal" principles. They were driven rather by the spirit of conflict with the opposing camp. Society and thought on both sides of the hostile divide aimed first and foremost not to resemble the "enemy."

Hence, during the Cold War, the United States ceased in practice to be most concerned with the principles of Jeffersonian democracy and instead became obsessed with being an "anti-

Marxist" society.[1]

In the totalitarian society which was the Soviet Union, such tendencies were even more pronounced than in the comparatively open societies in the West. Anything and everything that could be ascribed to "bourgeois" influences was rejected, including music, fashion, even hair styles.[2] This was carried to the point of rejecting "assistance" of all kinds from those in the West who wanted to be "friends" and perhaps build bridges between Soviet-style society and Western democracies, something which was in hindsight clearly self-defeating for those who had wished to maintain themselves in power. This was especially true of artists and intellectuals who did not toe the line set down by the Communist Party of the Soviet Union, such as Sartre, as well as advocates of "Western Marxism" or "Eurocommunism." In many such ways, the Soviet Union ceased being primarily a "Marxist" society, and instead became obsessed with creating an "anti-anti-Marxist" world.

In such circumstances an examination of one of the most unique and yet typical aspects of Soviet-style Marxist philosophy, that is, its aesthetic theory, may make it possible to more clearly identify and better understand central ideas and tendencies in the theoretical foundations of Soviet-style society, particularly those concerning the formation of the sphere of the "taken-for-granted" that underlies meaningful perceptual thought and action. This, in turn, may help us better understand those basic values which formed the fabric of the perceptual and social reality that was Soviet-style society. If it is also noted how Soviet-style aesthetic thinking and activity developed in specific opposition to the "anti-Marxist" world, the former may provide a key to seeing how Soviet-style society as a whole developed as an "anti-anti-Marxist" world. Hopefully, this will serve to begin an accounting of the gains and losses suffered by both opposing camps of the Cold War so that the first steps can be taken in moving intellectual life, and especially philosophy, forward once again.

AESTHETICS AND SOCIAL LOYALTY

What positive insight can be gained from a consideration of aesthetics in specific reference to Soviet-style society? For many years it has been almost too easy to argue that it is quite inappropriate in respect to the totalitarian regimes of the former communist block — if not strikingly misdirected — to expend much effort in analyzing the field of aesthetics. The view of "Socialist Art" most common among observers has been to claim either that aesthetics simply did not exist in Soviet-style society as a serious branch of philosophy, or that Soviet-style art never amounted to much more than an exercise in political didactics because of its particular aesthetic orientation. But the nature of aesthetics as traditionally defined is to be a science dealing with the nature, creation and appreciation of beauty. If so it provides more challenges, and perhaps has more promise for revealing the nature of the paradoxical reality that was Soviet-style society, than any other area of study.[3]

Whatever sympathies or animosities one may have had toward the former communist world, perhaps the last thing a Western observer would say about society there as a whole, especially in respect to relationships between people and the power structure, was that it was in some sense "beautiful". However, non-Soviet observers are also often struck by the fact that, for very many years, very many of the people living in Soviet-style societies, particularly Russia, accepted as normal, and often with more or less sincere enthusiasm, a way of life and a type of social reality which the observers themselves viewed with a host of negative evaluations. It cannot be denied that the Party leadership, their social and economic policies, the political orientation of the government and the very fabric of society commanded deep respect and loyalty from the vast majority of the citizens especially of the Soviet Union for much of the Stalinist period. It was not until 1956, when the process of "de-Stalinization" quickly gathered speed following Khrushchev's famous "secret speech" at the 20th Party Congress, that serious questions began to be raised among certain segments of the population, the intelligentsia in particular, about the nature of Soviet-style socialist construction.[4]

In fact, the loyalty and admiration of the population at large did not begin to waver to a dangerous degree until well into the Brezhnev years, when such factors as corruption on a growing scale and the perceived unfavorable comparison with the West, brought to light the vapidity of socialist values. It is almost as if the people there were living in a different reality from that which those on the outside could see, and it would thus seem to be obvious that their very perception of reality had to have been basically different in some sense from that which was accepted by outside, "objective" observers. Ideology is often described as a pair of glasses that people wear by which reality is seen in a particular, different way. With respect to the Soviet-style communist world, the question might then be what kind of glasses were prescribed and worn so that the actual quality of social life and of the human condition were seen to be other than what would be seen from the West?

Such facts of life in Soviet-style society as the absence of free political activity and an ubiquitous police apparatus were not the glue which held society together. It would certainly be a mistake to underestimate the mark that these factors left on society, but neither should we be overly zealous in taking them to be more than they were. They do not and cannot explain the unmistakable fact that the vast majority of the population of Soviet-style society for significant periods of time sought to be loyal citizens who were quite willing to "play by the rules" in forging their personal lives and public careers. If we wish to understand and explain the nature of Soviet-style society, we must search for those mechanisms by virtue of which the meanings and values perceived in social reality became more or less identical with those of the Bolshevik-led program to create a type of society and a type of human personality substantially different from Western democratic society.

One of the most representative modern views of aesthetics, initiated by Baumgarten in order to correct the omissions and limitations of modern philosophy, emphasizes the importance of sensory and perceptual cognition as a complement to conceptual cognition.[5] With this distinction in mind, an examination of aesthetics and art may create important opportunities for bridging the gap between conceptual and perceptual cognition in respect to the formation and organization of social reality; for conceptual knowledge may be judged to be of secondary importance in this regard in comparison to the ways in which reality is perceived. What I wish to say is that an examination of what can be called the "aesthetic dimension" or "perceptual dimension" of social life may reveal those values and principles upon which the organization and formation of the sense and perception of social reality is based, Thereby the relations of power in a given society become the implicit, taken for granted, more or less unquestioned elements of daily life.

This may provide a way to grasp how the meaning and organization of social reality in a given society is inseparable from the ways in which people in that society perceive reality, This is so much so that they may in fact live within a world whose values, principles and significance may be radically different from what an outside observer is capable of seeing using commonly accepted analytical tools, procedures and methods. As social values become "internalized" in this way, the fabric of society is rewoven and the meaning of social reality is changed.[6]

I propose that aesthetics may be used as a social science in order to uncover the ways in which non-cognitive types of awareness serve to organize the perception and meaning of social reality, particularly in cases of societies that are markedly different from that of the observer. I would further suggest that an adequate analysis of the aesthetic dimension of Soviet-style society is especially useful for opening new perspectives for taking aesthetics as a social science because of the post-Cold War circumstances in which we now live. In addition, the many obvious and manifest differences between Soviet-style art and aesthetics and those that have been commonly accepted in the West provide a starting point that is both convenient and potentially fruitful for a comparison of anti-Marxist society with anti-anti-Marxist society.[7]

My assumption in this regard concerns not "good" works of art, which correspond to aesthetic criteria and whose value is beyond question, but rather those works that were created according to the approved Soviet formulae and which often challenge our abilities for aesthetic appreciation. It is that such works provide a type of valuable insight into the inner workings of Marxist society that is surprisingly at variance with much of accepted aesthetic theory. The best example in this regard is undeniably socialist Realism, which both stands upon the values and achievements of the aesthetic avant-garde in Russia, and also seeks to develop a kind of aesthetics that rejects much of what modern European culture assumes to be self-evident about art.[8]

The ultimate reference point in respect to the basic ideas of "socialist art" was also the ultimate goal of every communist party program, namely, to overcome social inequalities based on social classes by means of the creation of a new type of human being, the new "socialist man." This new type of human being can be represented as a statistical norm with supposedly equal abilities in every kind of artistic and creative endeavor. He/she is a "collective" personality in which the power of creativity would be harnessed to the reproduction of the ideologically specified conditions necessary to realize the ideal of communism.[9] That which emerged as the most representative type of Soviet-style "socialist aesthetics" is directly connected with this "totalized idea" of equality. It rejects the value for aesthetic satisfaction of contrast, theme and variation in aesthetic activity.[10] The examination of Marxist society in this respect raises the question of whether it is possible to build a notion of beauty, not to mention a society as a whole, on standardization, uniformity and a set of equal, interchangeable elements; for it must avoid what Santayana referred to as "aesthetic monotony" or "aesthetic fatigue." Indeed, this raises the question whether such "fatigue" is to be avoided at all in a "socialist type" of aesthetic experience (not to mention the corresponding type of social reality), even though Santayana, for one, viewed this as one of the main goals of artistic design.

One important element of the Bolshevik-style technology for building a just society was the elimination of the difference between, on the one hand, creative and uncreative spheres of activity and, on the other, between the various spheres of creative activity themselves. In this spirit it was argued that salvation from the viciousness of capitalism could be found only in standardization, in the uniformity of the products of practical activity, and in the technologizing of thought and aesthetic criteria.[11] This planned construction of standardized relations to every type of spiritual and material production was to be accomplished through the social organization of activity on the basis of an ideologized philosophy. This would fulfill the role of a supra-empirical criterion of truth, social usefulness and social significance.[12]

The implementation of this program would have far-reaching consequences for the quality of life in Marxist society, or rather, in anti-anti-Marxist society. It undermined traditional standards of professionalism and creative endeavor, not least of all in intellectual life and in the scientific disciplines. It is my contention that the "standardization" of creative activity, along with the suppression of imaginative diversity that resulted from this on a broad scale in society, served to transform Soviet-style society from a society capable of innovation and creativity in public life to one capable of only reproduction of existing norms and standards. This severely restricted its ability to develop in an expected fashion and compete successfully in the international arena.

Finally, the very nature of Soviet-style society may be sought in its works of art, if taken not as a true picture of reality, but as expressing the values and the principles that governed social life and indicated the goals society was directed to achieve.[13] But obstacles to this approach arise when Western aesthetic criteria are simply accepted as universal and are applied uncritically to the evaluation of Soviet works of art. What seems more important in this case is to try to understand what in fact were the guiding rules for the creation of Soviet-style art; what kind of moral, ethical and aesthetical criteria did they both express and also have to meet.

If the two blocks of the Cold War, viewed from the perspective of ideology did not share one and the same set of Cartesian "clear and distinct ideas," that is, conceptual knowledge, were they divided also in their perceptual knowledge? Is there any sense in which the peoples of especially the Soviet Union were educated to see the beautiful and the pleasurable where no one from the West would even consider that it might exist?

Non-Soviet observers have often viewed the aesthetics of Socialist Realism as perhaps the least sophisticated area of Bolshevik-style philosophical thought. In spite of this opinion, and regardless of the lack of consensus in Western philosophy concerning the nature of aesthetic experience and the determination of aesthetic value, a more objective observer might be able to appreciate the extent to which aesthetics was an "active combatant" in so-called "socialist construction." It was perhaps even more closely related to ideology and the construction of the social environment than was science itself. Indeed, given the importance of aesthetics, it was not by chance that before many areas of science, "bourgeois aesthetics" was recognized as being one of the primary "enemies" of the proletariat.[14] This attitude was prominent not only under the early Bolsheviks, but also throughout the Stalinist period and until the end of the Brezhnev years as well.

THE PROCESS OF SUBJECTION

Perceiving the "Taken-for-Granted"

The point of discussion of most concern at the moment involves the perception of reality that defines an individual, along with the social group of which he is a member. In particular, it concerns the way in which this may be more or less deliberately chosen and implemented by the authority that has responsibility for the horizon of perception and consciousness. Of special interest are the basic ways in which art and aesthetic activity may play important roles in this process.

When speaking of authority over the horizon of perception and consciousness, I in no way have in mind the common place (and commonly abused) notions of propaganda and political indoctrination. I view these as relatively simple ideas that do not touch upon the actual process whereby the possibilities for perceiving and thinking become situated within a world horizon that defines the location of any possible consciousness. Not only do these notions not indicate this process, they are incapable of doing so. Because they take it for granted, they conceal it even as their own activity reveals it.

Indeed, "taking something for granted" is one of the key elements of the process in which the horizon of perception and consciousness is defined and established. The "taken-for-granted" establishes the framework for all possible discourse insofar as it serves, so to speak, as the fabric of communications or the "least common denominator" of all possible meanings. Any discrepancy from the taken-for-granted in a given moment of intended communication or discourse will not be permitted to become meaningful and, thereby, an actual instance of discourse. The exception is that it be prepared for and/or presented in such a way that it can be drawn into the taken-for-granted context. That is not to say that it must in fact be situated within that context, but it must at least be seen to be related to that context such that a meaning appropriate to the context can be ascribed to it by the interlocutors. Even the possibility that the intended communication be misconstrued or perhaps eventually seen as incomprehensible in respect to the taken-for-granted demands that it initially be seen to have a relevance to that context. No discourse is possible, not even the discourse of misunderstanding, if an intended communication cannot at the very least be misconstrued as lying within the horizon of the taken-for-granted.[15]

A human subject engages Otherness, which is radically transcendent and cannot be reduced to the ontological state of possession by the subject, by virtue of his/her embodiment or inherence in the sensible.[16] Such inherence creates the possibility for a human being to perceive and be conscious.[17] Inherence is not a question of an "internal" subject "gazing upon" an "external" world. Subjectivity as the synthesis of perception, cognition and praxis emerges from and resides in the reciprocity that occurs between embodied beings. Neither is there subjectivity outside of such interaction, nor is there an exclusively private sense of self-consciousness. That which any subject considers to be most his/her own is always constituted through and defined in the orientation to Otherness. This includes the complex of physical and social circumstances (such as language) in which subjects locates themselves and are located by forces that they do not control.[18]

Furthermore, it is not only that perception and consciousness do not occur without Otherness. Our inherence in the sensible creates the very possibility of the historical "nature" or "essence" of subjectivity, that is, its possibilities for perception, action, reflection and communication. It also allows them to be manipulated through the creation of a determinate Otherness in order to elicit a determinate subjectivity.[19] Indeed, it is precisely our inherence in the sensible which makes it possible for those having authority over the horizon of perception deliberately to create the historical nature or historical "essence" of subjectivity. This is done through manipulation of the "ontological reciprocity" that defines the inter-relationship between subject and Otherness. Such manipulation of the reciprocity between subject and Otherness on the basis of control over the concrete possibilities of perception and cognition enables a "supreme agent" to project his intentional organization upon a world. This has such power and thoroughgoing efficiency that the relationships to Otherness of a mass of human subjects are forced to emerge within more or less clearly and narrowly defined parameters in specific periods of time.

The "supremacy" of such an agent is determined to a great

degree by his/her control of the power structures in society. This includes political and social authority, which extends to control over entry into and egress from the community in question. The power thus controlled makes it possible for the intentionality of that agent to be brought to bear upon other subjects. This can have virtually irresistible force through the mediation of the Otherness which has been "created" or is under his/her dominance.[20]

An agent is able to utilize the power structures in society to project with a high degree of efficiency his/her intentionality upon the world. Thus the world comes increasingly to be organized in accord with his/her intentional aims or those of the group he/she is the controlling, or at least representative and executive, member). This means that the agent in question comes to exercise control over the possibilities for perception and cognition. Human "subjects" normally have the experience of their relative independence (of the autonomy of their intentionality) in respect to the sensible world in which they dwell. Usually they do not thematize their dependence upon that which they perceive and experience. Of course, both autonomy and dependence work together in determining and identifying the essence of both subjectivity and objectivity, both at a particular moment, and also throughout the duration of "subjective" existence. But their roles are not constant, and they may indeed vary within a considerable range.

A "supreme agency" then can be in effective control of the possibilities of perception and cognition, including access to and egress from society. The ontological reciprocity of the embedded subject and sensible world can be oriented by social factors more or less beyond the control of the subject, in such a way that the "ontological dependency" of the subject upon the sensible world is maximized. This results in the subjugation of the subject's possibilities for perception and cognition to the agency of force in society. This does not have to be a process of which the subject is aware in order for it to be effective and efficient. On the contrary, the impression of the perceptual and cognitive autonomy of the subject may not only easily accompany an increased subjugation to social and political power structures — as is readily suggested by the development of pop culture, mass marketing, mass media and mass advertisement in advanced Western countries — it may actually facilitate this.

The phenomenon of totalitarian society demonstrates a high degree of perfection in this process. A truly totalitarian society does not rely on force and violence as the glue which binds it together. These factors are present to some degree in any society, and totalitarian society is particularly efficient in maximizing them and using them with brutal efficiency against those elements of society which, for whatever reason, are judged to exist outside the parameters of acceptability. However, force and violence do not command the loyalty and subservience to authority that are essential for the very functioning of totalitarian society as such.

The combination of fear and loathing which is a universal result of a brutal exercise of violence — not to speak of the lack of initiative and suppression of motivation which may accompanying it — does not satisfactorily to account for the agency of that violence itself.

For example, it may be assumed that fear of punishment was one element driving the behavior of the SS camp guard or NKVD executioner, but, perhaps more than anything else, the soldier who stood on the train platform at Birkenau and selected those arriving who would be sent to immediate death in the gas chambers was likely driven by a sense of "mission" and loyalty to a "higher cause." The NKVD officer who continued to execute Polish military prisoners in Katyn Forest even as the rumble of the approaching front grew loud did so because he believed he was following the course of history, not because he was afraid of what his superior might otherwise do.

And if those who commit such unspeakable acts of bestial violence on a mass scale are not motivated by something akin to belief in a higher moral or historical cause, then their actions are driven by an absence of belief in anything at all. The choice in this regard is not between action based on fear and action based on principle, but between action based on principle and action based on a lack of any principles whatsoever. However, the latter state of affairs is self-destructive to the highest degree and can in no way serve as a solid foundation for a stable society. Indeed, a widespread absence of belief in some sort of moral standards, however loosely defined, destroys the possibility that the social formation in question can long survive.

The point in this regard is that the extremes of brutality and violence in totalitarian society are of such a magnitude that those who carry them out cannot possibly be motivated solely by fear. Their active and willing commitment and participation is necessary for the system of terror and murder to operate. The question is whence does this commitment and choice arise.

It is not only the elite of dedicated extremists in totalitarian society but the ordinary citizens too must, at the very least, willingly cooperate with the structures of power and authority if society as a whole is to more or less efficiently function. Not even the smallest social units, such as the family, can long be held together if the only force for doing so is fear. A society can function in a normal and stable fashion only when its members implicitly believe in and accept the standards of behavior and, more importantly, the parameters of perception and consciousness which it demands of them. This is first and foremost a question of the horizons of possibility for perception and cognition. In other words, totalitarian societies function efficiently to the extent that the horizons of perception and cognition which they mandate are internalized by their members such that they are implicitly accepted as the "normal" parameters of everyday existence. This transforms everyday existence into the glue which holds that society together.

The Self as Virtual Other

It is the embeddedness of the subject in the sensible world which makes it possible for the "character" or "value" of the "object" to influence and determine to varying degrees the "character" or "value" of the subject. The autonomy of the subject within the process of ontological reciprocity cannot be reduced to zero, particularly in respect to the multiplicity of subjects. But, at any given moment within a given society, it can be significantly reduced in respect to forces which work for the ontological dependency of the subject on the object. The paramount example of this reduction of autonomy is totalitarian society.

The greatest possibilities for maximizing the reduction of the cognitive and perceptual autonomy of the embedded subject are to be found at the non-reflective or pre-reflective levels of conscious life. There is always an abyss between our fundamental reciprocity with the world as embedded subjects and our attempts to express that reciprocity explicitly at the level of reflective discourse or in theory. Consequently, theory cannot be the most effective "tool" in constructing the emergence of a particular, determinate relation to otherness involving other subjects because it is unable to bridge this abyss. Art and aesthetics have unique power in this regard.

The power of art as a fusion of the sensuous with the conceptual means that art is charged with semantic and conceptual energy.[21] However, this means also that, under certain conditions, that same energy can be directed in a deliberate fashion in order to create a determinate type of reciprocity between the subject and Otherness. This process is intensified as that "energy" is more extensively and consistently brought to bear across the full ranges of the conceptual and the sensuous. This is done on the basis of the control exercised by the agent of power in society over access to and egress from the community concerning subjects, possible perceptions and possible cognitions.

The point in question can be stated as follows: The agency in which power is concentrated is capable, under certain circumstances, of "reversing" the cycle of expression/externalization, recognition from the Other and self-recognition through the Other. Here that the projection of a determinate self-recognition by the Other before the actual fact of self-recognition is capable of forcing the emergence of such a manipulated "self-recognition" by the "self." The subject/self then emerges as a "virtual Other," that is, the self becomes the "Other" in respect to himself by virtue of the action of the actual Other (the agent of power) upon him. Thereby the self-identity of the subject is replaced with the identity the Other desires him to possess. This may be viewed as the constitution of the "self" as a virtual "Other" through the intentional power of an actual Other who is in command of the horizons of possible perception and possible cognition. In other words, this is an instance of "reversed" or "subverted" ontological reciprocity.[22]

In the case of such subverted ontological reciprocity it is the object which is "forceful" and "powerful". The object now embodies the "power/energy" of a "Supreme Agent" such that when it "shows itself as it is" it forces its "truth" upon the "self." This is not what is often considered the usual case, in which the "object" is viewed as being resistant to the action/intention of the subject. When ontological reciprocity is subverted in the fashion described, it is the "truth" of the "object/other" which drives the "constitution", or "emergence," of the "self." The "truth" of the object thereby becomes the "truth" of the subject as well.[23]

This is a situation in which the "other/object" has to overcome the "resistance" of the "self/subject," which is the same thing as saying that the "truth" of the "other/object" has to overcome the "truth" of the "self/subject." What may be spoken of as the hermeneutic circle is thus made to function from the perspective of the "empowered object/other" that has become dominant in the "ontological reciprocity" between embodied subject/self and Otherness. The relative autonomy of the subject is thereby reduced to the sphere of ontological dependence. It is the "object/other," which now appears as both the mediation and the medium of the intentional power of the "Supreme Agent," that has become ontologically dominant and autonomous vis-à-vis the subject/self.

What is important here is the generation of a specific semantic and conceptual energy by the totalizing agency of power in society, and that agent's objectification of such energy as overwhelming power in the ontological environment of the subject. This transforms the ontological reciprocity between subject and object into the ontological subjugation of the subject to the agency of power. The mediation is through the empowered object that has been endowed with the overwhelming force of the agent of power.[24] In such circumstances the agent of power is not compelled to exercise force (terror) directly over the subject. For the object, which he has endowed with his power, exercises his power in his stead. This minimizes the need for the exercise of force in that the domination of the subject by the object serves to restrict the possibility that acts of perception and consciousness may emerge with a significance which is at variance with the preferences and/or requirements of the agent. This heightens and reinforces the efficiency of the social control which has already been established.

The semantic and conceptual energy with which the object has been endowed thereby works to entrap the subject in a world which has been more or less deliberately designed to serve the purposes of the agent of power. The power of the object does not enable the subject to be engaged in the bringing forth of truth. Rather it plunges the subject into a lifeworld in which submission is the paradigm for the relation of the subject to the object and, through the latter, to the agent of power. This binds the subject's horizons of perception and consciousness to the power structures in a given society such that he/she internalizes those structures, becomes subject to them, and undergoes a marked reduction in the ability to experience acts of perception and consciousness at variance from them.

Department of Aesthetics
Uppsala University
Sweden

NOTES

1. A number of examples immediately come to mind: McCarthyism, one major aim of which was to emasculate the power of left-dominated organized labor; the formation of the AFL-CIO; foreign aid in general and the Marshall Plan in particular; the fashion in which West Germany was created; the organization of the U.S. as a war economy, a still dominant if somewhat diminished orientation whereby important sectors of the economy and important areas of the country, such as Massachusetts and California, suffer greatly from the current restriction of military budgets.

Most important in respect to intellectual life was that in practice it became impossible to discuss a whole range of ideas that had become identified as "communist", such as social democracy or even national health care. This was a rather marked change even for intellectual life in the U.S., which had always been rather conservative. A comparison with the 1930s and 1940s, when what could justifiably be called a working class ideology was a prominent element in the arts and certain other spheres of intellectual life, is revealing in this regard.

Western Europe was "anti-Marxist" too, only to a lesser degree. The fate of Italian governments (the aim being to exclude communists from national government) is one sign of this, as was the fact of "tolerable" fascism in Spain and Portugal. Another such indicator is the level of military production and the defense posture in a country like "neutral" Sweden, where a company such as SAAB (originally founded to guarantee the production of aircraft for the military) has become an important social and economic factor.

2. Even the value of specific foreign languages was

determined by the political orientations of the respective countries in which they were spoken. English, for example, was singled out for special treatment in certain countries, being considered as the "language of the enemy" before being considered as the "language of Shakespeare."

3. A valuable work in this regard is Åman 1992, originally published as *Arkitektur och ideologi i stalinstiden Östeuropa. Ur det kalla krigets historia* (1987). This book is a well-documented and illustrated study of the application of Socialist Realism in architecture and of its overall significance in respect to the worlds of both politics and art. It addresses in detail key aspects both of Soviet-style aesthetics in general, and also of the history of its development. A recurrent theme concerns the way that Socialist Realism in architecture was defined in explicit opposition to the ideas and styles dominant in the "enemy camp" consisting of anti-Marxist states.

4. The undesired (from the Party's viewpoint) effect of "de-Stalinization" on social and intellectual life is discussed in an insightful and accurate fashion by Kolalowski 1972, vol. 3.

5. It may be expected that philosophy will continue to have the honor of dealing with this "clear but confused" body of non-cognitive awareness as long as the latter escapes thorough conceptualization, thereby not being differentiated from philosophy as a separate science.

6. I do not wish to suggest that social reality is reducible to the way in which it is perceived. However, the meaning of social reality as it is actually lived cannot be grasped by an outside observer unless he/she is aware of the values and principles around which it is organized. He/she must grasp the sphere of the "taken-for-granted" that is the basis upon which all meaning and significance arise, including the sphere of deliberate, reflective thought and action. Some general awareness of cultural differences or of structural differences in society is not sufficient for this purpose. What is required is, among other things, a grasp of the aesthetic values, taken in a general sense, by virtue of which the perception of reality takes concrete shape. This is particularly true in respect to revolutionary programs to create a new type of society insofar as the possibility of success demands that people come to literally see and experience social reality in a revolutionary new kind of way.

Changing the substance of social reality goes hand in hand with changing the perception of social reality.

This was recognized by both the Communists and the Fascists. On the one hand, the Bolsheviks placed primary importance on art and aesthetics, not on ideology, in educating the population in "communist" values from the earliest days of their regime. This is evidenced, for example, by Lenin's decree on "Monumental Art." On the other hand, no less a figure than Mussolini maintained that ideology (conceptual thinking) is a "luxury, and for intellectuals only." He was explicitly aware that addressing people on the level of ideas could not strike to the heart of the matter in reorganizing society. Much the same is true of Goebbels, who often suppressed the release of motion pictures which he judged to be overtly political in content. Indeed, perhaps 90 percent of the films produced in Germany under Goebbels's control were of an entertaining, rather than overtly propagandistic, nature.

7. Several general types of questions arise at this point in respect to Soviet-style, anti-anti-Marxist society and include the following: First, which of the values at the heart of Soviet-style society which served to determine its manner of functioning and its eventual fate are revealed through an examination of Soviet-style art and aesthetics? Second, what role did art and aesthetics play in establishing relations of power in society; can we find precedents in the history of aesthetics? Third, how did aesthetics and art serve to formulate and control the perception of social reality in Soviet-style society? Fourth, what role did Soviet-style aesthetics, especially Socialist Realism, play in the development of Soviet-style society as anti-anti-Marxist society?

The most useful way of proceeding in addressing these questions involves an examination of the role played by the Russian tradition of avant-garde aesthetics and art in the formulation and implementation of the most important Bolshevik-style cultural and social policies, including Socialist Realism. This avant-garde tradition not only developed the main concepts, values and views that later became dominant in the Soviet-style tradition of art and aesthetics, but also promoted the view that art plays a leading role, side by side with politics, in any process of social transformation by virtue of its unique power to educate the population in a new view of society and in new social and moral values. The views that later became typical of the Soviet-style tradition in this respect in fact incorporated the views, values and ideas of avant-garde aesthetics to such a degree that Soviet-style social reality cannot be adequately understood without addressing its aesthetic dimension. This point merits attention in and of itself as the main topic of a separate study.

8. The fact that Socialist Realism dominated the sphere of art and creative expression in the communist countries has led many Western commentators to ignore Soviet-style aesthetics in general. It was judged to be ambiguous, unsophisticated, significantly self-contradictory, overtly ideologically bound, and didactic. Examples of these undeniably negative traits are amply provided by such works Leizerov 1974, Dubrovin 1977, and Kulikova and Zis' 1980. A valuable Soviet examination of an inherent theoretical ambiguity within Socialist Realism is Borev 1975.

However, precisely because Socialist Realism is so challenging for many views of aesthetic theory commonly accepted in the West, an unbiased examination of it may help define issues of central importance regarding the formation, functioning, decline and collapse of Soviet-style society. It could be argued that the otherwise vague principles of artistic creation and expression as related to creative thought and creative activity in general in Soviet-style society took final, clear shape in the process by which Socialist Realism became established as a dominant policy in Soviet social and cultural politics. This is particular of the ways in which it took up the Russian traditions of avant-garde aesthetics and art. For example, a discussion of how Marxist society was organized such that its reproductive potential was emphasized at the expense of its creative powers could easily take Socialist Realism as its legitimate point of analytical departure. This would make explicit reference to the way the ground for this was prepared by avant-garde aesthetics.

9. Konstantinov 1978 is a standard presentation, later prepared for an international audience, of the Soviet view concerning Marxist philosophy as a whole, including the general role of art in the creation of a new "socialist" human being.

10. The dominant opposing non-Marxist views in this regard are perhaps best expressed in Santayana's hedonistic theory of aesthetic forms. See, for example, *"The Sense of Beauty,"* first published in 1896.

11. A broad and uncritical discussion of these points typical

of official views until virtually the end of the Soviet period, and which contains also numerous references to the literature, may be found in Bezklubenko 1982, chapters 1 and 2.

12. Because Bolshevik-style thinking presents the communist theory of history as expressing the absolute objective truth of social reality, the type of connection mentioned here between the empirical world and an ideal world, which is the source of aesthetic meaning and value, makes it possible to present the empirical standards of party ideology as supra-empirical aesthetic criteria. A representative Soviet-style discussion of how this issue lies at the center of the theory of reflection developed in Soviet philosophy, which aimed in part to develop the idea that it was possible to reflect that which did not yet exist in the real world, is found in Andreev 1981, pp. 15-35.

13. A degree of inspiration in this regard could be taken from Hegel's *"Lectures on Aesthetics"*. Its central theses is that beauty and truth can be understood only in terms of their systematic coherence by virtue of both being ideas. This implies that: (a) art itself really is both the Idea and a form of knowledge of the Idea, both Truth and a mode of knowing Truth, (b) art embodies the beliefs and morals of a given society in which the aesthetic judgements are rooted, and moreover, (c) art constitutes the subject's identity (concepts which dominate Hegel's aesthetic theory). Hence, there can be no more appropriate starting point for the discussion of Soviet-style society than art taken as the expression and knowledge of the highest governing principles of social reality and social life.

14. Nor was it by chance that a primary element in Gorbachev's policies of *glasnost* and *perestroika* was the relaxing of controls over artistic expression, especially insofar as these policies represent a program of "democratization from above." This relaxing of controls implicitly involves the recognition that the transformation of social views and social practices presumes the corresponding transformation in aesthetic views and artistic activity.

15. An analogous situation holds true for perception as well, although this issue will not be discussed here. Suffice it to say at this point that an object which is perceived emerges against the background of the taken-for-granted. It is perceivable only to the extent that a possible meaning can be ascribed to it. Even for it to emerge as a perceived object means that it has already been ascribed an "assumed" or "categorical" meaning.

16. Bernet 1988 provides a useful discussion of the complex relations between the concepts of intentionality and transcendence in respect to the work of Husserl and Heidegger.

17. These questions are focused upon and discussed in an insightful fashion in Crowther 1993. Pages 1-11, where the basic terms and framework for the study as a whole are presented, are immediately relevant to the theoretical outline of the present study. In respect to the transcendence of Otherness, Crowther notes that this may most simply be understood as indicating that not only are embodied beings finite, but that it is always possible to perceive more, discuss more and do more than is the case at any particular moment. Crowther states that the view he develops is substantially in the spirit of Merleau-Ponty's *Phénoménologie de la Perception*.

18. This view is articulated at the very beginning of the introduction to Crowther 1993.

19. Otherness may be spoken of in this context as the ontological environment or medium of subjectivity that enables consciousness to appear in a specific instance of historical space and time.

20. It is impossible for reflection, thought and knowledge to be effective means for exercising such force because they do not address the actual, unitary originality of the ontological reciprocity but instead take it for granted. They arise by virtue of the ontological reciprocity whereby conscious (perceptual) intentionality becomes bound with the sensible world in which it is embedded.

21. Crowther speaks of this fusion as the "concrete particular" and refers it to Hegel's discussion of art as a mode of self-understanding that lies "half-way between the concrete particularity of material phenomena and the abstract generality of pure thought." See Crowther 1993, 5. See also Chapter 7, especially pp. 122 ff. However, I would add here that art may be not only the expression of that which is fundamental in the human relationship with the world, but that its power can be utilized to drive the creation of that relationship. In the latter case it is as if the Spirit is driven to become self-conscious in a determinate way through the deliberate presentation (by the agent of power in a society) of an Otherness of a determinate type.

22. The ideas expressed here can be fruitfully discussed in relation to certain of the basic concepts in the dialectical philosophy

of Sartre's later period, such as *practico-inerte, passivité* and *sérialité*. For Sartre's primary presentations of these concepts see *Critique de la Raison dialectique*, tome I, p. 363 ff. and p. 546 ff., and tome II, p. 300 ff. More suggestive for the present discussion, however, is his exploration of totalization in a given society through the agency of a single absolute sovereign. This may be found in tome II, livre III, section B, "La totalization d'enveloppement dans une société directoriale; rapports de la dialectique et de l'anti-dialectique." Of particular interest are Chapters 1-3, "Singularité et incarnation dans la praxis souveraine," "Incarnation du souveraine dans un individu," and "La totalization d'enveloppement, incarnations des incarnations."

The emphasis in the present study differs significantly from Sartre's insofar as I wish to establish a theoretical framework for investigating how dialectical deviation, alienation and, especially, the power of the *practico-inerte* may deliberately be fostered and utilized on the ontological level by the agent of power, at least for specific periods of time. Here its purpose is to create a perceptual and cognitive realm of such character that the aesthetic elements of conscious existence come to subdue thought and reflection to the power of the Other which they embody.

23. This notion differs in an important fashion from the tone of Heidegger's discussion in the Introduction to *Being and Time* of the significance of capturing the meaning of an object "when it reveals itself on its own as it reveals itself on its own." The case of subverted ontological reciprocity does not concern the emergence of the Truth, which is a constant theme throughout the body of Heidegger's work in all of its various stages, not least of all in such essays as "The Essence of Truth" and "The Origin of the Work of Art." Quite the contrary, the aim of subverted ontological reciprocity is the forceful imposition upon the subject/self of what may be referred to as a determinate "truth substitute" through the action of an object/other which has been endowed with the aesthetic power of the agent of power. The concern of subverted ontological reciprocity is the "truth" of the object precisely as it may be forced upon the subject, not the Truth as it emerges through the ontological reciprocity between subject and Otherness. This ironically compares with Heidegger's notion of the "thinking of Being" as it is first presented in "On the Essence of Truth" insofar as "Being" forces

itself in the condition of subverted ontological reciprocity upon the subject in such a fashion that the possibility for the emergence of "opening" is itself subverted and the state of truth as concealment is maximized. Being now indeed assumes primacy over There-being, but not at all in the fashion for which Heidegger eventually calls.

24. When the object/other that has been empowered by the agent is considered as an art-work, then the aesthetic characteristics which Heidegger promulgates in "The Origin of a Work of Art" are seen to be lacking in social relevance. The case in question represents a type of creation in which truth is not at work and which originates neither Being nor truth, even though a world emerges. Richardson 1963 provides perhaps the best available examination of the relevant issues in Heidegger's work as a background for the present discussion. See especially Part II, Chapter I; Part III, Section A, Chapter V; and Part III, Section B, Chapter 1.

REFERENCES

Andreev, A. A. (1981) *Khudozhestvenniy obraz i gnoseologicheskaia spetsifika iskusstva*. Moscow.

Åman, A. (1992) *Architecture and Ideology in Eastern Europe: An Aspect of Cold War History*. New York, Cambridge, MA, and London: MIT.

Bernet, Rudolf (1988) "Transcendence et intentionnalité : Heidegger et Husserl sur les prolégomènes d'une ontologie phénoménologique." In F. Volpi et al. (eds.). *Heidegger et l'idée de la phénoménologie*, pp. 195-215. Dordrecht: Kluwer.

Bezklubenko, S. D. (1982) *Priroda iskusstva*. Moscow.

Borev, Iu. B. (1975) *Estetika*. Moscow.

Crowther, P. (1993) *Art and Embodiment. From Aesthetics to Self-consciousness*. Oxford: Oxford University Press.

Dubrovin, A. G. (1977) *Kommunisticheskoe mirovozzrenie i iskusstvo sotsiologicheskogo realizma*. Moscow.

Hegel, G.W.F. (1974-75) *Aesthetics: Lectures on Fine Arts*, T.M. Knox trans. Oxford: Clarendon.

Heidegger, M. (1977) *Basic Writings*, ed. J. Glenn Gray. New York: Harper and Row.

Kolalowski, L. (1981) *Main Currents of Marxism*, vol. 3. Oxford: Oxford University Press.

Konstantinov, F. V., ed. (1978). *Osnovy marksistko-leninskoi*

filosofii. Moscow.
Kulikova, I. S. and A. Ia. Zis' (1980). *Marksistko-leninskaia estetika i khudozhestvennoe tvorchestvo*. Moscow.
Leizerov, N. L. (1974) *Obraznost' v iskusstve*. Moscow.
Merleau-Ponty, M (1964) *Phénoménologie de la perception*. Paris: Gallimard.
Richardson, William J. (1963) *Heidegger: Through Phenomenology to Thought*. The Hague: Martinus Nijhoff.
Santayana, George (1960) *The Sense of Beauty, Being the Outlines of Aesthetic Theory*. New York: Dover.
Sartre, J.-P. (1985) *Critique de la Raison dialectique*. Paris: Gallimard.

PART II

THE COMPLEX TRANSITION

CHAPTER III

DEMOCRACY AND HUMAN RIGHTS IN THE AFTERMATH OF THE TOTALITARIAN CHALLENGE

MILOSLAV BEDNÁŘ

The dramatic, ongoing encounter of democratic civilisation with totalitarian regimes is the decisive philosophical and political event of the twentieth century, the impact of which has shaped the very essence of the movement of history. In its current form it consists of the bias to minimize, and in fact to displace, all of the unsettling findings concerning the nature of this conflict and its consequences.

To the west of the former Iron Curtain, this encounter involves two main tendencies. On the one hand, it amounts to a continuation of Cold War perceptions in the public opinion of western democracies. The prevailing character of those times, which seemingly has been permanently ingrained into the memories of ordinary citizens, was peace and stability, coupled with the acceptance of peripheral wars (Gambles, 1995, 26-35). In other words, the era of the Cold War was largely associated in Western public opinion with the peaceful everyday character of an affluent life-style. The routine of life, whose foundations and origins were hidden, remained unquestioned and unshaken. This was the decisive experience of the period.[1] The acute and drastic spasm of World War II was thus followed by a soothing, self-isolating defence from the chronic danger to democracy posed by the totalitarian communist regime.

Moreover, the peaceful serenity of "the Golden Age" of the western democracies during the greater part of the Cold War (1945-1973) can legitimately be explained as the unequivocal success of the United States in her efforts to turn the catastrophe of two world wars into a democratic "Century of America" for herself and into a "Golden Age" for other nations (Kurth, 1995, 11).

On the other hand, there are justifiable grounds for questioning whether the democratic world has actually come to grips with the totalitarian menace, and whether the Cold War actually came to an end with the democratic changes in Eastern Europe and the crumbling of the Soviet Union. A range of reasons substantiate such misgivings. Politically, for example, it is obvious that totalitarian regimes have not perished from the earth, and their flexible vitality can be seen in the most practical terms on the vast territory of continental China. This large communist power applies a differentiated approach to the various regions of the country and the many strata of the population with regard to the usage of communist terror (the substance of totalitarian regimes) and to ideology as the principle of action. No less characteristic of this approach is a nationalistic mixture of Marxist ideological schemes with the traditional Chinese rhetoric of Confucianism.

An analogous trend exists *mutatis mutandis* in certain East European countries, which at first had conformed to the wave of anti-communist upheavals and revolutions that took place in 1989. These include most parts of the former Yugoslavia, Slovakia, and the greater part of the former Soviet Union. A visible turn in the direction of a nationalistically tinted totalitarianism recently became evident in Russia itself during the Spring of 1996. The phenomenon has also appeared in such Asian and Africa countries as North Korea, Vietnam, Laos, Burma, Iran, Iraq, Libya and Sudan. There we find various combinations of the totalitarian aversion to principles of human rights and democracy with both nationalistically and superficially religious approaches to propaganda. By the same token, the religious and national significance of local traditions, along with their possible conjunction with the principles of human rights and the democratic option of the rule of law, are losing ground to totalitarian ideological distortions.

When investigated more closely from a philosophical perspective, the presumed coping with the totalitarian danger is revealed to be an alarming failure. Both the currently prevailing theoretical notion of human rights and democracy as well as the consequent practical views originate in a half-hearted understanding of liberalism as the given fact of individual liberties which require no preliminary conditions for either their possible or actual existence. This is how there has come about an unjustified rejection of the verifiable preconditions and grounds for the emergence of the concept of human rights and democracy, the latter being based on the former in terms of dwelling in the natural life-world. Such an approach is the culminating movement of modern dilettantism, whose key theoretical expression consists in systematically ignoring the only possible basis for the existence of natural human rights, namely, the phenomenon of the law of nature.

The basic principle of the law of nature was articulated by Augustinus Aurelius, one of the most distinguished early Christian philosophers, who wrote, "What you will not to be done to you, do not do this to others" (Augustinus, 7).[2] This is the decisive point of departure for natural law and natural rights, which later stood at the origins of the Anglo-Saxon notion of human rights and democracy. Its fundamentals had already emerged clearly within the Greek tradition of poetry, drama and philosophy as the eternal law, which provides the origins of human legislation.[3] The source of the modern tradition of democratic stability, including its basic concept of human rights, consists in the conviction that, "[T]he law of nature is that which God at the time of creation of the nature of man infused into his heart, for his preservation and direction; and this is the *Lex aeterna*, the moral law, called also the law of nature" (Coke, 1957, 45-46). This tradition became the basic framework for the modern conception of natural human rights, including the demand for religious tolerance and the ideas of democratic political consensus and civic virtues, first formulated by John Locke.

JOHN LOCKE

The development of the Lockean conception of the law of nature demonstrates a preference for the irreplaceability of its religious grounds, instead of the initially one-sided emphasis on its ability to be known rationally (Sinopoli, 1992, 39-51). Lockean philosophic realism is germane not only to the meaning of philosophy as such but to the Christian religion as a distinct phenomenon of world history. Locke agrees that, apart from knowing God as the creator of all things, humankind is capable of clearly knowing its duties. Locke maintained that it was precisely this aspect of knowledge which, although scrupulously cultivated by the ancient philosophers, had not taken secure hold among people (Locke, 1958, 60).

Nevertheless, Locke does not give in to the tendency to accuse mankind of moral corruption. He writes:

> All men indeed, under pain of displeasing the gods, were to frequent the temples, every one went to their sacrifices and services; but the priests made it not their business to teach them virtue. . . . Few went to the schools of the philosophers, to be instructed in their duties and to know what was good and evil in their action. The priests sold the better penny-worth, and therefore had all their custom. Lustrations and processions were much easier than a clean conscience, and a steady course of virtue (*ibid.*).

The force of natural reason cannot fully provide what Locke speaks of as a natural, morally adequate religion. He states that:

> It is too hard a task for unassisted reason to establish morality, in all its parts, upon its true foundations, with a clear and convincing light. And it is at least a surer and shorter way, to the apprehensions of the vulgar, and mass of mankind, that one manifestly sent from God, and coming with visible authority from him, should, as a King and law-maker, tell them their duties, and require their obedience, than leave it to the long, and sometimes intricate deductions of reason, to be made out of them: such strains of reasonings the greatest part of mankind have neither leisure to weigh, nor, for want of education and use, skill to judge of (*op. cit.*, 60-61).

The Lockean point of departure at the creation of the modern conception of human rights and liberalism is the philosophical legitimation of both the Christian and ancient origins of natural law. Proceeding in this fashion, Locke saw a harmony between verifiably true insight, understandability and practical usage. In addition, Locke took into account the obvious danger of a too narrow, egoistic grasp of the natural law. He criticized such attitudes by emphasizing that:

> [S]elf-interest is not the foundation of the law of nature, or the reason for obeying it, although it is the consequence of obedience to it. . . . Thus the test of the rightness of an action is not whether it is self-interested; but rather a moral action is also self-interested, but only because it is right (Wooten, 1993, 183).

The Lockean religious-ethical grounding of the natural law as the basis of human rights is clearly evident. For Locke, the conceptions of the law of nature and of human rights are unequivocally anchored in the philosophical and Christian tradition of the natural law as the identification of Right with Good within the framework of human participation in the eternal by means of the law of nature. This is not at variance in its basic intention with Hegel's philosophical-political conclusions regarding the topic of natural law (Hegel, 1972, 419-420).

As the Founding Father of the modern conception of human rights, John Locke sought an harmonious synthesis of the classical concept of natural law with the modern emphasis on the irreplaceability of individuals. For Locke, the rise of the body politic as political civic society in the form of the state comprised a safeguard of the rights to life, freedom and property on the basis of an application of the law of nature that was more consistent than in the state of nature (Wooten, 1993, 309-10). The basic modern concept of human rights and democracy thus differs essentially from the political philosophies of Thomas Hobbes and J. J. Rousseau on this crucial point. These thinkers presented unbalanced and one-sided conceptions of the state of nature as either arbitrariness or the absence of property, and they depicted the state as the subordination of the population to the Sovereign or to the General Will.

As a result of the predominant modern fascination with mathematical natural history, and in the aftermath of the drastic events of the European religious wars, a distorted interpretation of the Lockean concept of human rights became routine, which displaced it from its religious and ethical foundation in the law of nature. Given the parallel impact of Rousseau's theory of the social contract, the conception of religiously and ethically indifferent liberalism took root initially in France, Belgium, and Germany as a secular, deductive, normative and all-encompassing system of law and political institutions based on law. Its origins are related to the close of the French Revolution, and its full-fledged development is connected with the aftermath of 1848 in Europe.

In contrast, the Anglo-Saxon tradition of democratic civilisation preserved the decisive continuity with natural law and human rights to a much greater extent. The still-growing liberal opposition to this tradition consists first of all in the prevailing tendency to consider the public civic sphere a realm of strict rationality and objective validity, and to separate it sharply from the spiritual dimension of human life, including religion and ethics, which it presents as a sphere of privacy, subjectivity and, on the whole, irrationality.

In this way, the modern conception of human rights and democracy lost its force, foundation and life-world horizon, all of which are expressed in the recognition of the validity of natural law. Along with the abandonment of the latter, the primary element of both self-control and public control, which is intrinsic to public dialogue about basic orientations and decision-making in the common world of human life, was also discarded. As a result, totalitarian movements and regimes were provided the means for raising the claim that this core element of human rights and democracy should be totally eliminated from within the framework of their thoroughgoing efforts to liquidate individual moral responsibility and eliminate it as the point of departure for human reflection, decision-making, and action. Totalitarian regimes thereby eliminated the unnatural separation of morality and public life characteristic of the half-hearted continental type of liberalism through their ideological postulate of objective laws of nature and history and through their omnipresent mass terror. Thus, the shallow dilettante elements and origins of religiously and ethically indifferent liberalism actually served to foster the enthroning of totalitarian regimes, mainly in countries with conspicuously weak and doubtful democratic traditions. These regimes represented, and in many places in the contemporary world still do represent, a viable alternative form of human existence.

The relative defeats delivered to both totalitarian Nazism in World War II and Marxist Communism in the Cold War have merely negative significance. A genuine coming-to-terms with totalitarianism in terms of education and democratic civilisation can take place only as a result of a thorough re-evaluation of religiously and ethically indifferent liberalism. This must include its untenable projects for dividing up human existence into separate units as the ground for a distorted conception of human rights and democracy. The extremist totalitarian challenge to democracy and human rights has so far triggered only superficial, negative and limited aggressive reactions. Evidence of this is provided by the contemporary range of extreme forms of liberalism that culminate merely in its deficient version, i.e., its discontinuous polarization of, and subsequent abstract parcelling out of, human existence *ad infinitum*. Leftist communitarianism also belongs here as an updated version of the post-communist revision of Marxism (Walzer, 1989; Mouffe, 1992).

On the other hand, the conservative strand of communitarianism, which characteristically stresses the traditional ethical-religious environment of the moral virtues of democratic civilisation and its authentic development in terms of natural law, has met a weak response. This tenor of communitarian thought places the primary emphasis on a sense of civic responsibility in terms of the political articulation of community, involving civic education understood as duty. Consequently, this sense of responsibility amounts to a sense of dutiful mission representing that which binds democratic civilisation together (Johnson, 1995). Ethics is conceived as the leading scheme of laws such that civil law should be directed in harmony with the law of nature (Kirk, 1994). Conservative communitarianism fundamentally argues against the present currents of positivism and realism in law. It maintains that the origins of the positivist science of law lie in the interpenetration of 19th century nationalism with scientific mechanism and materialism. As a consequence, legal positivists and realists conclude that laws are mere commands issued to human beings. In such a conception, there is no necessary coherence between law and morality, i.e., between laws as they exist and how they ought to be. It is thus presumed that value judgements are not defensible by rational arguments.

Conservative communitarians see this as the first stage of a general contempt for laws. That is why they argue for the necessity of reviving a general understanding of both ancient and Christian teachings on justice (Kirk, 1993). It appears obvious that the spiritual climate of the United States in the mid-1990s endorses a rejuvenated synthesis of the conservative and liberal bases of American democracy. This development was necessitated first of all by the impasse, long verified both theoretically and practically, facing materialistically-grounded liberalism (Heineman, 1994; Lowi, 1979). Its modern origins date back as far as Hugo Grotius, who declared that he would deduce the law of nature solely out of the humanist condition of a purely secular contract between men independent of the divine mind or will, i.e., apart from any divine framework whatsoever. Grotius's point of departure contradicted the notion of any absolutely valid law of nature and the existence of God; in fact, it renders God superfluous. Grotius wrote:

> Measureless as is the power of God, nevertheless it can be said that there are certain things over which that power does not extend. . . . Just as even God cannot cause that two times two should not make four, so He cannot cause that which is intrinsically evil be not evil (Grotius, 1925, I, i).[4]

Grotius's alluring efforts moved the unclear distinction between law and morality into the sphere of the self-important Absolute of human self-sufficiency. Human freedom as a crystally transparent freedom of the will, its relation to rationality, and the recognition of duty became isolated in "rational choice" as a self-sufficient frame of reference. Its philosophical-political outcome can only be a religiously and ethically indifferent liberalism. In contrast, the Lockean modern renewal of the original meaning of the natural law, along with its liberal and democratic culmination, emerge as the appropriate synthesizing and promising response to the challenge Grotius had presented to this notion.

Considering the global turn of events after 1989, we now stand before a task strikingly similar to the one with which John Locke had to cope in the aftermath of the catastrophic European experience of the Religious Wars. It is necessary today to stand up to the still challenging totalitarian alternative of human existence, which arose out of the empty, liberal, voluntaristic rejection of any moral vision, through a revival of the realist moral option as the basis for the movement of human life and the world. This option amounts to a cogent reconstruction of clear rational vision as "a result of moral imagination and moral effort" (Murdoch, 1970, 37). The will is not an arbitrary movement, and man is not a combination of impersonal rationality and personal will (*ibid.*, 40-41).

There is need for a true and authentic coming-to-terms with the totalitarian alternative of human existence at the level of the philosophy of politics. This involves conceiving human rights on the basis of a new synthesis of post-totalitarian perspectives in respect to the intrinsic union of individuals, community, the spiritual and moral tradition of "caring for the soul," and the institutions of the liberal democratic state. Such a conception of human rights and democracy is necessarily anchored in an essential unity of the spiritual-moral and public spheres of human existence, and it decidedly involves a hierarchy of values that revives the original meaning of the natural law.

JAN PATOČKA

The present impasse facing liberal conceptions and the one-sided arguments of the communitarian critique of liberalism demand a profound philosophical reflection upon the issues at stake. The current literature contains references both to this obvious necessity as well as to its orientation, which originate from the intrinsic nature of the everyday human experience that always precedes contemporary utilitarian culture (Paparrigopoulos, 1995). In particular, the recent development of the Czech tradition of political philosophy has outlined a valid conception and elaborated a viable terrain that comprise an appropriate response to that demand. This can be found in Jan Patočka's conception of the Third Fundamental Movement of human life, which is a philosophical restoration of the unity of human freedom and responsibility. This conception depends fundamentally on an individual's decision concerning whether one will disperse and lose personal integrity in particulars, or retrieve and realize oneself in terms of a genuine relation to other beings, the universe and one's own life. The latter involves a radical reorientation of one's life towards other lives: if an individual human life is lived according to its finality, the natural end of such a self-retrieval consists in self-devotion to others.

In this way, Patočka indicates a lifeworld sociality that is rooted in the shattering of the seemingly unshakable Second Fundamental Movement of human life, that alienated human beings from each other by self-extension of life through endless provision, competition and defence (Patočka, 1989, 280-284; Patočka 1970, 228; Patočka 1980, 1.2.190). This is the source from which arises Patočka's moral philosophy and his conception of human rights in the spirit of a phenomenological recovery of the natural law. Patočka writes:

> No society, no matter how well-equipped it may be technologically, can function without a moral foundation, without convictions that do not depend on convenience, circumstances or expected advantage. Yet the point of morality is to assure not the functioning of a society but the humanity of humans. Humans do not invent morality arbitrarily, to suit their needs, wishes, inclinations and aspirations. Quite the contrary, it is morality that defines what being human means.

From this perspective, the very concept of a "Pact on Human Rights" implies:

> that even states, even society as a whole, are subject to the sovereignty of moral sentiment: that they recognize something unconditional that is higher than they are, something that is binding even on them, sacred, inviolable, and that in their power to establish and maintain a rule of law they seek to express this recognition. This conviction is present in individuals as well, as the ground for living up to their obligations in private life, at work and in public. The only genuine guarantee that humans will act not only out of greed or fear, but freely, willingly, responsibly, lies in this conviction (Patočka, 1989, 341).

This philosophical insight reveals the verifiable and decisive reality that the very existence of the human being, society and the state stands and falls with its non-instrumental, spiritual and moral basis. The Czech tradition of the philosophy of politics has thus succeeded in grasping as a whole and clearly defining the authentic source and the decisive context of human dignity. The core of the possibility for a fundamental movement in both the private and public dimensions of human life is the verifiable recognition of their common unconditional end in terms of a transcending validity. Accordingly, the philosophical-religious and ethical reality of the natural law reappears disquietingly, but no less legitimately, at the centre of the philosophy of politics.

The problem of how to conceive of the comprehensive public good, which liberal philosophers and political economists since Thomas Hobbes have evaded, has once again been placed on the agenda, now with an imperative urgency due to the experience of totalitarianism. The frequent liberal flights into allegedly reliable mechanisms for maintaining social peace by means of generating prosperity have always failed in the long run. The reason is obvious: private, calculating interests lack the genuine prudence that can never be replaced by any social engineering (Sullivan, 1982, 29, 171). The original Aristotelian meaning of prudence consists of knowledge and purpose in bringing about what is unquestionably the best and most fair political order. It also involves real attainability, prevailing validity and absolute measure, i.e., measure which is not established according to concrete circumstances. The original notion of constitutional republican democracy (*politeia*) meets the basic assumption that civic freedom and equality comprise a permanent struggle for the virtuous life in terms of recognized natural law (Bluhm, 1962, 750-753). There is obvious need that these ideas, including the concept of human rights, must be restored. Together they comprise the authentic alternative both to the extreme totalitarian challenge of the 20th century, and also to mainstream, spiritually indifferent liberalism, including "post-modernism" as its offspring.

Different conceptions of power apply in these latter cases. Concerning liberalism and the post-modernism that arises from it, there is also an emphasis on freedom as the occasional absence of obligation in respect to any concrete purpose or end (Taylor, 1979, 177; Skinner 1986, 193-221). The present post-modernist inclination towards the definition of power as a diffusion without origin belongs to this same category. Its postulate that power is of an exclusively local nature represents a one-sided reception of the present exponential growth of diversity in communication during our technological era. Adherents of the "post-modern" view of the world supply merely directives and speculations about "strategies of survival" that lack virtually any normative responsibility. The only permissible, universally valid response they admit is the imperative of pluralistic justice, i.e., the command to maximize and multiply small narratives to the greatest possible extent (Lyotard and Thébaud, 1985, 59, 87; White, 1991, 132-38). The origin of the "post-modernist" inclination for this dogma of a false infinity of pluralistic otherness is the recurrent phenomenon of the original human entanglement with the neutrality of being, with its essential confusedness that always offers the comfortable recourse of routine in daily life (Patočka, 1980, 3.4.29; Patočka, 1990, 111). "Post-modernist" dogmatism basically represents a half-hearted modern regression to the level which precedes the understanding "that there is another possibility or possibilities of how to live than, on the one hand, toil for a full stomach . . . and, on the other, orgiastic occasions in public and private" (*ibid.*).

"Post-modern" philosophical claims are in principle in no position to transcend the originally positivist attitude towards philosophical thinking. This by no means entails, however, that it is not appropriate to strive for such a transcending of the modern situation. In our present times, the modern vision of life and of the world culminates in a technological civilisation which is based upon the general release of force and the ensuing universal being-subject-to-force, including the extreme option of totalitarian regimes that clearly ruptured the Western spiritual tradition.

It is without a doubt impossible to proceed beyond the modern tradition as it has existed until now simply by postulating that it is possible to do so; a demonstration of its evident legitimacy must be provided. In order to gain an appropriate insight into the legitimacy of distancing oneself from this tradition, it is first absolutely necessary to attain a thorough understanding of the grounds of its origins and of its subsequent development. In other words, it is necessary that its objective *raison d'être* be revealed. Only to the extent that a thoroughgoing insight is attained into the modern tradition, including its perspective upon the world and the whole of human life and the activities which may follow from it, will it be possible to go beyond the limits of that dominant tradition.

It is necessary to acknowledge the preceding spiritual tradition of modernity in its entirety and authentic essence, not merely in certain of its particular features or factors. The contemporary wave of declarative philosophical post-modernism, along with its accompanying congenial multi-culturalism, is in no position whatsoever to meet this call. That is why such philosophical post-modernism is incapable of giving rise to a genuine post-modernism; that is, to a verifiable breakout from the objectivising subject-object position that has reached its zenith in the present era of a universal, exponentially increasing release of force.

A philosophically grounded and truly post-modern project that overcomes the horizons of the preceding spiritual tradition, including the technological culmination of modernity, is rather to be found in the approach and attitude adopted by Patočka. This approach displays a self-consistent and radical understanding of the principle of *logos* within the determining context of *appearing-as-such* conceived of as the authentic origin of both Western spirituality and the fundamental movements of life. This gives rise to an essential revision of Heidegger's philosophical position of Being, as well as all subsequent levels of philosophical reflection. Patočka thus rehabilitates the problem of truth as the appearing of beings-in-themselves, an appearing which takes place within the phenomenological life-world on its ontologically corporeal, intersubjective, historical and accordingly political level of existence. Stated otherwise, "a self-consistent and thoroughgoing phenomenological reception of logo-centrism within the Western spiritual tradition gives rise to a genuine overcoming of the universal being-subject-to-force that characterizes the contemporary developmental tendency of the modern subject-object position" (Patočka, 1979, 159, 211-214).

Patočka's account of the principle of *appearing-as-such* emphasizes the not-matter-of-course nature of reality and, consequently, its inherent natural enigma. This in principle makes possible unbiased communication with non-Western, non-European cultural spheres as, *mutatis mutandis*, communication with other human beings as such. The phenomenological ontology of the lifeworld thus penetrates behind the limits of the preceding development of metaphysics through realization of the foundational metaphysical position of insight into its ultimate spiritual, ethical, and political consequences.

In regard to the ultimate phenomenological basis of *appearing-as-such*, which presents the only possibility for comprehending latency, one can hardly imagine a deeper precondition than an insightful life directed towards its own fulfillment. This crucial life-orientation could be defined as faith in terms of a religious attitude determining the temperament of life. The strength and inevitability of this position follows from the obvious fact that it is humanly impossible continuously to endure the plenitude of appearing-as-such that represents the ultimate stage of insight. Consequently, the principle of an indispensable logo-centrism is to be complemented by the principle of a religious attitude of faith that arises from the ultimate insight into appearing-as-such.

The religious principle as the human orientation towards insight into *appearing-as-such* is in basic accord with Patočka's Third Fundamental Movement in human life, and it perhaps makes the latter more precise. In this sense, the authentic phenomenon of religion appears as living in the truth of caring for one's soul on the level of an explicit surpassing of the modern project of life and world. It is a genuine transcendence of the non-technological essence of technology as the total release of force. From the point of view of human being-with-others, this can be seen as an expression of the original concept of Masaryk of religious democracy as a correlation of eternal souls in a style of life oriented towards God (Ludwig, 1937, 62-72, 217). Today this has special topical importance because of the ongoing encounter with the extreme, totalitarian alternative type of human existence that is breaking down the whole of Western civilisation.

The elementary democratic claim that human rights speak for themselves, that they be heard and that what is spoken be explicitly applied in the time and space of shared human life must have a solid philosophical foundation. This is especially so today after the destructive experience of a not entirely understood, and in fact unfinished, struggle of democratic civilisation against the totalitarian challenge. The results to date of the continuing polemic between neo-liberalism and communitarianism obviously do not meet this demand. However, the development of the Czech tradition of political philosophy in the course of the 20th century does seem to present one possible philosophical resolution of this crucial problem. This solution results in a reinterpretative renewal of the leading position of natural law in democratic political philosophy. The strength and future prospect of the idea of democracy and human rights does not reside in ideology, Utopia or some mere vacillation between them (Dunn, 1992, 265-266). Nor it is fair to circumvent the question of the Common Good by defining it as the common power of opposing forces while refusing to grasp it within the horizon of moral virtue (Kouba, 1995). The verifiable coherence of philosophy, religion, ethics, human rights and democracy is to be defined with all the pertinent risks instead of being avoided in a half-hearted fashion.

Institute of Philosophy
Czech Republic Academy of Sciences
Prague, Czech Republic

NOTES

1. This is a topical interpretation of an idea that Jan Patočka originally employed in another context. See Patočka 1990, 111.
2. See also St. Mathew's Gospel, 7, 12, and St. Luke's Gospel 6, 13.
3. A typical example is Aristotle, *Rhetoric*, 1373 b.
4. Also see d'Entreves 1967, 50-54; Henry 1995.

REFERENCES

Aristotle (1940). *Rhetoric*. In *The Works of Aristotle*, trans. J.A. Smith and W.D. Ross. London: Oxford University Press.

Augustinus Aurelius, "Enarr. in Ps. LVII", 7.

Bluhm, Wm. T. (1962). "The Place of the 'Polity' in Aristotle's Theory of the Ideal State." *The Journal of Politics*, No. 94, 743-753.

Coke, Ed. (1957). In Edward S. Corwin. *"Higher Law." Background of American Constitutional Law*. Ithaca, NY (reprint of 1928 edition; original from late 1760s).

d'Entreves, A.P. (1967). *Natural Law*. London: Hutchinson University Library.

Dunn, J. (ed.) (1992). *Democracy, the Unfinished Journey*. Oxford: Oxford University Press.

Gambles, I. (1995). "The Forgetting of the Cold War." *The National Interest*, No. 41, 26-35.

Grotius, H. (1925). *De Iure Belli ac Pacis*. Washington, D.C.
Hegel, G.W.F. (1972). "Ueber die wissenschaftlichen Behandlungsarten des Naturrechts, seine Stelle in der praktischen Philosophie, und sein Verhältnis zu den positiven Rechtswissenschaften." In G.W.F. Hegel. *Jenaer Schriften*, ed. Gerd Irrlitz. Berlin, DDR: Akademie-Verlag.
Heineman, R. (1994). *Authority and the Liberal Tradition*, 2d ed. New Brunswick, NJ: Transaction Publishers.
Henry, C.F.H. (1995). "Natural Law and Nihilistic Culture." *First Things*, No. 49, 54-60.
Johnson, P. (1995). "Freedom. Taking Account of Human Nature." *Crisis* (March), 19-24.
Kirk, R. (1994). "A Lecture on Natural Law." *Policy Review* 69, 77-82.
____. (1993). "The Meaning of Justice." *Heritage Lectures* 457. Washington, D.C.: The Heritage Foundation.
Kurth, J. (1995). "If Men Were Angels . . ." *The National Interest*, No. 40, 3-12.
Kouba, P. (1995). "Vule k politice" ("Will to Politics"). *Kritický sborník*, 1-2, 16.
Locke, J. (1958). *The Reasonableness of Christianity*, ed. I.T. Ramsey. Stanford: Stanford University Press.
Lowi, T.J. (1979). *The End of Liberalism*, 2d ed. New York: W.W. Norton.
Ludwig, E. (1937). *Duch a cin* (*Spirit and Action — Conversations with Masaryk*). Prague: Drustevní práce.
Lyotard, J.-F. and Jean Loup Thébaud (1985). *Just Gaming*. Minneapolis: University of Minnesota Press.
Mouffe. C. (ed.) (1992) *Dimensions of Radical Democracy*. New York: Verso.
Murdoch, I. (1970) *The Sovereignty of Good*. London: Routlege and Kegan Paul.
Paparrigopoulos, Xenophon (1995) "Theories of Justice: Past and Present." Paper from the Symposium "Greek Philosophy and Czech Thinking." Prague, November 20.
Patočka, J. (1990) *Kacírské eseje o filosofii dejin* (*Heretical Essays on the Philosophy of History*). Prague: Academia.
____. (1989) *Philosophy and Selected Writings*, ed. Erazim Kohák. Chicago and London: The University of Chicago Press.
____. (1980) *Přirozený svet a pohyb lidské existence* (*The Life-World and the Movement of Human Existence*), vol. I. Prague

(samisdat).

_____. (1970) *Přirozený svet jako filosofický problém* (*The Life-World as a Philosophical Problem*). Prague: Ceskoslovenský spisovatel.

_____. (1972) *Platon a Evropa* (*Plato and Europe*), vol. 2. Prague (samisdat).

Sinopoli, R.C. (1992) *The Foundations of American Citizenship*. New York and Oxford: Oxford University Press.

Skinner, Q. (1986) "The Idea of Negative Liberty: Philosophical and Historical Perspectives." In Richard Rorty, J. B. Schneewind, and Quentin Skinner (eds). *Philosophy in History*. Cambridge: Cambridge University Press.

Sullivan, Wm. M. (1982) *Reconstructing Public Philosophy*. Berkeley: University of California Press.

Taylor, Ch. (1979) "What's Wrong with Negative Liberty." In A. Ryan (ed.). *The Idea of Freedom*. Oxford: Oxford University Press.

Walzer, M. (1989) *Spheres of Justice*. Oxford: Blackwell.

White, S.K. (1991) *Political Theory and Postmodernism*. Cambridge: Cambridge University Press.

Wooten, D. (ed.) (1993) *Political Writings of John Locke*. New York: Mentor.

CHAPTER IV

LIBERALISM AND LIBERAL DEMOCRACY: PARADOXES AND PUZZLES

JOSEPH MARGOLIS

DEMOCRATIZATION

I trust it is not too late to enter a political demurer against the spread of democracy from the United States and Western Europe to Eastern Europe and Asia — and perhaps Africa, Central and South America and, beyond, to any lands that have not been mentioned. Talk of "democracy" is something of a coded discourse linked (nowadays) to facilitating access to, and enlargement of, new investments, trade, spheres of power, normalized markets and the price of admission to all that is ticketed as the endorsement of certain forms of representative government and security of property and person. I am not opposed to such measures as a matter of principle; but the easy spread of "democracy" masks its inevitable deformation. We have now, at the end of the century, entered a phase of recolonizing the world that we cannot fully fathom. "Democracy" is pretty nearly its political currency, just as English is its lingua franca. I make its beginning approximately from the end of the Gulf War, when, in a candid moment, the American President, George Bush, proclaimed, "We've won!" by which I understood him to have meant, in effect, that the world would henceforth find itself drawn, more and more explicitly, to trade in the two currencies just mentioned, in ways favorable to the imperial interests of the United States.

Of course, it would be a mistake to exaggerate the importance of the Gulf War. It could not possibly have had the significance I assign it if the World War II had not turned out as it did, if the resources of defeated Germany and Japan had not been recruited by the Western democracies, if the Soviet empire had not been dismantled, if American political and economic power had not been adequately sustained, if the oil states had not remained weak clients of the West, and if there had not been a nearly total dearth of fresh political vision and debate during the last 50 years of the post-War world. The looming importance of China and neighboring "lesser" states has had almost no conceptual bearing on the political philosophies of the West: the notion of liberal democracy has, in an unprecedented way, become (partly by default, partly by convenience) the fatigued but well-nigh uncontested idiom of humane politics around the world. Tienanmen Square, for instance, is a metonymy for an uneasiness that seeks reassurance from China that its political and trading intentions will not violate a certain threshold of gathering global tolerance. It expresses itself in terms of strong human rights and the rights of dissidents, but that is surely a verbal deflection from its true concern. Similarly, in Saudi Arabia and Kuwait, where disputes about democracy make no sense at all, the best strategy is to produce as much silence on the matter as can be managed. By contrast, Eastern Europe is eminently — even willingly — permeable to the West, a kind of complicit membrane altering its old chemistry for the sake of politically untried nutrients that it cannot now refuse. The promise is that, on a selective basis, Eastern Europe may yet participate in the new dreamed-of hegemonies the West is contemplating.

But what of liberalism and democracy and liberal democracy and human values? If, within the terms of the strange graftings and inseminations now being tried out, it pays to reflect on older conceptual questions regarding the human condition, then I may have some well-worn conversation beads to share. These may be collected in two baskets. One draws attention to the unpredictable effects of applying the abstract forms of one tradition to the alien practices of another; the other draws attention to the late paradoxes and inflexibilities of the same forms applied, at home, to new puzzles that they cannot easily be made to fit. The two baskets are rightly judged to have a good deal in common, once it is observed that the alien applications of the first resemble the new native applications of the second. There is a need for care, here, because, however cynical we may choose to be about what liberal democracy has come to mean, we cannot entirely ignore the fact that we must make the best of our political life. *Faute de mieux*, we must consider what is normatively possible in the liberal tradition.

Let me put my instructional beads before you as openly as I can. I concede they are all quite banal. What redeems them is that they seem to have been — and continue to be — largely neglected. That also reduces, of course, the likelihood that they are merely arbitrary or idiosyncratic. (That's a gain and a distinct advantage.) Everything I have to say stems from the truism that liberal democracy is an unstable mix of disparate elements: liberalism and democracy point in entirely different directions; so much so that liberalism may well subvert particular political "democracies," and "democratic" states may have little or no interest in "liberal" norms and values.

What more I have to say depends on the supplementary truism that there cannot be an assured fit between the utopian or ideal claims of liberalism and democracy, or of liberal democracy, and the historical actualities of political life. If you add to these indisputable distinctions the problems, already acknowledged, of attempting to apply the abstracted regularities (along liberal or democratic lines), drawn from some home tradition, to a very different tradition, you may reasonably expect to collect all the strains of our late age pertinent to absorbing Eastern Europe within the protective mantle of the West. Once again, the successful exemplars of this strategy go back to the end of the World War II — to the deliberate "democratization" of Germany and Japan.

More recently, the same democratizing effort has been extended to a newly minted Russia, where one sees (more clearly than in Japan and Germany) the awkwardness and alien quality of the intended fit. The United States has, for years, been intoning the victorious truth that, except for Cuba, the Hispanimerican world is now substantially "democratic"; but that same pronouncement affords fair warning that the criteria in question cannot fail to be distinctly relaxed. It could not be otherwise, if you reflect on the paradoxes of liberal democracy in the United States itself. And, of course, if you think of the meaning of the verdict when applied to Haiti or Guatemala (or Bosnia), you see the sense in which it pays to be as clear as possible about our supposed principles and what might count as their right application.

IMCONGRUITIES OF LIBERALISM AND DEMOCRACY

Consider the following incongruities, then. Liberalism is not initially occupied with the structure of any political state or government; democracy is essentially a form of government. Liberalism is primarily a theory of normative individual life; democracy is primarily a descriptive category: it need not be normative at all; and where it is it may (as with Rousseau) be read in collectivist as easily as individualist terms. In its classical Western forms (Enlightenment, Kantian, Habermasian, Rawlsian), liberalism is ahistorical, committed to an essentially changeless or species-specific model of reason apt for discerning the proper norms of human life; democracy is little more than a taxonomic category for a family of historically limited, very different exemplars in the ancient and modern world. Again, when democracies (in the modern sense) are pointedly construed as committed to the protection of human rights (or of positive rights approximating to human rights), democracy becomes a very different hybrid structure — a "liberal democracy" — which diminishes the collectivist or communitarian forms of "democracy" and ambiguously disallows applying the term to states that fail to feature individual human rights in certain formal (constitutional) respects (for instance, so-called "Confucian democracies"). Finally, liberalism — *a fortiori*, liberal democracy — is a utopian or ideal conception, whereas democracy is normally not utopian at all, no more than a procedural or descriptive conception. This last distinction bears in an important way (as we shall see) on some of the more baffling paradoxes of "democracy" and "liberal democracy."

Now, it is entirely possible to construe liberalism merely ideologically. On that reading, there would be no point to a philosophical defense of the American Declaration of Independence or its constitutional application in the Bill of Rights (appended to the American Constitution) or the French Declaration of the Rights of Man. But that would be absurd, seeing how important and controversial such documents are: we cannot possibly ignore the question of their legitimation, if we regard their validity as separable from the local historical times in which they were formulated. Nevertheless, the prospects must be slim indeed, now at the end of the century. For there is hardly a plausible defense of the double claim (whether theoretical or practical), viz. : (i) that human nature or human reason is changeless over history, and (ii) that natural or practical reason is apt for determining the objective norms of human life--in particular, essential human rights.

No doubt the theory has considerable appeal as well as a prudential and notably humane use. But is the doctrine valid? To insist that it is would signify that all those who deny the rational or ontic validity of the claim — even if they were willing to support positive rights — would be backing a demonstrably false claim, possibly a necessarily false claim. That certainly seems unlikely.

Notice that if liberal values were treated as artifacts of history, we could never legitimate liberalism in its classic form. For, if it were historicized, it could not be changeless; there would be little reason to suppose that the different forms of enculturing "human nature" would effectively converge to support any single or any favored set of changeless norms. It would be implausible to suppose that societies with very different histories from those of our would-be exemplars could straightforwardly accommodate full liberal values, except on very loose, very dubious grounds or at very considerable cost to their own entrenched practices. The Czech Republic, for instance, might well be a more tractable candidate than, say, Russia or Bulgaria.

There is no compelling argument confirming the fixity of practical reason or its capacity to discern or decide the universal validity of liberal norms (or, for that matter, any alternative such values). At the end of our century, the project has been called into fundamental question. There is no assured changeless structure of humanity or its changeless norms! The sheer variety of the world beggars its pretensions. The Hegelian critique of Kant (and the companion critique of Hegel) still stands: that is, first, that any purely formal version of universalizability (the Kantian view) can be made to support any internally consistent policy; and, second, that if the norms of practical reason are culturally variable, the very search for universal norms must be misguided or mischievous.

Of course, theorists like Jürgen Habermas and John Rawls, the current champions of liberalism, have succeeded in capturing versions of the generic liberal doctrine. But they cannot legitimate their own ideologies. Eastern Europe, attracted to one or another form of compliance with the West's hegemony, can hardly pretend that whatever "version" it may favor could possibly legitimate its moral "choice" by "rational" means or by reference to its counterpart history.

What is the implication of all this? Certainly, at least our practical norms cannot be entirely independent of the *sittlich* structures of our history and that history cannot be enough to those or any norms. To suppose the *sittlich* requires no further justifying rationale than would instantly obviate the entire legitimative question. As soon as one acknowledges the consensual support of Nazism and Stalinism, one sees the difficulty for any ideology, no matter how popular.

We must concede the following, then: (i) there are no evident, "natural," neutral, objective, universalized, essential or necessary norms of moral and political life; (ii) there are also no plausible grounds for promoting political revisions that are not legibly grounded in our *sittlich* sources; and (iii) there is no way to admit (i) and (ii) that would justify construing the legitimation of our liberal norms as any less improvisional or any more reliable than our original *sittlich* norms. The upshot of accepting (i) - (iii) is tantamount to accepting Plato's advice (in *Statesman*) that political and legislative visions and reforms, whether utopian or not, can never be more than "second-best."

Any neutral vision of essential human nature is beyond our powers and utterly meaningless. If so, then liberalism and democracy must submit to the same verdict. That political norms are "second-best" — no more than second-best — signifies (in Plano's terms) that they can never be confirmed by reference to the eternal Forms of what is good and right or the fixed essence of human nature or human reason. There cannot be any uniquely correct way of proceeding in human affairs; and whatever we judge to be a fair revision of our political practice cannot fail to depend on some projection from the same sources from which the questioned norms had originally issued.

We are not at an impasse here, however; the verdict is neither circular nor paradoxical. It simply diminishes the presumption of political and moral philosophy. Would-be "applicant" societies from Eastern Europe and elsewhere are hereby forewarned.

LIBERALISM AS UNIVERSAL

Beyond all this, there are difficulties of a more insistent gauge. They return us to what I had earlier dubbed two "baskets" of political beads. One concerns liberalism as such; the other, liberal democracy.

Each bears on the reasoned critique of acknowledged liberal societies as well as societies that aspire to be liberal by dint of a considerable transformation; but they do so in two entirely different ways. One draws attention to puzzles that lie beneath the level at which liberalism normally functions; the other draws attention to unforeseen complexities that go beyond the expected range of liberal policy. Their joint admission suggests that liberalism and liberal democracy may yet prove to be transient forms of wider political conceptions that have not sufficiently congealed to attract us in their service. Merely to broach the possibility is to suggest that the improvisational art by which societies claim to confirm their democratic or liberal credentials — now at the end of the century, when every society aspires (on the optimistic argument: George Bush's, for example) to be liberal or democratic or both — signifies that the new alliances that the next century will permit or require may be better served by alternative inventions that we have still to hit on. The history of Western liberalism and democracy may actually be too shallow, too confined, to guide us plausibly in the next age.

There are some examples of the characteristic inflexibilities of liberal theory drawn from recent American political experience. In offering them, I mean to encourage application (by analogy) to the local practices of somewhat alien aspirant societies (Poland and Hungary, say) that must look to their own *Sitten* for similar potential complications.

It may come as a surprise to Europeans, for instance, that the notorious Rowe v. Wade decision of the American Supreme Court favoring abortion rights for women does not actually address the abortion issue directly in terms of fundamental human rights. It could not, according to the formalities of liberal thought! The curious reason is this: there is (and can be) no admissible way — as matters now stand in the United States — to defend abortion rights as such. One must subsume them, *qua* rights, under a guise that has nothing to do with the abortion question. The trouble with the defense of abortion as a possible fundamental right is that its defense would have to make reference to the biological differences between men and women; but that would mean construing the rights doctrine in terms of sub-species-wide distinctions. On the usual Constitutional interpretation, that would "signify" denying the equality doctrine!

As a consequence, the defense of abortion in Rowe v. Wade is crafted in terms of an individual's (any individual's) right to privacy! Which is to say, crafted in a way that ignores the biological complexities of pregnancy and abortion in order, precisely, to make it possible to defend it on liberal grounds.

Similarly, in the 1996 Presidential, Congressional, and state-wide elections in the United States, a certain referendum (known as Proposition 209) passed in California, which, it is claimed, effectively repudiates all forms of so-called "affirmative action" — which is to say, all public policies that seek to restore a measure of politically effective equality in the face of extreme inequality among the races and between men and women in terms of educational and economic opportunity. The defeated corrective practices proceeded by way of "reverse discrimination": by introducing "corrective" inequalities meant to dislodge deeper forms of resistance to equality. The referendum therefore does concede longstanding *de facto* inequalities but adopts a "strict" or utopian view of the rights doctrine — which effectively thwarts its own realization and is known to do so.

What you see here is an unavoidable dilemma: in the name of basic rights, proposition 209 has the effect of stiffening resistance to the actual recovery of equality. It makes the inequality of rights invisible to the political eye, and it actually defeats the correction of inequalities by the use of the rights doctrine. There seems to be no way to break out of these reversals, once we admit a principled disjunction between abstract rights and quotidian politics.

Liberalism and liberal democracy are completely utopian conceptions. They defeat their own political purpose when "strictly" applied. If, then, you think to extend the rights doctrine to the treatment of homosexuals, or in support of assisted suicide for the terminally ill, or for the special treatment of genetically impaired offspring, or even (less controversially) to reduce poverty, to provide for medical needs, to make education affordable, you begin to see that the rights doctrine cannot be relied on (cannot even be strategically adjusted) for the new contests that are taking form.

All this has to do with sub-species-wide distinctions. The trouble is that, now, at the end of the 20th century, there are fewer and fewer contests that are likely to confirm the adequacy of the strictest forms of liberalism. I have no wish to deny the immense humanity historically codified in documents like the American Bill of Rights and the French Declaration of the Rights of Man. Constraints against arbitrary imprisonment, torture, confiscation of property and conviction for crimes without benefit of trial cannot fail to remain among the permanent targets of enlightened states. The paradigms are reasonably in place. But, plainly, on the argument offered, there is no reliable prospect that further constitutional formalisms of the same sort can be extended to the newer disputes — about abortion, gay rights, assisted suicide, euthanasia, racial and gender equality — or to come to the most telling challenge, the elimination of the enormous global inequalities involving the control and use of the material goods of the earth. These obviously escape the resources of the rights doctrine and rely almost entirely on captive perceptions of justice.

Consider, for instance, of the internment of United States citizens of Japanese origin during the World War II, nor is there need to draw parallels to recent Bosnian history. The point is simply that if, say, Eastern Europe has had, as indeed it has, an altogether different constitutional history from that of the United States and Western Europe (allies in the Second War), then whatever may be made of liberalism and liberal democracy in Eastern Europe will be more a function of *sittlich* habits and the drive to recover power, under altered circumstances, than of utopian or constitutional intentions.

LIBERALISM AND THE HISTORICAL SITUATION

You may see this as cynicism, but it is not. For, on the one hand, there is no principled defense of any essentialist or rationalist version of liberalism; and, on the other, there are plausible ways of recovering something of the values and more that the liberal tradition has regularly favored, without attempting to restore putatively necessary rights. The doctrine of "unalienable" human rights belongs to the intellectual ethos of the Enlightenment. At a certain moment in history, the overthrow of the privileged estates plausibly led to the doctrine of universal reason and essential human rights. That is certainly what marks Kant's important standing in the liberal tradition — and marks it still in the philosophically dampened ("heroic") liberalisms of Habermas and Rawls two centuries later.

Yet, already in the eighteenth century, the comparative linguistic and anthropological inquiries that attracted Humboldt had fatally questioned the fixity of human nature; the intuitions of Rousseau had found an insuperable paradox at the very heart of democratic doctrine — *a fortiori*, at the heart of the radical individualism that liberal democrats would never dislodge. By the end of the eighteenth century, de Maistre had already attacked the pure fiction of essential "man" in the Declaration of the Rights of Man appended to the French constitutions of the 1790s; and the very concept of democracy (that is, the "identity" of rulers and ruled) would henceforth be obliged to shuttle between *les volontés de tous* and *la volonté générale*.

There is a sense in which democracy need not be liberal at all — the sense in which, following the perception of figures like Karl Schmitt and Heidegger, the World War II, as well as the struggle between the Soviet empire and the West, might reasonably be construed as two phases of the same contest between radically opposed visions of democracy! The possibility is all but absent from the American political horizon.

When, after the Gulf War, President Bush pronounced his fateful finding, "We've won!" he had no idea of the deeper "communitarian" pressures "democracy" would bring to bear on the supposedly stable elite liberal democracies of the West. He did not realize — in general, Americans do not realize — that the sheer mobility and mingling of diverse ethnic peoples (having few, if any, historical ties to 18th century liberalism) would, as immigrants, threaten to drown the individualistic model of liberalism (and liberal democracy) in a sea of multicultural forces.

The point is this: there is no accessible liberal canon for accommodating in our time the collective "entitlement" of multicultural— would-be communitarian— democracies within the terms of liberal democracy itself. The idea is an oxymoron. The only option liberal democrats admit is one of temporizing, of assimilating ethnic populations by political reduction (the "melting pot"). If the human rights doctrine holds, they believe, then immigrant populations— Pakistanis, Cubans, Haitians, Mexicans, Palestinians, Koreans, Cambodians, Russians, Nigerians, Chinese, Vietnamese, Turks, Serbs, Sikhs and Amerindians— must bring their local *Sitten* into compliant accord with the conditions of entitlement regarding essential rights. That means the new immigrants must subordinate their ethnic solidarity to individualism. But they are resisting more effectively than ever before.

We already have seen the weakness and inflexibility of the natural rights doctrine as well as the ambiguity of what to count as democracy. Political prudence could hardly fail to favor communitarian interests. Now, notably in the "English-speaking" world, we face the prospect of accelerating forms of immigration that favor the forces of ethnic solidarity, favor values hitherto unfamiliar with, and to, political liberalism, convictions that cannot fail to challenge or obscure, even if innocently, every liberal effort to extend the rights struggle beyond the usual scope of 18th and 19th century events, movements that increasingly pit the forces of "communitarian" democracy against the forces of liberal democracy. So the prophetic tensions of the French Revolution are, for the third time in the twentieth century, gathering for an unheard-of struggle for global hegemony. It is in that setting that the advocates of liberal democracy contemplate the local extension of their favored order throughout Eastern Europe — through the whole world, if possible.

The novelty of the present practice of liberalism in the United States — by all odds the most extreme champion of liberal democracy — lies with its deliberately intruding the human rights doctrine, however opportunistically enlarged and distorted, into all its dealings regarding international trade. Recall the Contras's adventure in Nicaragua; the embargo on Cuba; the attempt to use the dissident issue, state abortion policies, the prison labor question, in trade negotiations with China, when the obvious priorities lay with opening up Chinese markets to American exports. American liberalism has, now, in its latest phase, begun to experiment with enlarging its canon — most adventurously, in pressing the abortion issue (for instance, in shaping economic aid to India) — that reflects not so much the classic human rights issue as the politico-economic incorporation of *sittlich* or communitarian or even explicitly religious concerns. These maneuvers are only very dubiously connected with individual rights.

We need not make too much of particular episodes, of course. But the fact remains that, both in the United States and abroad, American liberalism is being increasingly interpreted in terms that depend on the same "communitarian" issues of American history (remember godless communism!) that Tocqueville had already noted at the beginning of the nineteenth century. Adding to this the import of new immigration patterns and the paradoxes of liberalism at home and one begins to see that the extreme individualism of the classic liberal thesis may not be able to withstand the onslaught of the ascendent forms of ethnic solidarity, without yielding ground at the close of the century.

It may be that the attempt of the Western liberal democracies to ensure their global standing politically and economically may oblige them to submerge more and more of their liberal convictions in the service of policies that are obviously "communitarian" in a hegemonic sense. The Europeans have always been more inclined in this direction than the Americans: that is surely the lesson of the World War II and the shifting fortunes of the old contests involving the Soviet empire. Now, at the end of the century, American liberalism begins to seem more and more arbitrary and parochial as well as more and more somnambulistically informed by its own peculiar *sittlich* solidarity. In any event, the international community is not likely to be hospitable if it can effectively resist American muscle.

It needs to be remembered that although human beings cannot be convincingly denied in our time some minimal measure of political protection regarding "life, liberty, and the pursuit of happiness" (or "property") , such provisions need not be cast in terms of "unalienable" rights or the individualistic language of liberalism. There are many other idioms in which positive rights or protections may be promulgated in states that enjoy a measure of uncoerced loyalty; yet that loyalty may have nothing to do with the peculiar essentialism invoked to legitimate liberal claims.

If you grant that much, you will see at once that there is nothing intrinsically sinister, politically, in the growing implausibility of classical liberalism. By the same token, "communitarian" thinking need not be strengthened by liberalism's decline if, by communitarian thinking, one means either (i) to endorse a genuinely collective "entity" having its own normative needs, interests or "rights"; (ii) to subordinate in a principled way the norms and values governing individual lives to the norms and values of collective entities; or (iii) to claim that there are rational or revealed grounds for championing either (i), (ii) or both. Communitarian provisions tend to be totalitarian (fascistic in extreme cases) wherever items (i)-(iii) are strongly favored. Still, so-called "Confucian democracies" (Singapore, for instance) are communitarian, lack a natural rights doctrine, provide humanely for individual citizens and subjects (at least on comparative grounds), without being fascistic.

Generally, such states are not fascistic when, in the deepest sense, communitarian matters are confined to predicative concerns. What that means, quite simply, is that collective properties are rightly assigned to aggregates of individual citizens or subjects. We must do the same when we attribute linguistic aptitudes to ourselves. There are no selves or persons but the apt members of *homo sapiens* who have suitably internalized the language and practices of their native societies. If so, then the denial of a "communitarian" dimension to human life is, effectively, the denial of human "nature" itself — the denial of that "second-natured" nature that emerges from our biological aptitudes and transforms them.

To admit selves and human nature, then, is to admit the endless diversity of *sittlich* life, without benefit of any essential norms by which political alternatives can be strictly shown to be right or wrong. Here we touch on the deepest stratum of the puzzle. For, if essentialism — in particular, an essentialism regarding political and moral norms — cannot he vindicated, then the regulative fixities of both liberal and communitarian democracy will be placed at risk. That is not to say that political habits will unravel, only that no modal legitimation will prove viable or even "possible".

The short argument is plain enough: give up Platonism among norms, and you will (as Plato remarks, in *Statesman*) be bound to fall back to a "second-best" state, that is, a state validated only by the frank construction and reconstruction of whatever norms our *sittlich* history deems "objective," "neutral," "reasonable," "rational" for a time. Liberalism is more vulnerable, here, than democracy, for there is no way to legitimate the first if Platonism is false. Any form of democracy may be legitimated, as a "second-best" state, if it can be legitimated at all. Hence, positive rights or positive protections can be equally managed by liberal and communitarian means. Nothing need be lost. What is lost is liberalism's pretension to be more than ideology. We now see that to be impossible. Hence, the drift toward 21st century history cannot be counted on to strengthen liberalism specifically. Its fortunes will be the fortunes of the global market.

LIBERALISM AND MULTICULTURALISM

I come now to a final set of puzzles. These have to do with the effect of trying to accommodate "multicultural" rights (or, more narrowly, collective or communitarian goods) within the terms of liberal democracy. Straight off, one realizes that, strictly speaking, there cannot be any collective rights within the terms of the classical formula; there would be a contradiction at once. Still, once we admit the *sittlich* standing of rights and norms — in effect, the artifactual "nature," the "second nature" of selves (or persons) — we see that the very institution of norms and values cannot fail to have a "communitarian" cast. The aporia goes to the very heart of human life: viewed predictively, individualistic norms are as communitarian as multicultural norms. They are *sittlich* in origin: they are norms claiming multicultural validity, pretending, by Platonist devices, to be grounded in something quite other than our collective practices. They could not otherwise claim independent standing. But the fact remains, we cannot possibly legitimate Platonist pedigrees.

The picture is a muddled one. For one thing, if selves are "second-natured," that is, first formed by submitting the infant members of *Homo sapiens* to the enculturing processes of a natural language — so that a self (a human subject or human agent) is the apt site, biologically individuated, for the exercise of certain collectively defined competences — then persons are individuals only by virtue of sharing collectively defined powers. That is already incompatible with a purely liberal ontology. Once granted, theorists as diverse as Hobbes and Locke and Jefferson and Kant and Mill and Rawls and Habermas may well have been summarily defeated.

Liberalism has no ontological validity: natural rights make no sense except when transmuted into positive rights, that is, when they are historically promulgated and enacted. But then, the success of a rights policy does not depend on the autonomy or normative fixity of reason, but on the convergence of historical critiques along prudential lines. If so, then there is no principled conflict between the doctrine of individual rights and the admission that rights have a *sittlich* source. But there is a conflict between the historicized grounds for actually advancing a rights policy and the liberal vision of the universalized neutrality by which reason necessarily endorses it. Philosophical liberalism is completely indefensible. Liberal democracy, however humane, is little more than a fictionalized political practice officially blind to the dynamics of actual political life.

Multiculturalism fares no better than liberalism. The presumption that there are or can be collective rights defined in multiculturalist terms, or communitarian goals that can function legally and politically, as liberal rights, is a conceptual monster. For one thing, to legitimate multiculturalist rights is to assign a veto power (in effect, an overriding right) to some determinate subpopulation within a states's jurisdiction, on the prior grounds of respecting its *sittlich* norms; secondly, there can be no autonomous or rational basis for favoring, as such, one contingent history over another; thirdly, the practice leads in the direction of the fascist possibilities of communitarianism; and, fourthly, it makes a shambles of any would-be critical review under which, democratically, *sittlich* norms might be reasonably altered.

Beyond that, multiculturalist rights cannot possibly be reconciled with liberal rights. Imagine for instance that the right of divorce were defended by an application of a liberal reading of the rights of freedom and privacy. (This mimics the abortion argument in the United States.) Might it not happen that an immigrant population religiously opposed to divorce might sue for the right to practice in accord with its own tradition and, as a consequence, for the right to forbid divorce among its own adherents? It is said, for instance, that the Catholic hierarchy in Poland has been campaigning for a reversal of the legal right of divorce. How could such a conflict possibly be countenanced in liberal terms? Surely, the game would play itself out in the same way with respect to abortion, suicide, physician-assisted suicide, euthanasia, homosexual marriage, separation of church and state.

There are hidden difficulties here. Liberal theorists tend to be "proceduralists" rather than "substantivists": that is, they believe that the advocacy of natural rights and a liberal conception of justice in no way commits a society to any substantive view of virtue or the good life. They think of liberalism as occupied with purely formal or procedural ("rational") goods serving every tolerable form of life. That explains the importance of Kant (of a blind loyalty to Kant) for the liberal cause; it is the point of convergence among the bestknown contemporary liberal theorists: Rawls and Ronald

Dworkin in the United States, Habermas and Karl-Otto Apel in Germany. It accounts for the liberal penchant for neutrality and objectivity.

But, of course, the paradoxes of liberalism betray the fiction: there is no determinate procedural payoff in supporting formal rights separated from actual history. That is the lesson one draws equally well from Hegel's *reductio* of Kant's Categorical Imperative and from the self-defeating features of American Constitutional policies on racial equality. Liberals are caught in a dilemma: they fear to countenance the relevance of history because they cannot then confirm any strict neutrality; and they cannot commit to any contingent vision of the good life, for then reason would be hostage to ideological contest.

In this one can see how the proceduralist reading of the liberal doctrine must have been particularly well-suited to the early "melting pot" conception of American democracy. It worked in a fashion because, for one thing, the diverse *sittlich* practices of immigrant peoples up to about the end of the World War II did tend to dissolve or yield in favor of liberal notions of rights and justice (which is not to confirm the actual victory of liberal values in the same period); and, secondly, because the *sittlich* values of the politically dominant subpopulation did, during the same interval, provide the effective ground for interpreting liberal doctrines. That has all changed now: liberal theory is confronted with its own paradoxes, under unforeseen circumstances; and immigrant populations can no longer be counted on to yield to the primacy of liberal values in the old way. The result is that, even in the United States, the potential conflict between liberal policies and *sittlich* actualities can no longer be ignored. Granting all that, the preposterousness of late German liberalism (Habermas's, preeminently: pure procedural justice, for instance) stares one in the face. Nothing seems to have been learned from the legal trickery surrounding the Reichstag fire! Humane theorists like Dworkin and Habermas cannot possibly be more than the innocent sports of a utopian imagination.

Nevertheless, liberals have, in recent years, attempted to incorporate multiculturalist norms into liberal theory itself. This is an honest effort, let it be said, admitting the import of recent immigrant patterns. The threatening racism of Britain and France and Germany can only be exacerbated by Common Market policies:

mounting unemployment at home can only count against absorbing "foreign visitors" (ethnic labor); the rising tide of Turks and Serbs and Bosnians and North Africans and Eastern Europeans threatens to alter permanently the *sittlich* salience of "native" populations in Western Europe in the same way the influx of Asian and Latin American immigrants threatens the *sittlich* balance of American life. There is surely no way to halt the trend. But that is precisely the blind spot of utopian liberalism.

Apart from the melting pot concept, liberalism has favored two distinct policies regarding the compatibility of multiculturalism and basic rights. All of the options are really broken-backed, however, since they all implicitly concede a potential conflict between "inalienable" rights and the survival of one or another form of cultural or ethnic solidarity. The inevitable failure of the undertaking — reconciling rights and ethnic survival — lies with the utopianisms of the supposed *sittlich* neutrality of the defense of natural rights policy and the prudential interests of the immigrant ethos. The truth is that the primacy of the rights doctrine requires the primacy of the historically associated *Sitten* of the population responsible for the first. There cannot be parity among the diverse "communities" that happen to have gathered together within a liberal democracy: on the liberal argument, the demands of "cultural survival" must yield to the requirements of fundamental rights; but, against the liberals, that cannot obtain unless the *sittlich* priorities that ensure such rights also take precedence, at least effectively. Theorists like Charles Taylor, therefore, who profess to favor liberal values but mean to reconcile such values with the survival of ethnic sub-societies within the compass of a liberal state (Québec, for instance, within Canada; possibly the Flemand and Walloon communities, within Belgium) do not quite grasp the potential conflict between such values. Where collective values prevail, liberalism (but not democracy) must give way; and where liberal values prevail, multiculturalism cannot but be subordinate to the other.

The multiculturalist policies of liberalism, therefore, run as follows: (i) give no quarter — the melting pot model; if immigrants can accept liberal rights and liberal justice, then fine; there is no other admissible accommodation: (ii) protect diversity as far as possible — but not more; priority goes entirely in the direction of the liberal notion; and (iii) admit parity between liberal and communitarian values — hence, admit that liberalism may have to yield to the needs of cultural survival.

The first is championed by Rawls and Habermas; the second, by Michael Walzer; and the third, equivocally, by Charles Taylor. The first is completely utopian; the second is politically realistic on the side of what is dominant in the *sittlich* way, but utopian on the neutrality of liberalism itself; and the third is unwilling to come to terms with conflicting priorities. In this regard, Taylor's deliberate avoidance of the central difficulty marks the insuperable weakness of the liberal's position in the face of a rising communitarian challenge. To acknowledge the validity of ethnic or cultural "survival" as a liberal right is a completely incoherent maneuver. No competent "communitarian" (Alasdair MacIntyre or Michael Sandel, for instance) would ever dream of bringing the two systems together.

It may be, therefore, that liberalism — or liberal democracy strictly conceived — is a hothouse doctrine that has seen its best inning and is likely to dwindle more quickly now than ever before. After all, the very concept of a self has undergone a fundamental change since the time of the French Revolution. The curious thing is, the English-language tradition in philosophy and politics has largely favored the notion of an autonomous, essentially ahistorical, reliably rational agent through the entire two centuries that have elapsed. If Hegel may be thought to have had liberal sympathies — or, more broadly, Enlightenment sympathies — then you must grant as well that Hegel also effectively historicized reason and human nature and, as a result, has obliged us to construe selves as cultural artifacts. The European tradition that runs from Hegel through Marx through Nietzsche through Dilthey through Heidegger through Horkheimer through Gadamer through Foucault has, in the post-Gulf War period, been largely set aside (for more fashionable or merely opportunistic liberal values), all the while its deeper collectivist and constructivist themes have prospered.

It is obvious, therefore, that if the culturally preformative dimension of human existence is not entirely abandoned in the foreseeable future, it is likely that its historicist and contingent implications will be recovered in due time. There is at least one essential truism that will surely dawn on us again: viz., universalism and historicism are incompatible — politically as well as philosophically. At the moment we are in that strange limbo in which a piece of the historicist conception has been detached from historicity itself, namely, the *sittlich* dimension of human life; so that Western theorists committed to something like democracy, if not liberalism proper — the communitarians: Taylor, Sandel, MacIntyre, possibly even Richard Rorty — are, ultimately, as ahistoricist as the liberals they oppose.

If, as many now foresee, the greatest market activity of the new century will be centered in Asia, then there can be no question that the contest between liberalism and democracy and between individualism and communitarianism will require a revival of historicist distinctions. For, insofar as the United States is now expected to take a leading role in East-West exchange (which, until very recently, had not been anticipated by Asia or Europe) the idiom of early 21st century political debate is bound to be a continuation of the idiom of the past. And then, the ideological reinvention of Eastern European countries along "liberal" or "democratic" lines is bound to define itself in terms of the paradoxes and puzzles of Western political history and theory. It is a good idea to travel with a map in hand.

Temple University
Philadelphia, Pennsylvania USA

REFERENCES

Dworkin, Ronald. (1978) "Liberalism." In Stuart Hampshire (ed.). *Public and Private Morality.* Cambridge: Cambridge University Press.

———. (1971) *Taking Rights Seriously.* Cambridge: Harvard University Press.

Foucault, Michel. (1977) "Nietzsche, Genealogy, History." In Donald F. Bouchard (ed.), Donald F. Bouchard and Sherry Simon (trans.). *Language Counter-Memory, Practice: Selected Essays and Interviews.* Ithaca: Cornell University Press.

Fraser, Nancy. (1989) *Unruly Practices: Power, Discourse, and Gender in Contemporary Social Theory.* Minneapolis: University of Minnesota Press.

Habermas, Jürgen. (1990) "Discourse Ethics: Notes on a Program of

Philosophical Justification." In Christian Lenhardt and Shierry Weber Nicholsen (trans.). *Moral Consciousness and Communicative Action*. Cambridge: MIT Press.

———. (1994) "Struggles for Religion in the Democratic Constitutional State." In Amy Gutmann (ed.). *Multiculturalism: Examining the Politics of Recognition*. Princeton: Princeton University Press.

———. (1996) *Between Facts and Norms: Contributions to a Discourse Theory of Law and Democracy*, trans. William Rehg. Cambridge: MIT.

Holmes, Stephen. (1993). *The Anatomy of Anti-liberalism*. Cambridge: Harvard University Press.

Kymlicka, Will. (1989) *Liberalism, Community, and Culture*. Oxford: Clarendon.

MacIntyre, Alasdair. (1984) *After Virtue*, 2nd ed. Notre Dame: University of Notre Dame Press.

Margolis, Joseph. (1986) *Pragmatism without Foundations: Reconciling Realism and Relativism*. Oxford: Basil Blackwell.

———. (1996) *Life without Principles: Reconciling Theory and Practice*. Oxford: Basil Blackwell.

Rawls, John. (1971) *A Theory of Justice*. Cambridge: Harvard University Press.

———. (1993) *Political Liberalism*. New York: Columbia University Press.

Rorty, Richard. (1989) *Contingency, Irony, and Solidarity*. Cambridge: Cambridge University Press.

Sandel, Michael. (1982) *Liberalism and the Limits of Justice*. Cambridge: Cambridge University Press.

———. (1984) "The Procedural Republic and the Unencumbered Self." *Political Theory*, XII.

Strauss, Leo. (1953) *Natural Right and History*. Chicago: University of Chicago Press.

Taylor, Charles. (1989) *Sources of the Self*. Cambridge: Harvard University Press.

———. (1994) "The Politics of Recognition." In Amy Gutmann (ed.). *Multiculturalism: Examining the Politics of Recognition*. Princeton: Princeton University Press. An expanded edition of Charles Taylor (1992). *Multiculturism and "The Politics of Recognition."* Princeton: Princeton University Press.

Walzer, Michael. (1994) "Comments." In Amy Gutmann (ed.). *Multiculturalism: Examining the Politics of Recognition*. Princeton: Princeton University Press.

CHAPTER V

VALUES, NORMS, INDIVIDUALS: MODERN AND/OR POST-MODERN
(Twenty Theses On Post-Totalitarian Individualism)

ASEN DAVIDOV

1. All of today's liberal or so-called developed democracies claim to guarantee each of their members the possibility of a healthy and happy, free, yet moral and religious life. There is nothing surprising in this fact since the problem of human rights is clearly defined as the very root of the drive of humankind for a happy society. The *Magna Charta* of 1215, which was forced upon King John by the English nobility, the *English Bill of Rights* of 1689, the *United States Declaration of Independence* of 1776 and the *United States Constitution* of 1787, the *French Declaration of the Rights of Man and Citizen* of 1789, and the European democratic revolutions of 1848 are but a few of the more prominent examples of this fact. Not the least of such examples are the democratic political structures of the 20th century and the respective, internationally acknowledged documents (such as those of the UN) that have provided a basis for efforts to build and maintain, all over the world, democratic societies based on the principles of happiness and freedom for everyone. All democratic ideologies maintain the principle that, limited as it may be, the individual's self-assertion is, in John Stuart Mill's terms, one of the elements of both society's and the individual's welfare, happiness and humanism.

THE INDIVIDUAL

2. "Totality *versus* Individuality," "Law *versus* Accident," "Necessity *versus* Arbitrariness," "Unquestioning Obedience *versus* Free Decision," "One Party's (or the One Leader's) Commands *versus* Free Will and Creative Activity," "Terror and Fear *versus* Mutual Trust and Tolerance," and so forth. All of these now seem natural. It has become commonplace in all types of anti-totalitarian

ideologies that the values and norms of individualism are both necessary preconditions for and the results of a genuinely humane and truly democratic society. It could hardly be otherwise since all types of totalitarianism share an immanent feature, namely, the either implicit or, which is the usual case, explicit suppression of the major possibilities for a free development of the components of a society from institutions through particular individuals. The goal is the creation of socially utilizable and completely "functional" persons lacking all individuality whatsoever. The type of personality that most conveniently fits a totalitarian regime has always been the one described by Theodor W. Adorno's team in the 1950s, the so-called authoritarian personality. This type of person is obediently submissive in regard to those who are "superior" and cruelly oppressive in regard to those who are "inferior."

3. But as Hannah Arendt has cogently shown, if one would speak in general of a totalitarian personality or mentality, one should keep in mind that one of its outstanding characteristics is its extraordinary ability to adapt and its absence of continuity. That is why a people's "forgetfulness" and inconstancy does not at all mean that they are "cured of the totalitarian delusion . . . the opposite might well be true." This is of extreme importance in regard to the building of an optimal model of democracy, since people could hardly attain genuine liberty but for historical memory (both social and individual). History lives through memory since, from a phenomenological point of view, memory *is* reality. A proverb says that those who strive to forget simply prolong their exile, and that the key to salvation is memory.

4. However, it is obvious that, in spite of the crucial role of freedom, freedom alone is not sufficient for progress in post-totalitarian liberation. First and foremost, unlimited freedom for *everyone* would prevent freedom for *all*. The so-called "free individuals" of the developed (liberal) democracies have been "formatted" by a long-term process of mutual agreements of various kinds (political, economic, social) that has placed limitations on each individual's freedom. To put it in Moses's words, there is no liberty without law. Every law, formal as it is, places limits upon individualism lest it turn into dangerous arbitrariness; it prevents individuals from breaking loose from all restraint. The latter would be a sure road to anarchy that would destroy all social institutions as well as the very

freedom of the individual.

5. One should add to the above-mentioned controversies certain new types which pervade developed (liberal) democracies and have recently become quite clearly visible, such as "Discipline *versus* Self-expression and willfulness," "Limitation *versus* Emancipation," "Social Justice *versus* Effectiveness," "Compromise *versus* Success," "Tolerance *versus* Prejudice," and so forth. The old problem of values and norms, of free activity and motivation, has thus taken a new form in the post-totalitarian situation. The problem here concerns the price individuals must pay to reach a way of being that would correspond to human dignity, to build their own *conditions humaines* and, by the virtue of this alone, to be deserving of them. The ideologies current in the post-totalitarian countries concerning modernization (liberalization, industrialization and so forth) have a "backward-looking" orientation in respect to "Western" patterns. In fact, they present models of yesterday rather than of today's Western developments (cf. G. Schoepflin). Because of this orientation, the current "modernization," "liberalization" and "Westernization" of East European countries faces the problem of avoiding certain shortcomings found in the historical evolution of Western (liberal democratic) values, ideas, ideals, motivational structures, institutions and so forth. Above all, as certain thinkers maintain, the human condition itself may well be characterized by an "incurable ignorance," leading to a lack of substantial progress in knowledge and thereby leaving always open "the road to serfdom" (Hayek). Moreover, late 20th century democracies, both old and young, ought to keep in mind the infernal experiences of both the Bolshevik and National-socialist types of totalitarian regimes, along with all the other dictatorships of our century. The latter have proven that individuality and freedom are quite fragile values. Stated otherwise, pluralism as it now exists may not provide a guarantee of individual freedom and civil liberties, and neither may democracy as such. It was quite clear even in the times of Plato and Aristotle that democracy, however it was understood, was but one of the many possible, and not one of the most stable, ways of governing society. Tragic witness to this truth is provided by this century's social-political transitions, both illegal (the Bolshevik overthrow of Kerensky's provisional government) and legal (the Nazi replacement of the Weimar Republic).

6. A new type of critique of ideology (*Ideologiekritik*) is indispensable. The too popular and too-pompous-to-be-true funerals of ideology have been products of wishful thinking which themselves comprise another ideology. Even followers of visions of the end of ideology, not to mention visions of the end of history, have to admit that ideology may start up again just as readily as it ended. Moreover, new ideologies, both anti-totalitarian and anti-anarchistic, may present alternative ways of building and maintaining democratic societies, and may also help in organizing *normal*, truly liberal politics. Without ideologies there would be no effective connection between, on the one hand, professionally elaborated ideas and revealed ideals however admirable and wise they may be, and, on the other, the mass consciousness that is the motivational sphere of the activities of individuals. Democracy and liberty "from above," artificial as they are, may well be a new kind of authoritarianism and dictatorship.

7. Insofar as *individualism* may be regarded as a leitmotif of liberal democratic discussion, it is crucial to place it once again in the limelight so that its metaphysical and ontological grounds can be elucidated theoretically. The notion of the autonomous and self-sufficient individual, which provides the horizon of liberal thought and shapes the core of political, moral, economic and cultural existence in a truly democratic society, implies that each person has equal value. In liberal literature, however, it is almost a commonplace that there are different types of individualism. Examples are John Dewey's distinction between the early 19th century's "abstract individual" and the individual of a "communal type," Hayek's "rationalistic individualism," which is seemingly false, and "true individualism," which fits well with the framework of market society. The point here is that the classical notion of the individual does not work today.

8. The *modern individual* has proven to be far from the classical ideals because the progress of modern society has made obsolete the values that were supposed to have provided the grounds for individual motivation. Reduction to the merely individual level of absolute sovereignty, full autonomy, desires, passions, responsibilities and personal good contradict the notion of public goods and the very institutions that are designed to introduce and maintain the liberal forms of social life. Moreover, it also contradicts certain basic norms of property values and the market economy. Along with the

freedoms of speech, association and access to information as necessary preconditions for an individual's self-aware involvement in communal decision making, the right to welfare could well be regarded as a basic "civil liberty." However, no individualist, classical or otherwise, would ever agree to include this right into the realm of the "genuine universal rights" of the individual, since its satisfaction may, more often than not, entail the abrogation of other rights of the individuals. At this point, the problem of human rights expands into a more metaphysical realm or, to be more specific, an *axiological* one.

VALUES

9. Value is a form in which human inter-relations in any society crystallize. The notions of values usually comprise visions of a moral, aesthetic and cognitive character, such as the place of human beings in the universe, the meaning of the world, the sense of human life, and conceptions of dignity, honor, beauty and truth. The realm of values also includes phenomena of *moral consciousness*, including concepts of good and evil, right and wrong, moral and immoral, justice and injustice, happiness and so forth. A given action has a moral meaning to the extent that it impacts, in one way or another, the social and cultural environment of a person, his or her community's activities and life. People regard actions that are in accordance with their moral principles as *good* and those which contradict them as *evil*. That is why moral actions may imply either functional or dysfunctional changes in the life of the person, all the way up to community on the broadest scale, and hence have social meaning. From this perspective, values play a *normative* role.

10. Norms may function either as social *frameworks*, that is, as *paradigms* for people's activity, or as *principles*, that is, as the *goals* or *ideals* of their activity. The former are necessary in regard to organizing social life, thus subsuming the private to the social; the latter act as inner drives, orientations and milestones for an individual's activities. Taken in their paradigmatic meaning, norms ensure the *normal* order, limitations, expectations and life of society. All types of institutions and so-called public opinion give it their sanction, by virtue of which they function as norms of an officious morality. Insofar as this normative paradigm is always of an external

character, insofar as it always intends to interiorize norms from without, all types of "ethicization" of social, political and economic spheres have proven unsuccessful. Two pertinent examples of such failures are the utopian *ethical-socialist* project of the Marburg neo-Kantians and the disastrous later attempts to "humanize" communism. The most radical post-Modernistic deconstruction of, along with everything else, the very notion of *normality* reveals only the relative content of the latter, which depends on the historical situation, traditions, mores, the stage of civilization and so forth. But it can never eliminate the *ideal* of normality as such. That is why the relativity which is thus revealed does not necessarily mean value relativism, moral nihilism or anything of the kind.

11. From an individualistic point of view, the Whole (the state or the collective, for example) is an intrinsic danger to a person's individuality. Despite the constant pressure of the former upon the latter (through an *interiorization* process), normative frameworks always face an inner resistance on the side of a person's sphere of values. Here lay the roots of the incessant, unabating tension between the individual and society. One may regard the respective conflicts as immanently tragic insofar as there is no individual beyond society, nor society beyond individuals. Marx's attempt to insert "sociality" into the very essence of human being turned out to be unsatisfactory and reductionist. See the *Sixth Thesis on Feuerbach*, in which Marx states: "Feuerbach resolves the essence of religion into the essence of man. But the essence of man is no abstraction inherent in each single individual. In its reality it is the ensemble of social relations." This approach was a complete failure in light of both the evolution and the involution of post-Marxian mankind. In the long run, individuality is a permanent danger to totalitarianism, which is why the latter hates the former so much.

12. *Positive* approaches to values comprise the following aspects:

a) *Ontological*: only those values can be labeled as genuine which are reducible to concrete persons, who are the only ones who act and choose in concrete situations, and whose acts and choices can be exactly measured and verified.

b) *Methodological*: the only genuine values are the ones that can be, in principle, reduced to scientifically meaningful propositions, that is, "logically reducible to actions, dispositions and volitions," either those of individuals (methodological individualism), or collective entities (a sort of "conceptual realism," regarded by some thinkers as a grave error from a strictly scientific point of view).

c) *Political*: genuine liberal democracy is only possible on the ground that individuals are to determine by themselves, and only by themselves, their own choices in practical, moral and economic activities. No external factors should interfere. Regardless of whether this aspect has a naturalistic (*natural rights, common humanity*, and other similar concepts) or utilitarian (*common good, harmony of interests, happiness* for each and for all, *solidarity* or *pleasures* of a "higher" order, etc.) foundation, in all cases one encounters evaluative judgments that have no empirical referents (such as *justice, happiness, good, dignity* and *honor*, as well as their respective antonyms). That is why it is quite reasonable to ask how consensus and communal (from a small group to the whole of society) coherence could emerge out of purely personal judgments, or whether there is any way out of the dogmas of ethical subjectivism. It seems at least suspicious, if not altogether dangerous, to identify the political aspect with a moral one. Such were Hegel's examples of the State regarded as: the highest principle of Morality, the unquestionable Good, both the political and moral embodiment of the Totality of the Absolute Idea. The totalitarian implications of such an equation, which lately have been explicated in practice, are known too well to be dwelt upon here. In any case, if right (*Recht*) was morality, the formal character of law should be eliminated, which would transform judges into executors, to use Franz Neumann's terms.

ONTOLOGY OF VALUES

13. Regardless of the unquestionable importance of the natural, methodological and political aspects of the post-totalitarian problem of individuality, the aspect which is usually labeled as *ontological* deserves more attention. By this, however, I am far from indicating any common meaning of the term, which has usually been linked to some "non-controversial metaphysical doctrine" of the primal "substance" (individual or collectivistic) of any social reality; nor do I here mean some specific *ontos* of the latter. It is rather an

axiological ontology which I am trying to reach within a *philosophical (metaphysical)* analysis of values as highlighting *norms* which are to be satisfied by every individual willing to contribute to the *normal* life of a *normal* society, that is, to a kind of society which is most adequate to the human dignity of each and all. It is much easier to stress, *in abstracto*, the need for individuals to develop a more communal perspective upon their everyday, social, economical, political and theoretical lives than to outline, *in concreto*, the meaning-giving field of values.

14. A *philosophical* approach to values/norms: the mutual ground where the philosophical and moral levels of consciousness meet is the layer of so-called *ultimate* problems, that is, problems concerning the place of humans in the world. Such problems are usually answered by means of considerations, or by *theory* in the widest sense of the term. In the case of morality, however, theory takes an explicitly *practical, concrete* stance, while in the case of philosophy it is of a much more *speculative, abstract* and even aloof character. In both cases, nevertheless, there is above all an intention, which is the *active* attitude of the individual towards the Whole (of the world and his or her *socium*). The ancient *Sofos* may be a good sample in this respect, whose way of living and behavior was identical to doctrine, for whom philosophy was a genuine *modus vivendi*.

But what is *the nature of the Whole*? It would be more instructive to formulate the question in another way, namely, what *ought* the nature of the Whole be in order to maintain the constant intention in human actions, within a transcendent horizon, for a genuinely humane co-existence — with nature, with other beings, with self?

15. K. Wojtyla emphasizes *living-with-others* as an aspect of human being that is both a natural (anthropological) and a social feature of a person's existence. The empirical reality of this co-existive aspect of human nature may be discovered in the phenomenon of *participation*. Only through the prism of participation may a human being be regarded as a person, as a true individual, who has a social, cultural and historical meaning from one's own and from others' points of view. Through participation, a human being acquires a profound significance; individuality is acquired only by sharing-life-with-others. Both individualism and

totalism alike impede participation, thereby hindering a person's "formatting" as an individual.

An organic unity of the traditional *metaphysical* (in Wojtyla's case, Thomist) and the *phenomenological-existential* types of anthropology is needed in order to outline the *topos* where values as principles and values as norms coincide, that is, the "location" where human beings experience reality even before knowing and/ or evaluating it. The former is the necessary, transcendental precondition of the latter. In philosophy, world-view is not just an *aspect* or *type* of perspective, but rather an active orientation on the side of the subject. In the long run, philosophy taken from a practical perspective coincides with morality and just being (cf. Aristotle's *practical philosophy*). In contemporary philosophical thought, this intrinsic unity between idea and activity has been cogently re-discovered by thinkers like Schopenhauer, Kierkegaard and Nietzsche. Thus, the socio-cultural function of morality can now be traced back to general world-view (philosophical, in a postclassical sense) paradigms as an active factor of the general picture of the human world, not only in its ideal *ultima*, but also as a transhistorical dynamic of the *is*, where all the tensions between good and evil are merely means for an approximate progress towards the *ought to*.

16. The Baden neo-Kantians (Windelband, Rickert, Lask) attempted to outline and overcome the duality of *Naturwissenschaften* and *Geisteswissenschaften*, thereby making a genuine philosophy of values and philosophical axiology not only possible but real. This failed in the final analysis, in spite of all their brilliant intellectual achievements and those of all under their influence in this respect (Dilthey, Simmel, Weber, *et al.*) The reason for this failure was, to use Husserl's words, their traditional (modern) naturalistic, that is, non-transcendental, attitude. Thereby they forgot or simply were blind to the fact that even natural science "is a culture" which belongs within the cultural world of the civilization "which has developed this culture and within which, for the individual, possible ways of understanding this culture are present." In other words, the neo-Kantians remained caught up, like many others before and after them, in a limited *naturalistic objectivism*. For Husserl, an *objective science of the spirit*, an *objective science of the soul*, has never existed and will never exist. This is because the

belief in an *objective* or *positive* knowledge, "in the sense that it attributes to souls, to personal communities, inexistence in the forms of space-time," is the grave mistake of Modernity.

RELIGION AND COMMUNITY

17. What is the *practical point* of all these seemingly too abstract metaphysical and phenomenological speculations? Briefly stated, it is impossible to build and maintain a genuinely democratic society beyond the *individuality principle*. It is hardly possible, however, to follow this principle in traditional ways. A certain post-modernist emphasis on difference, on otherness as an aspect of human existence worthy of respect, is of some importance inasmuch as it may help reveal the field of mutual tolerance and forgiveness. In my view, the post-modern attitude, with its accent upon a sort of *radical plurality* and *unlimited tolerance*, may be of good service to contemporary mankind (regardless of its past and present) in getting rid of the original human (or even Satanic) sin of *hubris*, which is the root of all the dangerous self-deceptions of humanity. In a certain respect, we here are facing a typically Modern vision of human dignity: individuals who are autonomous and free in their actions, the human person as the active subject of his or her own destiny.

18. It is just on this point that the other side of the coin has been hidden throughout the history of humanity. I here mean what is perhaps the most dangerous of all human errors, the one which has constantly pushed people in the direction of feeling themselves to be *creating* history and society, whereby they also feel themselves to be the genuine creators of the world. This is an over-extension of everything that is "human, all too human" into the sphere of the Divine. Stated otherwise, this is a case of what is all-too-human deifying itself, that is, a dangerous substitution of an anthropocentric picture of the world for the theocentric, which has been only too typical since the European Renaissance. It is a conceit that Hayek promptly labeled as *fatal*, in which all the errors of socialism (and, one may add, of every kind of totalitarianism whatsoever) have been deeply rooted. This does not mean that either liberal or conservative thought, whether classical or contemporary, would embrace a post-modern idea of individualism. In their view, a total

adoption of the post-modern stance would lead to a disaster, and they might well be correct. I wish only to say that one specific aspect of post-modern experience, namely, a commitment to treat others as ends in themselves, might be quite helpful in the making of new democracies.

19. The post-modernist hushing of the individual's specific voice, despite its noble (radically tolerant) intentions, is still unsatisfactory and dangerous in that it can easily lead to a kind of personality who is deprived both of his or her actual rights and of the legitimate claims to rights. On the other hand, regulating human relationships and attachments by impartial moral principles may cause a sense of loss, tension and conflict within the individual rather than a sense of community and participation. In this way, too, individuals may again be susceptible to the cunning force of totalization. An effective way out may perhaps be described as *activity-with-and-for-others*. The only horizon that could give meaning to this kind of activity would be of a transcendent rather than merely transcendental (which is the case with Karl-Otto Appel's and Habermas's communicative ethics) nature. This means that a type of horizon capable of providing not only an individualistic, but a humane meaning to an individual's existence must be of an essential nature. Such is the perspective of the Divine; hence, the role of religion in the making of democratic society.

It is certainly no coincidence that the Orthodox Bulgarian Church became a target of purely political interest, especially on the side of the former communist (now self-renamed "socialist") rulers. One of the most serious results of this intervention is the deep crisis and schism which the Bulgarian Orthodox Church has faced since the fall of the overtly communist dictatorship in November, 1989. There is an apparent paradox in this respect, namely, the institution of the Catholic Church, typically opposed to the existing secular rule, preserved its independence (even if only in a relative and comparative sense) throughout the totalitarian period in countries like Czechoslovakia, Hungary and especially Poland. Moreover, it played a significant role in all the movements of dissent and opposition in those countries. With some rare exceptions, this has never been the case with the Eastern Orthodox Church, which has always avoided open conflict with the powers that be. In spite of this fact, the latter have more often than not been destructively hostile to the former.

20. In conclusion, a philosophical attitude organically combined with religious insight may help overcome the shortcomings of both modern and post-modern individualisms. As Nikolai Berdyaev put it, Spirit is freedom, and freedom by nature is always Becoming, never Being, insofar as genuine freedom, as well as the human spirit itself, are emanations of the Divine Spirit. That is why only the spiritual is genuinely creative. Furthermore, any objectivistic explanation of the spirit is a *contradictio in adjecto*. Berdyaev says that, "Nature comes from without, but Spirit emerges from within. So, one can understand God in man through the spirit only." The next step, however, would be from *I* to *you*, and then to *they*. Since this was a step that Berdyaev himself was not confident enough to make, the Spirit remained a rather lonely life for him. The Church as a nexus of spiritual community may provide the post-totalitarian individual with the right direction and the step to make. The kind of Church and the kind of religion (whether "traditional" Orthodoxy, Catholicism or Protestant Christianity) the individual might choose are theological and dogmatic rather than philosophical questions. Not least of all, such questions are a matter of free personal choice and decision, which is why I will not dwell upon them here. Suffice it to say that here lies the corrective which is needed to impede the rise of new waves of totalizing, authoritarian, partoctratic, nationalistic or other such movements. It contains the corrective that is to keep people vigilant against the constant dangers of Totalitarianism, whether it be old, new, pre-modern, modern, post-modern or whatever else in nature.

University of Sofia "St. Kliment Okhridski"
New Bulgarian University, Sofia

CHAPTER VI

IDENTITY AS OPENNESS TO OTHERS

GEORGE F. McLEAN

SEARCHING FOR THE NATURE OF FREEDOM

At the turn of the century there is reason to rejoice and reason to fear. Unfortunately, the two may be so intimately related that it is impossible simply to jettison our fears and proceed with our hopes. Instead, it would appear that there is urgent need for work in philosophy in order to achieve the progress in understanding needed for an era that will be truly new. This progress might be that of a dialectic understood, not in the Hegelian sense of continued progress, but in that of Tillich which sees the catastrophes which force us to the very borders of life as enabling being to unveil Being itself (revelation) at new levels and in new ways.[1] This is not far from the models of metaphysical development in Seligman[2] and Dubarle.[3] It suggests not that metaphysics alone can prevent conflicts from arriving, but that even such conflicts make possible more profound metaphysical reflection, which in turn becomes an integral part of our free creative response to the challenges of our times.

In this light the triumphs and tragedies of humankind in our lifetime are deeply — even metaphysically — instructive. The great celebrations of the last fifty years all reflect the explosive power of human freedom. They are instances of the liberation of the person and the emergence or reemergence of peoples old and new: the liberation from fascism in the '40s, the liberation from colonialism in the '50s and '60s, the breaking down in the '70s of structures oppressing minorities, and the bursting of the Iron Curtain in the '80s — all these landmarks of recent history are steps in the liberation of peoples.

However, these steps now appear to have opened new and equally threatening challenges for the future. In the most recent years and even months, we have found that authentic liberation is not merely a matter of establishing new economic systems — though that cannot be low on the long list of things to be done. More directly, it is the task of living freedom. This requires understanding the new sense of identity on the part of peoples, finding ways to promote this identity and relating it with other peoples in a new fusion of strengths, rather than of destructive confrontation.

Toward this end the present paper will first attempt to situate the social issue as a matter of the exercise of freedom and then to locate the proper mode of operation of the different levels at which freedom operates. Second, it will study the nature and formation of cultural traditions as works of a third level of human freedom. Finally, it will look to that level of freedom for the foundations not only of passive tolerance, but of positive cooperation between peoples of different cultures.

In the ideological context of the Cold War freedom was sought in strange places. On the one hand it was said to be the arbitrary self-affirmation of a supposed atomic individual without family or history, goal or values. On the other hand, it was considered to be the impersonal dialectic of economic forces in search of profit or of political forces in search of power.

With the collapse of this artificial and extreme polarization there now emerges anew a more natural pattern of association among peoples in unities which reflect real needs and especially the decisions of people as to which associations to form in order to respond to these needs and to implement civil society in our time. As the concretization of freedom in our day this reconstitutes a new *locus philosophicus* in full reality of human freedom. We will begin by looking to its earliest thematic articulation in Aristotle, and then move synchronically to its deepest reality. In these terms we will be able to consider cultural identity as the creation of human freedom as it emerges in and through relations to others. But these relations could still be pragmatic ones related to manipulating others. Hence a metaphysical reflection will be required in order to inquire regarding the basis of human freedom and consequently the manners in which it is properly exercised.

CIVIL SOCIETY AS THE NEW *LOCUS PHILOSOPHICUS*: UNCOVERING THE REALITY OF FREEDOM

To identify the basic nature of freedom in society it is helpful to look back to the majestic work of Aristotle in first providing each part of philosophy with a scientific structure. Aristotle begins his politics not historically but by thematically delineating the elements in which political life consists.[4] Both however bring us to the same point, namely, that to be political means to govern and be governed as a member of a community. Most properly the political bespeaks governance or directive action toward the goal. Significantly this is expressed by the term *arché* which originally means beginning, origin or first source. Secondly, this is extended to governance in the sense of sovereignty, that is, of directing others toward a good or a goal while not oneself being necessitated by others. This point of the beginning or origin of social action, which takes responsibility for the overall enterprise is characteristically human; it is the exercise of freedom by individuals and groups through originating responsible action. Though most actions of humans at the different inorganic and organic levels can be performed by other physical realities, it is precisely as these actions are free that they become properly human acts. This issue of corporate directive freedom — its nature and range — is then the decisive issue as regards civil society. How this can be exercised effectively today is the key to the development of civil society for our times.

There is a second dimension to the issue of governance in Aristotle. It is indicated in what many have seen as a correction of his evaluation of types of governance. His first classification of modes of government had been drawn up in terms of the quantity of those who shared in ruling. When ruling is seen as a search of material possessions or property, this tends to be an *oligarchy*; rule is by the few because generally only a few are rich. Democracy, in contrast, is rule by the many who are poor.[5] Aristotle needed to improve on this basically quantitative division founded empirically on the changing distribution of property, for conceptually there could be a society in which the majority is rich. Hence, he came instead to a normative criterion, namely, whether governance is exercised in terms of a search not for goods arbitrarily chosen by a few out of self-interest, but for the common good in which all can participate.[6] In this light governance has its meaning in terms of the broader reality, namely, the community (*koinonia*) which comes together for the happiness or the good life of the whole. Community supposes the free persons of which it is composed; formally it expresses their conscious and free union with a view to a common end, namely, the shared good they seek.

The *polis* is then a species of community. It is a group which as free and self-responsible joins in governance or in guiding efforts toward the achievement of the good life. In this way, Aristotle identifies the central nature of the socio-political order as being a *koinōnia politika* or "civil society".

Civil society then has three elements. First there is governance: *arché*, the beginning of action or the taking of initiative toward an end; this is the exercise of human freedom. But as this pertains to persons in their various groups and subgroups there are two other elements, namely, communication or solidarity with other members of the groups and the participation or subsidiarity of these groups or communities within the whole. The key to understanding civil society lies then in the solidarity and subsidiarity of the community as its members participate in the governance of life toward the common good.

Solidarity and Community

Through time societies have manifested an increasing diversity of parts; this constitutes their proper richness and strength and brings quantitative advantage. It is important that the parts differ in kind so that each brings a distinctive concern and capability to the common task. Further, differing between themselves, one member is able to give and the other to receive in multiple and interrelated active and receptive modes. This means that the members of a society not only live alongside each other, but share the effort to realize the good life through mutual interaction.

Aristotle develops this theme richly in "On Friendship", in Book IX, 6 of his *Nicomachean Ethics*, stressing that the members of a civil society need to be of one mind and heart for the common weal.[7] Such solidarity of the members of society is an essential characteristic. Plato used the terms *methexis* and *mimesis* or participation for this, but Aristotle feared that if individuals were seen as but an instance of a specific type persons would lose their reality. Hence, he used the term 'solidarity' which recognizes the distinctive reality of the parts.

In the human body, where there is but one substantial form, the many parts exist for the whole and the actions of the parts are actions of the whole (it is not my legs and feet which walk; I walk by my legs and feet). Society also has many parts whose differentiation and mutuality pertain to the good of the whole. But in contrast to the body, the members of a community have their own proper form, finality and operation. Hence, their unity is one of the order of their capabilities and actions to the perfection of the body politic or civil society and the realization of its common good.

Aristotle does not hesitate to state strongly the dependence of the individual on the community in order to live a truly human life, concluding that the state is a creation of nature prior to the individual.[8] Nevertheless, in as much as the parts are realities in their own right outside of any orientation to the common good of the whole, society is ultimately for its members, not the contrary.

Subsidiarity and Community[9]

But there is more than solidarity to the constitution of civil society. Community in general is constituted through the cooperation of many for the common goal or good, but the good or goal of a community can be extremely rich and textured. It can concern nourishment, health maintenance, environmental soundness; it includes education both informal and formal, basic and advanced, initial and retraining; it extends to nutrition, culture, recreation, etc. — all the endless manners in which human beings fulfill their needs and capacities and seek "the good life". As each of these can and must be sought and shared through the cooperation of many, each is the basis of a group or subgroup in a vastly varied community.

When, however, one adds the elements of freedom as governance (*arché*) determining what will be done and how the goal will be sought, subsidiarity emerges into view. Were we talking about things rather then people it would be possible to envisage a technology of mass production in a factory automatically moving and directing all toward the final product. Where, however, we are concerned with a community and hence with the composit exercise of the freedom of the persons who constitute its membership, then governance in the community initiating and directing action toward the common end must be exercised in a cumulative manner beginning from the primary group or family in relation to its common good, and moving up to the broader concerns or goals of more inclusive groups considered both quantitatively (neighborhood, city, nation, etc.), and qualitatively (education, health, religion) according to the hierarchy of goods which are their concerns.

The synergetic ordering of these groups, considered both quantitatively, and qualitatively and the realization of their varied needs and potentials is the stuff of the governance of civil society. The condition for success in this is that the freedom and hence responsible participation of all be actively present and promoted at each level. Thus, proper responsibility on the family level must not be taken away by the city, nor that of the city by the state. Rather the higher units either in the sense of larger numbers or more important order of goods must exercise their governance precisely in order to promote the full and self-responsible action of the lower units and in the process enable them to achieve goals which acting alone they could not realize. Throughout, the concern is to maximize the participation in governance or the exercise of freedom of the members of the community, thereby enabling them to live more fully as persons and groups so that the entire society flourishes. This is termed subsidiarity. Thus civil society is a realm of persons in solidarity who through a structure of subsidiarity participate in self-governance.

This manifests also the main axes of the unfolding of the social process in Greece, namely,

- (a) from the Platonic stress upon unity in relation to which the many are but repetitions, to the Aristotelian development of diversity as necessary for the unfolding and actualization of unity;
- (b) from emphasis upon governance by authority located at the highest and most remote levels, to participation in the exercise of governance by persons and groups at every level and in relation to matters with which they are engaged and responsible;
- (c) and from attention to one's own interests, to attention to the common good of the whole.

LEVELS OF INSIGHT AND LEVELS OF FREEDOM

Aristotle's analysis says much about human freedom in society, but according to the glasses one wears — or, more properly, the epistemology one employs — his texts can be read diversely and yield a number of levels of insight and hence the number of levels of freedom outlined by Mortimer Adler and his team in *The Idea of Freedom: A Dialectic Examination of the Conceptions of Freedom* (Garden City: Doubleday, 1958).

Circumstantial Freedom of Self-realization

At the beginning of the modern stirrings for democracy John Locke perceived a crucial condition for a liberal democracy. If decisions were to be made not by the king but by the people, the basis for these decisions had to be equally available to all. To achieve this Locke proposed that we suppose the mind to be a blank paper void of characters and ideas, and then follow the way in which it comes to be furnished. To keep this public he insisted that it be done exclusively via experience, that is, either by sensation or by reflection upon the mind's work on the materials derived from the senses.[10] Proceeding on these suppositions as if they were real limitations of knowledge (i.e. taking the game too seriously), David Hume concluded that all objects of knowledge which are not formal tautologies must be matters of fact. Such "matters of fact" are neither the existence or actuality of a thing nor its essence, but simply the determination of one from a pair of sensible contraries, e.g., white rather than black, sweet rather than sour.[11]

The restrictions implicit in this appear starkly in Rudolf Carnap's "Vienna Manifesto" which shrinks the scope of meaningful knowledge and significant discourse to describing "some state of affairs" in terms of empirical "sets of facts." This excludes speech about wholes, God, the unconscious or *entelechies*; the grounds of meaning, indeed all that transcends the immediate content of sense experience are excluded.

The socio-political structures which have emerged from this model of Locke have contributed much, but there are a number of indices which suggest that he and others have tried too hard to work out their model on a solely empirical or forensic basis. For in such terms it is not possible to speak of appropriate or inappropriate goals or even to evaluate choices in relation to self-fulfillment. The only concern is which objects among a set of contraries I will choose by brute, changeable and even arbitrary will power, and whether circumstances will allow me to carry out that choice.

Such choices, of course, may not only differ from, but even contradict the immediate and long range objectives of other persons. This will require compromises in the sense of Hobbes; John Rawls will even work out a formal set of such compromises.[12]

Through it all, however, the basic concern remains the ability to do as one pleases: "being able to act or not act, according as we shall choose or will".[13] Its orientation is external. In practice as regards oneself, over time this comes to constitute a black-hole of self-centered consumption of physical goods in which both nature and the person are consumed. This is the essence of consumerism; it shrinks the very notion of freedom to competitiveness in the pursuit of material wealth. Freedom in this sense remains basically Hobbes's principle of conflict; it is the liberal ideology built upon the conception of human nature as corrupted, of man as wolf and of life as conflict. Hopefully this will be exercised in an "enlightened" manner, but in this total inversion of human meaning and dignity laws and rights can be only external remedies which, by doing violence to man's naturally violent tendencies, attempt to attenuate to the minimal degree necessary man's free and self-centered choice's and hence the basic viciousness of his life. There must be a better understanding of human freedom and indeed they emerge as soon as one looks beyond external objects to the interior essence and existence of the human subject and of all reality.

Acquired Freedom of Self-perfection

For Kant the heteronomous, external and empiricist orientation character of the above disqualifies it from being moral at all, much less from constituting human freedom. In his first *Critique of Pure Reason* Kant had studied the role of mind in the scientific constitution of the universe. He reasoned that because our sense experience was always limited and partial, the universality and necessity of the laws of science must come from the human mind. This was an essential turning point for it directed attention to the role of the human spirit and especially to the reproductive imagination in constituting the universe in which we live and move.

But this is not the realm of freedom for if the forms and categories with which we work are from our mind, how we construct with them is not left to our discretion. The imagination must bring together the multiple elements of sense intuition in a unity or order capable of being informed by the concepts or categories of the intellect with a view to constituting the necessary and universal judgments of science. The subject's imagination here is active but not free, for it is ruled by the categories integral to the necessary and universal judgements of the sciences. In these terms the human mind remains merely an instrument of physical progress and a function of matter.

However, in his second *Critique*, that of *Practical Reason*, beyond the set of universal, necessary and ultimately material relations, Kant points to the reality of human responsibility. This is the reality of freedom and spirit which characterizes and distinguishes the person. In its terms he recasts the whole notion of physical law as moral rule. If freedom is not to be chaotic and randomly destructive, it must be ruled or under law. To be free is to be able to will as I ought, i.e., in conformity with moral law.

Yet in order to be free the moral act must be autonomous. Hence, my maxim must be something which as a moral agent I — and no other —give to myself. Finally though I am free because I am the lawmaker, my exercise of this power cannot be arbitrary, if the moral order must be universal.

On this basis, a new level of freedom emerges. It is not merely self-centered whimsy in response to circumstantial stimuli; nor is it a despotic exercise of power or the work of the clever self-serving eye of Plato's rogue. Rather, it is the highest reality in all creation; to will as I ought is wise and caring power, open to all and bent upon the realization of "the glorious ideal of a universal realm of ends-in-themselves". In sum, it is free men living together in righteous harmony. This is what we are really about; it is man's glory — and his burden.

Unfortunately, for Kant this glorious ideal remained on the formal plane; it was a matter of essence rather than of existence. It was intended as a guiding principle, a critical norm to evaluate the success or failure of the human endeavor — but it was not the human endeavor itself. For failure to appreciate this, much work for human rights remains at a level of abstraction which provides only minimal requirements. It might found processes of legal redress, but stops short of, and may even distract from and thus impede, positive engagement in the real process of constructing the world in which we live: witness the paralysis of Europe and the world in the face of the Yugoslav dissolution of mankind's moral and hence legal foundations for life in our times.

This second level of freedom makes an essential contribution to human life; we must not forget it nor must we ever do less. But it does not give us the way in which we as unique people in this unique time and space face our concrete problems. We need common guides, but our challenge is to act concretely. Can philosophy without becoming politics or other processes of social action consider and contribute to the actual process of human existence as we shape and implement our lives in freedom?

When the contemporary mind proceeds beyond objective and formal natures to become more deeply conscious of human subjectivity, and of existence precisely as emerging in and through human self-awareness, then the most profound changes must take place. The old order built on objective structures and norms would no longer be adequate; structures would crumble and a new era would dawn. This is indeed the juncture at which we now stand.

Natural Freedom of Self-determination

Progress in being human corresponds to the deepening of man's sense of being, beyond Platonic forms and structures, essences and laws, to act as uncovered by Aristotle and especially to existence as it emerges in Christian philosophy through the Middle Ages. More recently this sensibility to existence has emerged anew through the phenomenological method for focusing upon intentionality and the self-awareness of the human person in time (*dasein*). This opens to the third task stated above, namely, that of deciding for oneself in virtue of the power "inherent in human nature to change one's own character creatively and to determine what one shall be or shall become." This is the most radical freedom, namely, our natural freedom of self-determination.

This basically is self-affirmation in terms of our teleological orientation toward perfection or full realization which we will see to be the very root of the development of values, virtues and hence of cultural traditions. It implies seeking when that perfection is absent and enjoying or celebrating it when attained. In this sense, it is that stability in one's orientation to the good which classically has been termed holiness and anchors such great traditions of the world as the Hindu and Taoist, Islamic and or the Judeo-Christian. One might say that this is life as practiced by the saints and holy men, but it would be more correct to say that it is because they lived in such a manner that they are called holy.

In his third *Critique*, Kant suggests an important insight regarding how this might form a creative force for confronting present problems and hence for passing on the tradition in a transforming manner. He sees that if the free person of the second *Critique* were to be surrounded by the necessitarian universe of the first *Critique*, then one's freedom would be entrapped and entombed within one's mind, while one's external actions would be necessary and necessitated. If there is to be room for human freedom in a cosmos in which man can make use of necessary laws, indeed if science is to contribute to the exercise of human freedom, then nature too must be understood as directed toward a goal and must manifest throughout a teleology within which free human purpose can be integrated. In these terms, even in its necessary and universal laws, nature is no longer alien to freedom; rather it expresses divine freedom and is conciliable with human freedom.

This makes the exercise of freedom possible, but our issue is how this freedom is exercised in a way that creates diverse cultures, i.e., how can a free person relate to an order of nature and to structures of society in a way that is neither necessitated nor necessitating, but free and creative? In the "Critique of the Aesthetic Judgment," Kant points out that in working toward an integrating unity the imagination is not confined by the necessitating structures of categories and concepts as in the first *Critique*, or the regulating ideal of the second *Critique*. Returning to the order of essences would omit the uniqueness of the self and its freedom. Rather, the imagination ranges freely over the full sweep of reality in all its dimensions to see where relatedness and purposiveness can emerge. This ordering and reordering by the imagination can bring about numberless unities or patterns of actions and natures. Unrestricted by any *a priori* categories, it can integrate necessary dialectical patterns within its own free and creative productions, and include scientific universals within its unique concrete harmonies. This is the proper and creative work of the human person in this world.

In order for human freedom to be sensitive to the entirety of this all-encompassing harmony, in the final analysis our conscious attention must be directed not merely to universal and necessary physical or social structures, nor even to beauty and ugliness either in their concrete empirical realizations or in their Platonic selves. Rather, our focus must be upon the integrating images of pleasure or displeasure, enjoyment or revulsion, generated deep within our person by these images as we attempt to shape our world according to the relation of our will to the good and hence to realize the good for our times.

In this manner human freedom becomes at once the goal, the creative source, the manifestation, the evaluation and the arbiter of all that imaginatively we can propose. It is *goal*, namely to realize life as rational and free in this world; it is *creative source* for through the imagination freedom unfolds the endless possibilities for human expression; it is *manifestation* because it presents these to our consciousness in ways appropriate to our capabilities for knowledge of limited realities and relates these to the circumstances of our life; it is *criterion* because its response manifests a possible mode of action to be variously desirable or not in terms of a total personal response of pleasure or displeasure, enjoyment or revulsion; and it is *arbiter* because it provides the basis upon which our freedom chooses to affirm or reject, realize or avoid this mode of self-realization.

Thus, freedom in this third existential sense emerges as the dynamic center of our life. It is the spectroscope and kaleidoscope through which is processed the basic thrust toward perfection upon which we shall see culture as the pattern of public life to be based and by which its orders of preference are set. The philosophical and religious traditions it creates become the keys to the dynamics of human life. Hence the possibilities of peace and cooperation must depend fundamentally on the potentialities of creative freedom for overcoming the proclivities of the first level of freedom for confrontation and violent competition, for surmounting the minimal criteria of the second level of freedom, and for setting in motion positive processes of peaceful and harmonious collaboration.

CULTURAL IDENTITIES AS THE WORK OF FREEDOM

Our next task is to uncover how human persons in exercising this third level of freedom emerge in the communities of family, neighborhood and people, and in so doing create their public life and its culture. This calls not merely for a sociological description of culture as the compilation of whatever humankind does or makes; it is rather the conscious weaving of the fabric of human symbols and interrelations through which a human group chooses to live its unique process of unveiling being in time. This requires attention to a number of specific issues:

1. the nature of values, culture and tradition;
2. the moral authority of a cultural tradition and its values for guiding life; and
3. the active role of every generation in creatively shaping and developing its tradition in response to the challenges of its times.

Cultural Traditions as the Cumulative Freedom of Peoples

If being stands against nonbeing, then living things survive by seeking the good or that which perfects and promotes their life in the sense of Kant's third *Critique* and its description of the work of the imagination. A basic exercise of this third level of human freedom therefore is to set an order of preferences among the many possible goods. Those are the "preferred" or "values" in the sense that they "weigh more heavily" in making decisions than do other possible goods. Gradually, one becomes practiced in the arts of realizing and/or achieving these values, which competencies are our moral strengths or "virtues". Cumulatively, our values and corresponding virtues set a style for our action. Together the values and virtues, artifacts and modes of human interaction constitute an integrated pattern of human life in which the creative freedom of a people is expressed and implemented. This is a "culture" taken synchronically as a context in which human life can be cultivated and perfected.

Through time there evolves a vision of actual life which transcends time and hence can provide guidance for our life-past, present and future. The content of that vision is a set of values which points the way to mature and perfect human formation and thereby orients the life of a person. Such a vision is historical because it arises in the life of a people in time and presents an appropriate way of preserving that life through time. But it is also normative because it provides a harmony and fullness which is at once classical and historical, ideal and personal, uplifting and dynamizing, in a word, liberating. For this reason it provides a basis upon which past historical ages, present options and future possibilities are judged.

What then should we conclude regarding the values and culture in which we have been raised, which give us dominion over our actions and enable us to be free and creative? Do they come from God or from man, from eternity or from history? To this question Chakravarti Rajagopalachari of Madras answered:

> Whether the epics and songs of a nation spring from the faith and ideas of the common folk, or whether a nation's faith and ideas are produced by its literature is a question which one is free to answer as one likes. . . . Did clouds rise from the sea or was the sea filled by waters from the sky? All such inquiries take us to the feet of God transcending speech and thought[14]

The Open Creativity and Interchange of Cultural Traditions

As an active process tradition transforms what is received, lives it in a creative manner and passes it on as a leaven for the future. Taken diachronically the process of tradition as receiving and passing on does not stop with Plato's search for eternal and unchangeable ideals, with the work of *techné* in repeating exactly and exclusively a formal model, or with rationalism's search for clear and distinct knowledge of immutable natures by which all might be controlled. Rather, in its application according to the radical distinctiveness of persons and their situations tradition is continually perfected and enriched. It manifests the sense of what is just and good which we have from our past by creating in original and distinctive ways more of what justice and goodness mean. J. Pelican said it well: "Tradition is the living faith of the dead, traditionalism is the dead faith of the living."

Further, if one takes time and culture seriously one must recognize that he or she is situated in a particular culture and at a particular time; hence all that can be seen from this vantage point constitutes one's horizon. This would be lifeless and dead, determined rather than free, if one's vantage point were to be fixed by its circumstances and closed. This points to the necessity of meeting other minds and hearts, not simply to add information incrementally, but in order that one might be challenged in one's basic assumptions and enabled thereby to delve more deeply into one's tradition and to draw forth more pervasive truth.

This hermeneutic mode of openness does not consist in surveying others objectively, obeying them in a slavish and unquestioning manner, or even in simply juxtaposing their ideas and traditions to our own. Rather, it is directed primarily to ourselves, for our ability to listen to others is correlatively our ability to assimilate the implications of their answers in order to delve more deeply into the meaning of our own traditions and draw out new and ever more rich insights. In other words, it is an acknowledgement that our cultural heritage has something new to say to us and that we are the ones who can enable it to speak.

Here hermeneutic, democratic and critical attitudes converge. The attitude is not one of methodological sureness which imposes its views, nor is it a mere readiness for new compromises or new techniques of social organization — for these are subject to manipulation on the horizontal level. Instead, it is readiness to draw out in open dialogue new meaning from a common tradition. Seen in these terms our heritage of culture and values is not closed or dead; rather, democratic interchange can enable life to remain ever new by becoming more inclusive and more rich.

CULTURAL IDENTITIES AS RELATIONS TO OTHERS: A PHENOMENOLOGICAL UNVEILING OF THE METAPHYSICAL NATURE OF FREEDOM

The previous sections have enabled us to locate the specific existential level of freedom at which we are able to create a culture and hence the origin, nature and content of a cultural tradition. We saw, as well, the essentially open and dialogic character of cultural progress. It remains now for us to look more closely at the open attitude toward other peoples and cultures to see whether this be a matter of self-enhancement in order to dominate and control others or of love and concern for others within an integrating horizon and, indeed, an integrating reality.

Kant himself could say only that to be authentically human life had to be lived "as if" all is teleological. But then its exercise would be restricted to the confines of the human imagination; freedom would be not only self-determining but self-constituting and self-limited. In contrast, if the human spirit strives deeply to realize the life of persons then the transcendent principle it requires must be the most real in heaven and earth; if freedom presents us with a limitless range of possibilities, then its principle must be the Infinite and Eternal, the Source and Goal of all possibility. This Transcendent is the key to real liberation: it not only gives absolute grounding to one's reality and certifies one's right to be respected, but evokes the creative powers of one's heart, frees them from the confines of one's own slow, halting and even partial creative activity, and plunges them into infinite possibility and power.

This can be approached through the steps of phenomenological reflection on the person as gift. First, our self-identity and interpersonal relatedness are not made by us, but are givens with which we work. Second, if we reflect on the character of a gift we note that it has a radical character: to attempt to pay for it in cash or in kind would destroy its nature as gift. As gratuitous, a gift is based primarily in the freedom of the giver, not in the merit of the one who receives.

There is here striking symmetry with the 'given' in the sense of hypothesis or evidence. In the line of hypothetical and evidential reasoning there is a first, namely, that which is not explained, but upon which explanation is founded. Here, there is also a first upon which the reality of the gift is founded and which is not to be traced to another reality. This symmetry illumines what is distinctive of the gift, namely, that the gift's originating action is not traced back further, that it is precisely free or gratuitous. Once again, our reflections lead us in the direction of that which is Self-sufficient, Absolute and Transcendent as the sole adequately gratuitous source of the gift of being.

Thirdly, as an absolute point of departure with its distinctive spontaneity and originality, the giving is non-reciprocal. To attempt to repay would be to destroy the gift as such. Indeed, there is no way in which this originating gratuity can be returned; we live in a graced condition. This appears in reflection upon one's culture. What we received from the Bible, the Koran or the *Vedas*, from a

Confucius or an Aristotle, can in no way be returned. Nor is this simply a problem of distance in time, for neither is it possible to repay the life we have received from our parents, the health received from a doctor, the wisdom from a teacher, or simply the good example which can come from any quarter at any time. The non-reciprocal character of our life is not merely that of part to whole; it is that of a gift to its source.[15]

In a certain parallel to the antinomies of Kant which show when reason has strayed beyond its bounds, many from Plotinus to Leibniz and beyond have sought knowledge, not only of the gift and its origin, but of why it had to be given. The more they succeeded the less room was left for freedom on the part of the human person as a given or gift. Others attempted to understand freedom as a Fall, only to find that what was thus understood was bereft of value and meaning and a source of violence in human life and its cultures. Rather, the radical non-reciprocity of human freedom must be rooted in an equally radical generosity on the part of its origin. No reason, either on the part of the given or on the part of its origin, makes this gift necessary.

Fourthly, the freedom of man as the reflection of his derivation from a giving that is pure generosity is the very image of God. Freedom thus received implies a correspondingly radical openness or generosity: the gift is not something which is and then receives, but is essentially gift. It was an essential facet of Plato's response to the problems he had elaborated in the *Parmenides* that the multiple can exist only *as* participants of the good or one. Receiving is not something they *do*; it is what they *are*.[16] As such they reflect at the core of their being not the violent self-seeking of the first level of freedom or the passive principles of the second level, but the open, active and creative reality of the generosity in which they originate.

The truth of this insight is confirmed from many directions. Latin American philosophies begin from the symbol of earth as the fruitful source of all (reflected in the Quechuan language of the Incas as the "Pacha Mama"). This is their preferred context for their sense of human life, its relations to physical nature, and the meeting of the two in technology.[17] In this they are not without European counterparts. The classical project of Heidegger in its later phases shifted beyond the unconcealment of the being of things-in-time, to Being which makes things manifest. The *Dasein*, structured in and as time, is able to provide Being a place of discovery among things,[18] but it is being which maintains the initiative; its coming-to-pass or emission depends upon its own spontaneity and is for its sake. "Its 'there' (the *da-* of *Dasein*) only sustains the process and guards it," so that in the openness of concealed Being beings can appear un-concealed.[19]

The African spirit, especially in its great reverence for family, community and culture — whence one derives one's life, one's ability to interpret one's world, and one's capacity to respond — may be uniquely positioned to grasp this more fully. In contrast to Aristotle's classical 'wonder,' these philosophers do not situate the person over against the object of his or her concern, reducing both to objects for detached study and manipulation. They look rather to the source from which reality is derived and are especially sensitive to its implications for the mode and manner of life as essentially open, communicative, generous and sharing.

Cultural Harmony and Creative Interchange

Seen in terms of gift, freedom at its third level has principles for peaceful cooperation, not only with my people whose well-being is in a sense my own, but with increasingly broader sectors, and potentially and in principle, with the whole of mankind. First, the good is not only what contributes to my perfection; being received, it is essentially out-going. The second principle is that of complementarity. As participants in the one, self-sufficient and purely spontaneous source, the many are not in principle antithetic or antipathetic one to another. Rather, as limited images they stand in a complementary relation to all other participants or images. This means that others and their cultures are to be respected simply because they too have been given or gifted by the one Transcendent source. This is the essential step which Gandhi, in calling outcasts by the name "harijans" or "children of God," urged us to take beyond the first sense of freedom which sees others only as contraries against whom we choose. Conversely, it means that as complementary we need each other.

Thirdly, as one does not first exist and then receive, but one's very existence is a received existence or gift, to attempt to give back this gift, as in an exchange of presents, would be at once hopelessly too much and too little. On the one hand, to attempt to return in strict equivalence would be too much, for it is our very self that we have received as gift. On the other hand, to think merely in terms of reciprocity would be to fall essentially short of my nature as one that is given, for to make a merely equivalent return would be to remain centered upon myself where I would cleverly entrap, and then entomb the creative power of being.

Rather, looking back I can see the futility of giving back, and in this find the fundamental importance of passing on the gift in the spirit in which it has been given. One's freedom as given calls for a creative generosity which reflects that of one's source. This requires breaking out of oneself as the only center of one's concern. It means becoming effectively concerned with the good of other persons and other groups, and for the promotion and vital growth of the next generation and of those to follow.

Finally, that other cultures are quintessentially products of self-cultivation by other spirits as free and creative implies the need to open one's horizons beyond one's own self-concerns to the ambit of the freedom of others and what they freely would be and would become. This involves promoting the development of other free and creative centers and of the cultures they create — which, precisely as such, are not in one's own possession or under one's own control. One lives then no longer in terms merely of oneself or of things that one can make or manage, but in terms of an interchange between free men and peoples of different cultures. Personal responsibility is no longer merely individual decision making or for individual good. Effectively realized, the resulting interaction and mutual fecundation should reach out beyond oneself and one's own culture to reflect ever more perfectly the glory of the one infinite and loving source and goal of all.[20]

Will this indeed eventuate? Can we overcome the violent conflicts which the recent emergence of a sense of self-identity appears to have engendered? To attempt to do so through suppressing freedom at this third level would destroy life as human. The history of the last half century consists in a studied and consistent rejection of such attempts at social engineering at the cost of freedom. The most recent history in Eastern Europe shows that even the most extreme attempts at forced socialization did not resolve problems of peaceful cooperation between peoples, but merely cov ered them over, isolated them from the requirements and achievements of human progress, and left them to reemerge in ever more intractable modes.

The alternative is to refuse to allow freedom to be reduced to its first level as an isometrics of violent conflict and not to stop at the passive and universalist formalisms of the second level. Rather to be human is to take up the burden of freedom at its existential level and to search deeply into its source and nature for principles of unity and open cooperation. The truth of these principles will be manifest most of all in their call for ever more inclusive patterns of social equilibrium, and the progress of cultures will consist in their genius in responding creatively to this call.

NOTES

1. George F. McLean, "A Dialectic of Liberation Through History: Paul Tillich," in G. McLean, *Tradition and Contemporary Life: Hermeneutics of Perennial Wisdom and Social Change* (Madras: Radhakrishnan Institute for Advanced Study in Philosophy, University of Madras, 1986), pp. 67-95.

2. Paul Seligman, *The 'Apeiron' of Anaximander: A Study in the Origin and Function of Metaphysical Ideas* (New York: Oxford Univ. Press, 1962), Ch. XIV & XV.

3. Dominique Dubarle, "Le poème de Parménide, doctrine du savoir et premier état d'une doctrine de l'être," *Revue des sciences philosophiques et théologiques*, 57 (1973), 3-34, 397-431.

4. *Politics* I, 1, 1252a22.

5. *Ibid.*, III, 7.

6. *Ibid.*, 8.

7. *Nichomachean Ethics*, IX, 6, 1167b13.

8. *Politics* I, 2, 1253a20-37.

9. John Mavone, "The Division of Parts of Society According to Plato and Aristotle," *Philosophical Studies*, 6 (1956), 113-122.

10. John Locke, *An Essay Concerning Human Understanding* (New York: Dover, 1959), Book, Chap. I, Vol. I, 121-124.

11. David Hume, *An Enquiry Concerning Human Understanding* (Chicago: Regnery, 1960).

12. *The Theory of Justice* (Cambridge: Harvard Univ. Press, 1971).

13. John Locke, *An Essay Concerning Human Understanding*, A.C. Fraser, ed. (New York: Dover, 1959), II, ch. 21, sec 27; vol. I, p. 329.

14. *Ramayana* (Bombay: Bharatiya Vidya Bhavan, 1976), p. 312.

15. Kenneth L. Schmitz, *The Gift: Creation* (Milwaukee: Marquette University Press, 1982), pp. 44-56.

16. R.E. Allen, "Participation and Predication in Plato's Middle Dialogues" in his *Studies in Plato's Metaphysics* (London: Routledge, Keegan Paul, 1965), pp. 43-60.

17. Juan Carlos Scannone, "Ein neuer Ansatz in der Philosophie Lateinamerikas," *Philosophisches Jahrbuch*, 89 (1982), 99-116 and "La Racionalidad Cientifico-Technologica y la Racionalidad Sapiencial de la Cultura Latino Americana," *Stromata* (1982), 155-164.

18. William J. Richardson, *Heidegger: Through Phenomenology to Thought* (The Hague: Nijhoff, 1967), pp. 532-535.

19. Joseph Kockelmans, "Thanksgiving: The Completion of Thought," in Manfred S. Frings, ed., *Heidegger and the Quest for Truth* (Chicago: Quadrangle Books, 1968), pp. 175-179.

20. Schmitz, 84-86.

CHAPTER VII

SOCIAL VALUES IN A TIME OF CHANGE? AN HEGELIAN APPROACH

TOM ROCKMORE

The complex issue of social values in a time of change raises the very problem of how, if at all, such values are related to the society for which they serve as a guide for action. This issue is not merely a philosophical curiosity, something philosophers do when they turn away from the external world to concentrate on their own interests, but is rather intensely topical in virtue of the enormous political changes brought about by the collapse of official Marxism in Eastern Europe since 1989. It is then of practical importance to know how to approach the many practical problems that have arisen in the wake of the widespread and still highly volatile series of ongoing political transformations that were set in motion by the nearly instantaneous disintegration of the official Soviet system and the subsequent disappearance of the Soviet Union itself.

One approach to the question I am raising is to invoke an already established system of values independent of actual events in order to orient the practical response. It is widely thought that there is a single set of socially relevant values that, like reality itself, are available and sufficient to guide our lives in all times and places, including times of change. Platonism, for example, which has never ceased to influence the later discussion, consists of the view that there is an independent reality of objective values known as the true, the good and the beautiful against which all our judgments can be evaluated.

The task of this paper will be to examine this approach with respect to the unprecedented changes now underway by virtue of the collapse of the Soviet bloc. Platonism leads to the idea that our abstract ideas are more important than any aspect of concrete reality, which, at best, only imperfectly reflects the independent reality that is our real concern. I will argue, on the contrary, that it is a significant error to hold that a general approach which fails to take account of the specificity of events can possibly be sufficient to come to grips with them. I will further argue that social values are relevant precisely to the extent that they are not elaborated prior to, but rather arise out of the events under consideration. I will finally argue that, although the existence of a single set of socially relevant values is routinely invoked, there is no reason to believe that this is anything more than a false description of what we in fact do.

This paper will be guided by the assumption that values embody expressions of possible social utility, of whatever kind. The term "value" will be understood very broadly as referring to the worth of something, where worth can be intrinsic, instrumental, inherent, contributory and so forth. The idea of social value will be taken as an undefined term referring broadly to whatever values are necessary, or at least useful, within such various levels of the social context as the familial or private and the public settings, including all the main areas of daily life. In this respect, there seem to be two main possibilities, roughly that social values are either invariant or variable in some as yet undefined sense.

If one holds, as many do, that social values are invariant, or at least roughly the same in all times and places, then very obviously one also has to hold that they are not dependent on or related other than incidentally to the context that they are intended to regulate. Those who believe that social values are invariant must also hold that they are formulated in a way independent of the social context. Here the difficulty is to arrive at a single set of social values that both hold across the board for all people in all societies and are more than incidentally relevant for life in society. If, on the other hand, one holds that social values are variable, not fixed or permanent, then the problem is to show that they are more than the expression of what a particular group or subset of the population happens to think at a given time and in a given place.

CONCRETE SOCIAL REALITY

It is obviously unproblematic to arrive at a single set of values covering all situations in a society where there is no change, hence nothing resembling real social time. It is highly doubtful that there has ever been a society in which nothing happens, in which there is no novelty of any kind. Depending on whether one thinks that structuralist descriptions are adequate to describe social reality, then a situation of this type is at least arguably envisaged in the writings of Claude Lévi-Strauss. In his structuralist anthropology,[1] there is properly speaking absolute social stasis, hence no real change, since society is organized so as to prevent any alteration in the basic consanguinal relations. In a society of this kind, it is at least possible to envisage being able to arrive at a single set of social values covering all situations since, in the absence of novelty, everything could be entirely predictable.

It is as easy as it is uninteresting to entertain the idea of a system of stable values in a society where nothing ever happens. It is considerably more difficult to do so in a society that is the theater of real change, Such a society presents new, often unforeseen and obviously unforeseeable situations, that on occasion are completely unlike anything that has earlier existed and which may or may not be amenable to analysis through a pre-existing conceptual framework. A conceptual framework adequate to a particular situation, whatever we mean by "adequate," is not placed in doubt as long as the series of events in the future remains sufficiently like those of the past. Obviously, this presupposes the existence of causal regularity over time. But this same framework may no longer be as relevant, or even relevant at all, if it turns out that the future is simply unlike the past.

Although theoretically possible, this seems practically implausible. Our views of physical reality formulated over a period of several thousand years continue to hold since nature as given in experience remains boringly repetitive. Bodies continue to fall toward the center of the earth, fire remains hot and the sun rises and sets in an entirely predictable fashion. The laws of physical theory would obviously cease to hold if any one of these familiar situations failed to recur. Yet if the planets no longer followed regular orbits but wandered aimlessly through the universe, modern physics would need to be rewritten. An analogous situation, which presents a real test for social values, has been occurring in Eastern Europe as a result of the nearly instantaneous political collapse and subsequent disintegration of the Soviet Union.

This situation was entirely unforeseen and probably unforeseeable, even had anyone speculated in this way.[2] Even the most pessimistic observers, those who thought that tensions were likely to increase within the Soviet bloc for political, economic, religious or other reasons,[3] did not forecast anything like the sudden series of events that actually took place. This is merely another reminder, should one be necessary, that, unlike the natural sciences, historical predictions however defined cannot be made with any reasonable degree of accuracy.[4] It is fair to say that the practical dimensions of the situation are without precedent in recent history, perhaps entirely without precedent. It is difficult to think of anything approaching the extraordinarily rapid political collapse of the important series of countries constituting the so-called Soviet bloc, including most importantly the Soviet Union with its member republics. This political collapse has affected a series of countries with close political and economic ties to it, including Bulgaria, Romania, Czechoslovakia, Poland, Hungary, the German Democratic Republic, and, more distantly, China, Cuba, North Korea, Cambodia, Vietnam and so forth. The dimensions of this political collapse are evident when it is realized that these countries comprise roughly half the population of the entire world. Although history records many examples of countries that disintegrated under intense pressure in time of war, most recently the former Yugoslavia, there is apparently no real precedent for the series of events that has befallen official Marxism in less than a decade in a time of peace, without so much as a single shot being fired. Hence, this presents an interesting test case for the problem of social values in a time of change.

CRITICISM OF A PRIORI MODELS OF SOCIAL VALUES

The issue of social values in a time of change is obviously a subset of the more general problem of whether there is a single specifiable set of values, for instance, moral or ethical commands such as the familiar golden rule, which can be said to hold in all times and places. Or on the contrary, are even the most familiar social values in some sense socially variable from one historical moment to another? The simplest approach is the widespread conviction that there is in fact a single specifiable framework of social values. In modern times, the outstanding example of this approach to practical matters is provided by Kant. His critical philosophy clearly turns on the conviction that the norms for morality and culture are to be drawn out of reason itself as the absolute guide for life. Kant maintains that reason, which determines the rules that govern action in particular circumstances, is wholly independent of any particular set of contingent circumstances. It is typical of Kant, whose intellectual probity was exemplary, that he was willing to admit that there has perhaps never been a moral person since his standards are so rigorous in practice that they simply cannot be met. At the same time, however, he insisted that these standards provide the minimal conditions for a rational political framework.

Religious Justification

Kant's approach to the problem is a secular form of the traditional religious doctrine that justifies itself through a claimed relation to divine authority. The most economical interpretation of this model is the claim that some among us have a privileged relation to God that may be either indirect or direct. When indirect, it is a case of an authorized representative, or privileged interpreter, of a body of writings that can reliably be regarded as divinely inspired. When direct, it is a case of divine revelation, such as in certain forms of mysticism. According to this model, the problem of reliably determining a set of social values reduces to the problem of identifying those whose role consists in transmitting a series of ideas that they and those who identify with them, such as the officials of an organized religion and those faithful to that religion, regard as faithfully representing God's views. The difficulty of knowing what to do in any particular situation lies merely in ascertaining what God would have us do. This is further ascertained either through invoking a series of general precepts oneself; or, as in orthodox Judaism, through consulting one learned in the main texts who creatively extends the doctrine to fit specific cases; or, as in Christianity and Islam, by following the authorized interpretation of the sacred texts.

Philosophical Justification

With respect to the traditional view of social values, the main difference between the religious and philosophical models lies in the effort to orient ourselves not merely through religious conviction, but rather through something rather grandly called reason. Conviction, including religious conviction, is presumably something that one has but cannot demonstrate or otherwise prove, whereas reason is self-demonstrating. Starting early in the discussion, a long series of philosophers have labored mightily to draw a distinction in kind between reason and belief, such as in the familiar Platonic view of knowledge as true belief plus an account.[5] Plato, for instance, maintains that some among us, call them men of gold, have a specific genetic endowment that, when properly developed, enables them literally to see the invisible, to grasp an independent conceptual framework adequate to measure the true, the good, and the beautiful.

The difficulty in this version of the philosophical model is that claims to know are by definition essentially private, not public, and are, therefore, not intersubjective, not subject to verification of any kind other than through the mere claim to "see." Obviously, there is no evidence for any claim to "see" reality other than the claim itself, which is finally indistinguishable from the claim of any religious believer to divine revelation. Kant improves on Plato in purporting to deduce rules for action in specific situations from reason itself. His aim is to deduce a general framework for practical action applicable to any and all particular situations. The difficulty, which Hegel quickly pointed out, is that any particular principle, such as the golden rule, is empty since it applies only in a general, non-specific manner. His counter-suggestion is that social principles are relevant to concrete situations to the extent that they take them into account.

Although a number of later thinkers have attempted to extend the Kantian line, no one to the best of my knowledge has yet answered Hegel's criticism. Kant claims that reason, hence practical reason (his name for morality), is specifically relevant for human beings since it necessarily incorporates human goals. In this way, he restates the Platonic conviction that philosophy is indispensable for the social context, even though it is totally independent of that context since it depends solely on rational arguments. The short version of this claim is that philosophy is a necessary condition for the good life. Yet it needs to be shown and not merely claimed that philosophy is really as socially significant as some philosophers claim it is.

This claim is scarcely obvious, even to philosophers. Aristotle notoriously thought that pure theory is socially irrelevant. Marx held that it was even a form of ideology. In Marx's wake, the Frankfurt School thinkers have suggested that some types of theory are socially irrelevant whereas other types are socially relevant. Yet the recent efforts of Apel and Habermas to provide a transcendental form of ethics fail to show either that ethics must be transcendental or that a transcendental form of ethics is socially relevant. In that sense, they fail to meet Hegel's criticism. Furthermore, Heidegger's view, which claims that social values are already embodied in the social past such that we only need to repeat it authentically in the future, fails to explain how to justify traditional social values.

Further Criticism of the Traditional,
a Priorist Model of Social Values

According to the traditional model of social values, there is one and only one specifiable system that is *a priori*, or independent of time and place. Religious efforts to establish this view through appeals to authority, even if admissible within a specifically religious frame of reference, obviously conflict among themselves. The result is that the major religions disagree with respect to social values. Claims for universality on the part of a particular religion, such as the Roman Catholic claim to be the sole universal church, must be tempered by the factual disagreements between the different religions. It is obvious, or at least should be, that this claim is accepted only by members of this particular faith and is not even potentially acceptable to the adherents of any other major religion.

Philosophical efforts to articulate this traditional model have the advantage of relying on reason, which in principle is universal in the sense that it is the same for all rational beings. If reason is universal, and if social values can be deduced or otherwise established through reason, then at least the idea of a single specifiable system of social values independent of time and place is plausible. Here, as in so many other areas, Kant is the central figure. More recent forms of Kantianism, such as Apel's transcendental pragmatism, are in fact weaker than the critical philosophy. Even if we grant Apel's assertion that all communication necessarily presupposes, at least implicitly, agreement among the members of an ideal speech community, nothing whatever follows concerning particular social values.

With respect to later, more abstract efforts to reformulate his theory, the advantage of Kantian morality lies in the claim to provide practical guidelines for action in every situation. Kant's view of the categorical imperative suggests that, based on an analogy between ethics and physical theory, there is a single way to analyze the social world. If this view is meant to support the idea of a univocal system of social values, the analogy is obviously problematic. Although critical of certain aspects of Newtonian mechanics, Kant thought that it would stand forever, like geometry or logic. Yet we now know that neither Aristotelian logic, nor Euclidean geometry, nor Newtonian mechanics is the last word on the topic. Although one may believe at any given time that a particular form of physical theory is correct, the history of science shows that there is more than one way to analyze the same external world.

The problem is even more acute with respect to the Kantian analysis of particular situations. The idea that in all cases particular situations can be brought under a single, univocally interpretable system of general rules for practical action presupposes that there is one and only one way to analyze them. Yet all, or nearly all, particular situations can be analyzed from a variety of different points of view that, as a result, yield different practical imperatives. A sick child who requires a transfusion from the standpoint of modern medical science requires only prayer from the standpoint of a Christian Scientist, whose religious beliefs preclude transfusion. This case, which is otherwise absolutely typical of the situations encountered in practice, illustrates a clash between different possible analyses that defeats anything like the Kantian assumption that there is one and only one rational analysis of concrete cases.

SOCIAL VALUES AND SOCIAL JUSTIFICATION

Social Justification of Social Values

In the discussion so far, we have examined approaches to social values based on authority, tradition, pure intuition and reason alone, all of which fail. This short list of approaches is significant in embracing the main strategies invoked to produce social values that are regarded as *a priori*, or independent of the social context.

Although for many observers it seems obvious that there can be no more than a single system of social values independent of time and place, in practice there seems to be no way to produce such a list.

If we are not to abandon the idea of justifying our social values, then we must seek another approach that is different from traditional but indefensible value a priorism. A clue as to how to proceed is suggested by the case very briefly examined, which suggests that, contrary to Kant, there is no interpretation as such in practice, no such thing as the only possible analysis of a concrete situation, but rather a variety of interpretations from different points of view that depend on prior presuppositions. So in the case briefly evoked above, the interpretation of the situation obviously depends on a prior commitment to modern medicine, the form of Christianity practiced by Christian Scientists, or still other points of view. The interpretation of this case is not independent of, but rather dependent on, a prior commitment, or a general conceptual framework that sanctions either or justifies a particular type of interpretation as opposed to other, rival interpretations.

In this respect, the problem is twofold insofar as it concerns the analysis of particular cases from a given point of view, as well as the formulation for a wider conceptual framework within which it is possible to do so. Now, the important thing to note is that the wider conceptual framework is not invariant, as might be thought, but rather a variable that results in practice from a process of social negotiation among the members of a given society.

An example, if one is needed, is the change in the idea of social solidarity. The Kantian idea that we must respect each person as an end in himself, which is clearly a secular reformulation of the Christian view that each person is made in the image of God, suggests that we have positive duties toward each other as human beings. This perspective can be used to support social solidarity of various kinds, such as notions of human dignity, altruism, charity or even socialism. It is obvious, however, that the idea that appeared obvious to Kant no longer appears obvious, or even plausible, to more recent "Kantians." For instance, Rawls holds that it is normal and in fact reasonable to expect human solidarity in concrete situations when all people directly benefit.[6]

Although the idea of social universals is frequently invoked, it is difficult to think of a single recognized instance. In our time, the most impressive effort has been Chomsky's generative linguistic theory, which is based on a distinction between the surface and the deep structures of language. In this theory, the deep structure that is built-in, or hard-wired, is the necessary and sufficient condition of acquiring language that simply cannot be explained on a behaviorist model.[7] Yet after many years of effort, not a single element of the so-called deep structure, hence not a single item of universal grammar, has to the best of my knowledge ever been identified. I suspect that the same remark holds true of other forms of cultural universalism. Actual acquaintance with different cultures reveals not that all people are the same everywhere, in a word, that we are all alike, but rather that there are fundamental differences that simply cannot be reduced to a single, simple model. Even such basic cultural traits as the so-called incest taboo seem to be restricted in application, not only through socially deviant behavior, but rather in particular societies, such as ancient Egypt.

Our problem is not whether there are cultural universals that do not require justification; it is rather how to justify the social values that permit us to analyze the particular situations with which we are routinely confronted in daily life. Obviously, if we cannot justify our social values in an *a priori* manner, either we must do so in an *a posteriori* fashion, or we must abandon the very idea of justification on pain of regarding values as merely arbitrary.

It would be a mistake to hold that we can justify our social values on the *a priori* plane, since we clearly cannot do so, as it would be to claim that they are merely arbitrary. But the alternative is not exclusive. In fact, as Hegel pointed out in his theory of spirit, our social values are the result of an ongoing process of social negotiation between members of a given society. A particular society is never static, but is rather constantly engaged in the process of defining and redefining itself through a vast participatory process in which the values it accepts as its own are constantly being revised. The criterion of justification is not that they are true, however understood, or that they are sanctioned by recognized authority, or that they are suitably derived from reason alone. It is rather that they are accepted by a given society as corresponding to its own understanding of itself at a given point in time. If this is true, social values are always temporary, never permanent, since they are always subject to revision at such time as a given society fails to recognize itself through them.

Social Values and Social Novelty

The simplest way to challenge the widespread idea that there is a single specifiable framework of social values adequate for any and all situations is to point to novel situations that have no real precedent. It has already been noted that the current situation in Eastern Europe, which simply has no precedent in recent history, is perhaps without any real precedent in recorded history. If this is the case, if we are confronted at present with real novelty unlike anything we have so far seen, it would be a significant error to believe that an adequate response could possibly be found through simply applying readily available formulas or other bromides, such as the golden rule, injunctions to rely on democracy, self-help and so forth.

It is obvious that some of the problems, such as food, shelter, basic medical care and so on, are simply too critical to await long-term solutions, but rather require urgent short-range action. Here lessons can be drawn from relevantly similar acute situations that continue to arise. It is considerably more difficult to understand how to react to a large series of longer range problems with which we simply do not have much, if any, relevant prior experience, such as rebuilding the social infra-structure, creating and strengthening a democratic political process, orderly transition between governments in a country such as Russia that has never had such a tradition, or converting from a command-style to a free market economy.

At the time of this writing, the form of unrestrained capitalism that is rapidly emerging in, say, Russia seems perilously close to undermining the very possibility of continuing efforts to achieve even reasonable political and social stability. For instance, the efforts to strengthen nascent democratic reform are clearly undermined by the difficulties of those living on fixed incomes, which have not kept pace with the rise of the cost-of-living. They often are attracted by the idea of returning to a more authoritarian but less socially precarious, form of life. Whether Russia can continue down the perilous road leading to an increasingly democratic form of politics may well turn on finding at least a provisional solution to this problem.

CONCLUSION

This paper has examined the widespread idea of a single set of socially relevant values. This approach is as widespread as it is naïve. It is further socially harmful since it leads in practice not only to false hopes concerning the existence of a single set of standards, but also to the rejection of the pluralistic approach that is probably the single most important methodological guarantee of even moderate success in any effort to address concrete social problems. On closer scrutiny, it turns out that there is no single set of social values on which all parties agree, which are socially relevant, and which are permanent or invariant. Values are a function of the sociocultural context from which they must arise if they are to be meaningful, and, in order to remain meaningful, they must change as the underlying context changes. The problem concerning social values is not to deduce inflexible standards from general principles that hold in all times and places. It is rather a question of finding a way to arrive at values that can be accepted by thinking through concrete problems in order to arrive at the widest possible consensus.

Duquesne University
PA, USA

NOTES

1. See Lévi-Strauss, 1958.
2. The most prominent effort to raise this question from the inside, namely, Amalrik's speculations concerning the continued existence of the Soviet Union in 1984, was not based on a detailed analysis of aspects of the existing situation. See Amalrik 1970.
3. An important example is the examination by Carrère-D'Encausse of the probable rise in tensions due to the hugely superior birth rate in the Moslem republics of the Soviet Union. See Carrère d'Encausse 1978.
4. One of the weaknesses of Hempel's covering law model of history is that it assumes an undemonstrated and indemonstrable basic analogy between history and the natural sciences. See Hempel 1949.
5. The most recent phase of the debate lies in Gettier's

counter-examples, which seem to have refuted the ideal analysis of Jaako Hintikka. For a discussion, see Ackermann 1972.
  6. See Van Parijs 1995.
  7. See Pinker 1995 for a discussion of Chomsky on this matter.

REFERENCES

Ackermann, R. J. (1972). *Belief and Knowledge*. Garden City: Doubleday.
Amalrik, A. (1970). *Will the Soviet Union Exist in 1984?* New York: Harper and Row.
Carrère d'Encausse, H. (1978) *L'empire éclaté*. Paris: Flammarion.
Hempel, C. G. (1949). "The Function of General Laws in History." In Herbert Feigl and Wilfrid Sellars (eds.). *Readings in Philosophical Analysis*. New York: Appleton-Century-Crofts, 459-471.
Lévi-Strauss, C. (1958). *Anthropologie structurale*. Paris: Plon.
Pinker, S. (1995). *The Language Instinct: How the Mind Creates Language*. New York: Harper.
Van Parijs, P. (1995). *Sauver la solidarité*. Paris: Cerf.

PART III

FEATURES OF DEMOCRATIZATION

CHAPTER VIII

BEYOND MODERNITY

VESSELA MISHEVA

EUROPEAN IDENTITY CRISES

The end of the 20th century in Europe is a time of transitions, a time of breaking old alliances, of collapsing boundaries and of closing old schisms. Europe as a whole is in a process of transition from being a continent that until recently was split into two hostile political camps to being a united Europe. The idea of a unified Europe is based most of all upon the idea of social sameness built upon existence in a common present measured by a uniform distance from a common past. The idea of European unification thereby emerges as almost completely devoid of historical sentiment and geographical connotation.

This process, however, is still far from being taken as the beginning of a unification of the present in which all European differences are melted down into a racial, social and cultural amalgamation. Rather, it seems much more as if the old European boundaries, which lived out their allotted time as useless stage settings within an historical drama that has been completed, are in the process of being dismantled in order for the stage to be set for the beginning of a completely different play.

The construction of a new boundary always involves the separation of "the different" from that which is "the same." That which is the European "different" can first of all be seen in the countries of Eastern Europe, whose "return" to Europe, to which they feel they belong, depends on their abilities to produce sufficient evidence of their cultural and social "sameness." The observation of differences concerning the success that different parts of Eastern Europe have enjoyed in this respect makes it clear that any generalized conclusions concerning this process as a whole will most probably be misleading. The impression is that their common immediate past and shared social experience of more than 50 years have not sufficed to eliminate the profound differences between

East European countries. Indeed, these differences apparently have not even been diminished, not to mention overcome. In such a case, that which is important for explaining the different degrees of success of these countries is rather to be found in their pre-Communist historical past and in their previous positions and roles on the political stage of pre-World War II Europe.

In this general picture, certain Balkan countries stand out as a paradoxical exception, as if the dramatic changes in Europe had there produced the most strange effect of opening the bottle where the "genie of old historical schisms" had been imprisoned. This powerful new wave of "Balkanization" and return to the past is quite opposed to the mainstream European orientation towards the future. One reason for such a profound difference is the fact that while most modern European countries look forward to dissociating themselves from their old identities and accepting new ones, certain Balkan countries have never had the opportunity to construct identities that could be replaced in the newly created favorable conditions. The problem is that societies build their identity through continuing reference to their own pasts (Luhmann 1992, 14), which means that only by drawing upon the difference between past and present can societies be capable of defining those points at which they differ in the present.

A long and tragic history has made it possible for a paradoxical question to be asked at the end of the 20th century: To what extent are the countries of the Balkans, conceived as the soil in which the roots of European civilization once sprouted, part of this Europe today? Can they be defined as "European-style societies" when it seems that their emotionally loaded social experience, their intellectual priorities, and their patterns of thinking and acting not only are not readily seen to exhibit "European" features, but in fact are generally considered to be inferior? To what extent can countries that have no other "capital" besides their overwhelmingly tragic social experience of a chain of continuous losses without any gains ever hope that their historical and social presence be acknowledged, especially if the success of their historical efforts lies mainly in self-preservation?

The Paradox of Observation in a European Context

The question of identity in the Balkans thus somehow has a different context than that in which it is located in the rest of Europe, being instead connected with the question of the identity of Europe as a civilization, not as a continent or a political and economic union. When considered in this respect, the question of identity may be said to concern the nature of the "Id" from which the idea of Europe once originated. Since the "Id" does not "travel," but belongs to a particular place that is unique, its "entity" cannot be borrowed from any other location. The "Id" is the medium in which the "idea of Europe" arose and, being designated as the past, gave it a heading. But can this heading assume an ever-growing distance from itself only in order to return to itself in a form of "Hegelian spirit"?

In the philosophical discourse of the last two centuries concerned with various aspects of the crisis of European civilization, the idea of crisis crystallized in the form of a crisis of the "European spirit" that cannot "return to itself in an Absolute Knowledge," as if it had forgotten its point of departure. This is a crisis of the *arché* that cannot name its *telos*, a crisis of the impossibility of reaching a "harbor" that does not have a "heading" because it is home.[1]

From the "heights" of the present, the spread of European civilization resembles a journey around the world undertaken in an effort to acquire a knowledge of "origins" through self-transcendence.[2] Now that all lands have been discovered, all temporal realities synchronized and all social space made accessible, it is clear that European civilization, regardless of the distance travelled, can never succeed in observing itself from without, thereby acquiring a full knowledge of itself, because all its observations necessarily remain one-sided and from within. It must then be assumed that the knowledge of modernity based on a transcendence of the limits of modernity must itself be sought not beyond the geographical limits of the continent, but rather beyond the history delimited by the historical stage of Europe, where live the non-actors, the non-subjects, the non-persons and the non-individuals of the non-modern world. Stated otherwise, this is the non-modern world of collective reason.

There has always been an unmarked social space beyond mainstream European experience taken as experience on a stage of action, an unmarked social space where the presence of Europeans has remained unacknowledged. This is the area of the social suffering of peoples who have lived in "virtual nation states," whose presence has never actually been acknowledged, who have been neither the subjects nor objects of action, and who have been deprived of any action for quite real historical reasons. The only possible role that could have been reserved for such peoples is that of observers, who watch the action in which they do not participate and remain compassionate sufferers with a suffering soul in a paralysed body and mind.

The difference between the role of compassionate observers and all other roles is that the former is never accepted as a personal choice and may not even be their own creation. In social life just as in theater, there can never be roles for every possible actor in every possible play. Some actors act while others sit and watch. In terms of social suffering, the essence of this fact lies in the nature of the social role that the individual has not chosen for himself, namely, the role of an observer for whom access to the stage where action occurs is denied. Indeed, the role of observer is no role at all, indicating rather the absence of a social role.

The question is whether the compassionate observer who never acts may acquire knowledge, and if so, what the nature of that knowledge might be. The very consideration that it may be possible to obtain knowledge that cannot be "learned" by any other means is by itself a challenge to the pragmatist's program idea of "learning by doing" insofar as the latter leaves unlearned a vast area of things that may be learned or known only by observation of action in which one does not participate. This consideration is also a challenge to modern sociological theory whereby the social world is conceived as a world in which there are only two interactive parties and no observers or audience.

To put it in Plato's terms, observers are those who were not taken on board the "ship of state" (Plato's metaphor in *Statesman* and *Republic*) but were rather left in the harbor, from where they watch the horizon in order to see when the ship will return. Suffering in this sense is quite contradictory to any experience in the realm of action. It is the deprivation of action that brings about the Promethean experience of hopeless waiting and lack of personal choice.

BELONGING AND NOT-BELONGING

If European nations can be divided into successful and non-successful nations, this fact can hardly be taken as a proof that peoples have inborn advantages and disadvantages. From a thoroughly sociological perspective, these differences should rather be analyzed as social constructions. The question that should then be asked concerns the factors that should be held responsible for the peculiarity of the Balkans as the most enigmatic portion of the European world.

From a Serbian perspective, the trouble with "this place" is that "it has too much history," as a Serbian poet one put it. From a Bulgarian perspective, the trouble with "this place" is its geographic location in that we built a country on a crossroads, "where no one would even build a hut." From a sociological perspective, both of these points are equally important. For example, it is possible to argue from a sociological point of view that the social fate of any given country may be heavily dependent upon and influenced by the historical roles it has previously adopted. In addition, the geographical location of a particular is of great sociological importance to the extent that it designates the point of observation from which the social world is observed. History and geography taken together can serve as a coordinate system in which the phenomenon of the Balkans can be thematized.

The point is, however, that the events of the immediate as well as of the observable past can hardly be blamed for Bulgaria's constant misfortunes. An analysis of the emergence of the Bulgarian state, along with the emergence of an historical pattern in her fate, create the impression that the continual recurrence of crises was in fact geographically and historically conditioned from the very beginning. Unfortunately, the lack of historical material and written records concerning this "beginning" make it impossible to perform a detailed analysis, but this does not necessarily mean that we cannot offer more than plausible speculations. In this sense, what is true for a human being is no less true for a social system such as a political state or a nation. We can thus talk about a people's fate as being to a great extent defined by the contacts they have developed with various cultural centers, from the "teachers" or "friends" which they have had, and from the "enemies" whom they have fought. In other words, the participation of countries in the process of European interaction is responsible for the shaping of their European minds.

But in a long historical perspective, no geographically bound system's position is better than any other since it is simply different. An important principle in contemporary macrosociological theory, which views the social world as a system, is that such differences can account only for the performance of different social functions. Europe can thus be viewed as a social system in which the many different political subsystems have played and continue to play different historical roles, none of which is more important than others according to the differences in their locations in social time and space.

The question then concerns the type of social position that represents a position located on the *geographical and historical boundary of Europe*, as well as the type of social function that can be ascribed to such a position.

A sociological explanation within the framework of contemporary systems theory in macrosociology (Luhmann 1982) can be found for why a pattern can be observed in the connection between geographic and historical boundaries. According to this theory, the political system of society is the only social system that uses territorial boundaries instead of communication criteria for demarcating its limits. It is then not surprising that geographical boundaries such as rivers and mountains not only frequently coincide with political boundaries, but also tend to recur once they have been established. Indeed, a thorough examination of the history of the place occupied by Bulgaria may convince scholars that history tends to repeat itself in certain particular places.

Support for this hypothesis can be found in the discussions in modern sociology concerned with the process of constructing social reality, according to which it is *unsuccessful socialization* that raises the question "Who am I?" (Berger and Luckmann 1967, 190). We may thereby speak about European countries that are unsuccessful today because of their historically defined *unsuccessful European socialization*. It is further important to note that primary socialization creates the pattern for further socializations, which in respect to the primarily internalized "base-world" are only partial realities or "sub-worlds" (*ibid.*, 158). Stated otherwise, the fact that it is apparently impossible for certain countries to assume any significant role is connected with the impossibility of a subjective identification with any of the particular existing roles. It can therefore be assumed that the resolution of this identity crisis may lead to the construction of a completely new role for which there previously has been no pattern.

Today, the signs of identity crisis are evident on almost all social levels. This equally affects individuals, peoples, nations, sciences and even the whole of European civilization, all being equally caught up by the inexplicable desire to know who they are. *Identity* has become the new catchword in modern social science, which itself is at pains to understand its modern origin. Such a situation, in which individuals, peoples and even entire nations acquire self-awareness, as belonging to a particular social whole according to certain criteria as well as being excluded according to others, is unmistakable evidence for what is known in sociology as an "identity crisis." Indeed, the question "Who am I?" does not seem to have occupied the consciousness of people on such a mass scale since classical antiquity, where *self-knowledge* had the status of a social imperative.

The conditions of social life in those days must have been quite similar in some essential aspect to those today if the question "Who am I?" has been so important in the two social realities so distant from each other in time. For example, these similarities may have something to do with the unsuccessful socialization of certain people with respect to their having been brought up in conditions of insuperable social conflict and yet feeling that they belong to both sides of it.[3] The simultaneous internalization of two conflicting worlds is a matter not of choice, but rather of social position, from which a conflict between two different worlds is presented as the only reality there is. In this regard, the process of primary socialization is a matter of fate to a greater extent than anything else in the social world. Neither can children choose the family into which they will be born, nor can people choose their mother tongue or the countries in which they are first socialized.

Although it seems reasonable to claim that any "birthplace" where primary socialization takes place is as good as any other, there is still one special place that is unlike any other because it lacks the basic privilege of any other place, namely, the privilege of granting identification. This is the place that can be defined as a boundary, i.e., as a place located between two worlds that is equally a part of both and yet belongs to neither. Such a state of "non-belonging" may easily be seen as leading to a special type of nihilism that is expressed in self-negation and is responsible for a *"neither/ nor, but both"* attitude towards a divided world.

According to Berger and Luckmann, the main result of the process of primary socialization is the construction of the *individual's first world*. But this world acquires a more complex structure with socialization in conflict systems than is the case with normal primary socialization. Although it is still a "theater," it is nevertheless quite different from that which Goffman described because it is a "tragic theater," i.e., it has not only a *stage* where the two interaction parties act, but also an *orchestra* where the observer or, as Nietzsche had it, the *ideal spectator* is situated.

In other words, upbringing in a conflict system, where there is no *dialogue*, but rather a *duel* between two equally right reasons, creates a compassionate observer who cannot take sides and yet suffers with the sufferings of both; who can neither take part in the action nor interrupt it because his presence is not acknowledged; who only can imitate the actions of both parties, being equally loyal and disloyal to both insofar as he belongs to both parties and yet can join neither of them.[4] These are the conditions in which the mind of *Chorus members* is constructed. They will have a role in the future although they have none in the present. For them the ancient Greek tragic theater preserved the role of pronouncing *the verdict of history*.[5]

Historical Excursus

The primary example that will be utilized in the present analysis is the place where Bulgaria is situated today. It is a Balkan country that has remained outside of mainstream European development for centuries, thereby becoming virtually completely invisible within the European context in which it is today situated. From the times of Plato, the essence of the passion and powerful emotion that represents the "Balkan spirit" has always been an enigma for the "civilized world" and has never been successfully decoded. Perhaps this is also one reason why the Balkans, which even the Enlightenment could not illuminate, still remain a "dark place" for advancing

European civilization.

The drive for self-knowledge has been quite typical of Bulgaria, which for centuries has gone through the agony of trying to "remember" who she was in order to gain the self-confidence that comes only with the knowledge of one's own history or one's own self. This creates the impression of a country that pretends to look forward to the future while actually having her gaze fixed steadily in the past. This apparently was true not only during the identity crisis that emerged after 1990, when she considered the possibility of having taken the wrong road, but even during the period in which Bulgaria claimed to be moving forward towards a Communist future.

The consequences of such a crisis are expressed by the fact that it is even impossible for the country to define her national interests, never having had a history of such interests, not to mention the impossibility of dissociating herself from the past and transforming feelings that have been cultivated over centuries into emotionless reason.

The importance of Bulgaria's particular geographical location can first be seen in the very creation of the Bulgarian state in the seventh century on a supposedly devastated and depopulated territory where the Thracian Odryssian state, which Thucydides had described almost ten centuries earlier as being most powerful and rich, had once been located. On this same territory, the heart of the ancient Thracian diaspora (Fol 1971), the Balkan Mountains became the boundary that divided the Latin from the Greek speaking worlds, making it a most convenient place for observing the difference between the two. Historians maintain on the basis of limited historical material that the Bulgarian state emerged as a result of a unique contract between two different ethnic groups having completely different cultures and patterns of life (Bulgarians and Slavs), who had chosen this European crossroads to begin a common settled life. Insofar as centuries-old popular Bulgarian cultural and ritual practices exhibit essential Thracian features to this day, it can be surmised that the remaining native population served as a kind of reconciliation force for establishing this union. Evidence for this type of social cooperation and cultural interpenetration is also provided by the particularity of the Bulgarian language as a construction of three diverse components, a fact that necessarily reflects the complex process of its formation.

It is very difficult to discover the traces of Thracian presence in Bulgarian history due to the fact that the main medium through which this culture realizes itself is oral tradition. From another point of view, however, it is precisely this type of culture that was most capable of survival during the centuries of Ottoman control, when the Bulgarian state ceased to exist and written tradition was long disrupted. It might thus be said that as the two cultural traditions of body and mind developed by Bulgarians and Slavs declined and almost vanished for a time, languishing without their own guardians, rulers and literate intellectuals, the only guarantor for the continued existence of Bulgarians as people was the invisible "third component."

This seems to have been the case at least when the initial signs of an awareness of the absence of self-consciousness emerged through the efforts of Paisii Hilendarski to write the first Bulgarian history. This history was apparently intended to be a "cure" for the gasping Bulgarian spirit, which had miraculously survived in spite of being divided between two different alien worlds. The "body" had been enslaved by the Ottomans and its physical power channelled through the Ottoman empire, while the "mind" had been enslaved by the Greeks and its communications forcibly channelled through the Greek language.

Under the pressure for assimilation, it is always possible that a people be preserved because of the difficulty in crushing and enslaving the invisible spirit. The spirit has no material expression, leaves no written records of itself, nor does it depend on particular social and material conditions for its maintenance. Apparently all that it required is a medium appropriate for channelling the feelings that no master can control. Regardless of the historical misfortunes some peoples may suffer, their history does not necessarily represent a chain of losses without any gains. But it is also not easy to perceive the "gains" that a preservation of the spirit may bring.

In this respect, historical conditions in Bulgaria have not always been appropriate for cultural development comparable to that of countries who have not shared a similar fate and did not experience a colonization of body and mind. Nevertheless they provided the opportunity for the continuation and flourishing of a culture that has long been considered to be an "extinct species" in the modern civilized world. The unique historical experience of a

European country that continuously maintained an observation position on the border of Europe, where two different civilizations were locked in struggle, may be seen as materialized first of all in the particularity of Bulgarian folklore as being representative of a highly idiosyncratic and symbolic culture. One of its most peculiar and unique features is perhaps its antithetical style.

From a systems point of view, there is the interesting question concerning changes in interaction rules that an oppressed society must introduce when it is faced with the necessity of talking not only with, but also about, those who are present.[6] For this reason, it may be said that the oral tradition of Bulgarian culture has a particular *style* that obviously had to be developed as the only means for constructing the social boundaries of an invisible state.

The Spirit as a Non-Person

This state of affairs demands a careful examination of the particularities of the place in question and its peoples because their current problems can no longer be viewed merely as results of chaotic circumstances whereby historical events in the Balkans always take the "wrong course." This in fact is the crisis of an oppressed European pre-history whose traces, having never completely withered away, constantly strive to become a matter of conscious awareness. This is the crisis of a place on the border between two continents, which cannot "borrow" an identity from any place else because it is identical only to itself. The Balkans have their own unique spirit, a European spirit that is stationary, remains true to itself and does not change.

During the 500 years of Ottoman control, Bulgaria lost her social and cultural presence in Europe. Although the Bulgarian state was restored at the end of the 19th century, today it is more clear than ever before that she is virtually not a subject within any context of European discourse. The countries that are present in such "European" discourse participate on the basis of accumulated cultural, intellectual, economic and political capital. The question then becomes whether there is something that has been accumulated and not dispersed which is of sufficient value to serve as a basis for exchange and interaction with other European countries.

Even among the Slavic countries, Bulgaria lost the prestige

and cultural importance that she once enjoyed by virtue of the creation and spread of Slavic literacy after her system of education was destroyed by invading conquerors. Indeed, it would be no exaggeration to say that she was transformed into a non-written culture and thrown back into the "darkness" from which she had emerged in her successful struggle against the almost overwhelming resistance of the Latin and Greek speaking worlds. As a result, the Bulgarian language not only lost its elegance, richness and grace, but also the honor of being the first written Slavic language (old Bulgarian), through which Orthodox Christian Slavic culture and the social, spiritual and artistic heritage of the Byzantine civilization had once been disseminated.

But an even greater tragedy for Bulgaria was that she lost her self-consciousness. In the 18th century she no longer knew why and when she was enchained, who she was, nor whence she came.[7] Since then she has been trying to remember and rediscover her lost identity because something in her unconscious memory does not quite correspond to the "memories" that the "other" has about her.[8] Because history is also a product human beings that have feelings and emotions, the question "Who is the historian, who is the storyteller?" cannot be put aside.

At the end of the 19th century, Bulgaria had to enter the modern world without the necessary cultural competence concerning the ways in which modern Western culture had been encoded. Bulgaria was neither venerated nor consecrated, regardless of the weight of her history, the extent of her suffering and the preservation of a quite old and unique European culture that dates from a time about which Europe has neither memories nor sufficient records. This situation has not changed much a century later, and the question concerning the place of Bulgaria in European culture is as acute as it ever was.

Bulgaria nevertheless succeeded during several decades of capitalist development to establish a stable economy based on her traditionally strong agriculture after she had been finally liberated by Czarist Russia in 1878.[9] However, Bulgaria lost even these economic advantages during the Communist period.[10] Social, cultural and economical disasters have also been accompanied by an ecological crisis. The beauty of the country, which has long been the source of inspiration and of deep emotions and passion, has been severely damaged, and one wonders if there is still anything left which can be lost.

It is true that Bulgarians survived as a people, that their state was not forever erased from the map of Europe, and that their language was preserved. But does the mere survival of a nation provide sufficient grounds in the modern world for earning recognition and prestige? Can we say that there are no longer any obstacles to the advance of the creative forces and the spirit of the Bulgarian people?

Ehrenberg observes in respect to certain outstanding and striking historical examples, such as the survival of an idea, a people or a civilization that "outlives all human expectations, and continues to maintain its historical existence in spite of the strongest endeavors to destroy it," that "it is perhaps here that the greatest heroism of human beings is displayed" (Ehrenberg 1974, 173). However, Bulgarians have never been counted among these "striking examples," regardless of the genocide waged against them in the second half of the 19th century which passed unnoticed, like so many other political events in Bulgaria's more recent history. In this sense, too, a pattern can be observed according to which not only the great days but also the great sufferings of Bulgarians have been passed over in silence.[11]

Looking back through their seemingly senseless, centuries-long history of life without freedom, Bulgarians find no other source of pride than the preservation of the "spirit" that is somehow firmly and inseparably attached to the "place." Now, while even a brief glance indicates that Bulgarians apparently believe that this spirit is a *treasure*, it is not clear what cultural value can be ascribed to it, nor how a "spirit" can play some socially important role. Furthermore, why should a "spirit" that demands endless sacrifice and suffering without any gain be preserved?[12]

ON THE QUESTION OF "BALKAN NATIONALISM"

In sociology, "nation" is considered to be a modern phenomenon. It is closely related to the concept of nation state, whose boundaries are either a matter of self-definition, an issue to be determined through negotiation with other nations or both. Nation formation is thus a process of self-definition and self-separation from other peoples, the grounds for which involve such shared features as history, experience, language or even a common enemy. A nation cannot be formed from without.

"Nationalism" is generally understood as a claim for priority or superiority over other nations and people. We talk about nationalism in cases where one nation exalts itself above all others, but in order to use this term we must first be sure that there already is and continues to be a nation. Against this background, the movement of a people for self-definition and nation formation can hardly be considered as an expression of "nationalism" insofar as the term has no legitimacy and meaning when there is not yet a nation. The Bulgarian National Revival, for example, can thus not be defined as a nationalist movement since it was rather a struggle to create the Bulgarian nation. Bulgarian historiography correctly refers to this process as a "movement for national self-determination."

In addition, the concept of "nation" must also be considered in respect to systems theory, according to which it is possible to talk about political systems and nation states only when their boundaries have been drawn from within. Because systems boundaries always belong to the system that establishes them, states whose territorial boundaries have been defined or delimited from the outside cannot be conceived of as social systems.

But it must be questioned whether modern terms can be applied to describe peoples who have never actually become modern, nor even had the opportunity to do so. It is necessary to consider the possibility that a nation may be dismantled under certain conditions, or that it may cease to exist as a system when stripped of the right to participate in interaction concerning its own boundaries.

And what is the "other" of the concept of nationalism?

It is no exaggeration to say that the question of boundaries has always been, as it still is today, the most acute question in the Balkans. The likely reason for this has been the fact that this is a place where many different European interests have clashed and become intertwined, giving rise to a myriad of often conflicting border designations. During the course of a long and complex history, establishing the existential boundaries of certain Balkan peoples has often been a matter of "other-determination" by external authorities rather than self-determination or negotiation. Today there are few existing boundaries that cannot be challenged, and it is virtually impossible to identify just criteria for redefining them that do not leave one or another interest unsatisfied. It is as inappropriate in this respect to appeal to the power of reason as it is to disregard the power of suppressed feelings. Perhaps the fact that peoples in the Balkans once again took a path completely different from that of most of Europe after the collapse of the Communist block is somehow connected with the popular wisdom that "In order to unite, we first have to separate." Nevertheless, still absent from the Balkans is the tradition of self-determination that other European peoples have long enjoyed.

Bulgaria today, in particular, can be considered neither a state nor a nation if we accept systems criteria as decisive. Formations whose boundaries have been drawn from the outside are not nation states, but rather "compulsory organizations" or institutions.[13] Bulgaria would then be not a nation, but rather a compulsory organization.

Nationalism as a concept cannot be used to signify both sides of one and the same difference. The "other side" of this difference can only be designated by a term that is virtually unknown in sociological literature. This term is *national nihilism*.

National Nihilism as a Sociological Concept

It is not necessary to convince anyone familiar with Bulgaria, her history and her culture that the situation she faces today is not the same as that of the other former Communist countries.[14] To talk about "Bulgarian nationalism" indicates a lack of any understanding of Bulgarian psychology. What we must discuss instead in this respect in precisely a kind of "national nihilism."

Although national nihilism obviously requires a process of self-thematization and self-examination, it is not merely a "private question" of little importance to the general body of scientific knowledge that deals with the particular in what is common and the repeatable rather than with the common and the repeatable in what is particular and unique. Indeed, I would argue that it is precisely a lack of knowledge of the "other" of nationalism that accounts for the lack of needed development in the contemporary theory of nationalism.[15] From this point of view, the concept of national nihilism as the "other" of the concept of nationalism is of special interest to contemporary sociology.

The concept of national nihilism can easily be regarded as a kind of paradox, being related as it is to a type of people's consciousness that "exalts" itself beneath all other peoples and nations. If national nihilism presupposes the existence of a nation, it rather points to the state of a nation whose identity, loyalty and devotion are built upon self-negation. From another point of view, national nihilism also implies an ironically high level of "national altruism" whereby people respect all other nations more than themselves and place primary emphasis on promoting other nations' and peoples' cultures and interests. Perhaps we should then say that national nihilism exists where a nation either no longer exists, or exists in some state of disintegration that hardly exhibits any collective features except a shared positive attitude towards "the other" and a lack of respect towards what is considered to be the same.[16]

If we accept Giddens's definition of a nation as a "collectivity existing within a clearly demarcated territory, which is subject to a unitary administration, reflexively monitored both by the internal state apparatus and those of other states," then we must conclude that the Bulgarian nation was formed in the ninth century insofar as the Bulgarian state then had "unified administrative reach over the territory over which its sovereignty was claimed" (Giddens 1985, 116, 119). It had its own language, script, laws, common religion, high degree of territorial integration under a central administration and ethnic integrity based on the amalgamation of Thracians, Slavs and Bulgars.

But if we accept his claim that "nations and nationalism are distinctive properties of modern states" (Giddens 1985, 116), then the Bulgarian nation could not have been formed before 1878. Given his definition, it is incomprehensible how certain historians could talk about "Bulgarian nationalism" or even "Macedonian nationalism" under the condition of the complete absence of states. Furthermore, insofar as Bulgarians themselves did not participate in the process of determining their state boundaries and Bulgarian interests were not taken into account in 1878, then the application of Giddens's definition becomes even more problematic. We could not justifiably speak of the Bulgarian nation because the demarcation of its territory was not a process of "reflexive monitoring" by internal and external forces and its boundaries were formed by the bureaucracies of other states. There is no place for the case of Bulgaria in such discussions of nationalism.

It is thus no coincidence that neither Bulgarophilism nor even Slavophilism strongly developed in Bulgaria after 1878, nor that she failed to overcome her past and to orient herself to the future. Political life instead became an arena of imported retro-romantic tendencies as expressed by the two strongest political parties, the Germanophils and the Russophils.[17] This was also the time when socialist and Communist ideas began to flourish, as if disproving all claims about their modern class characteristics.

This strange mode of political determination that is based upon disregarding a nation's own interests and preferring those of others has not been sufficiently studied. It reveals national nihilism to be a paradoxical state of self-denial, self-underestimation and self-dishonor which however, must be considered as being proceeded by a denial of the "other." National nihilism is a state most typical for a people in an identity crisis that has been brought about by a confused history of living on a boundary, a people who have always belonged to no less than two different worlds but have never belonged to themselves. This identity crisis is accompanied by an acute sense of shame, of being different, of being "other," that paralyses the mind and body and makes one incapable of social action.

The important question concerns the causes for this painful self-negation.[18] Studying the question of nihilism, Nietzsche found its roots in Christian morality.

In summary, the problem for Bulgaria is hidden in its past, the chains of which it carries along in any new future that it enters. The case of Bulgaria thus represents an ideal object in which national nihilism can be studied as a phenomenon having particular social causes and social consequences.

The Philosophy of Nihilism

Nihilism is one of the core problems in the works of Nietzsche. Although today there is a much greater need for an analysis of nihilism than there was a century ago, there have been no significant efforts after him to "decode" the spell that has been cast upon human beings, condemning them to permanent negation and a reproduction of the tragic.

Nietzsche distinguishes two types of nihilism, namely, an *active nihilism* and a *passive nihilism*. The former is the embodiment of strength and a "sign of increased power of the spirit," but it is also "a violent force of destruction," while the latter is the sign of weakness and is a "weary nihilism that no longer attacks" (Nietzsche 1968b, 13-14).

In its ordinary meaning, nihilism is often viewed as a "philosophy of negation" that rejects traditional authority and morality. It is thus taken to be a lack of faith in the existing order. But since no other order can replace the latter, the very foundation of traditional beliefs is challenged and existence thereby loses its meaning, even though it could be claimed that traditional morality, values and beliefs are not necessarily objects of negation. In respect to Bulgarian nihilism, however, it seems that the reverse is the case, i.e., it is the underlying tradition which negates through a continuous reproduction of certain basic eternal values in every type of new present that may come about. This is a nihilism carried out by an agent that does not accept any external reformulation and is oriented towards the preservation of a kind of "primordial" homeostasis. This is a negation of a present that always remains "inferior" to a social ideal that has been lost somewhere in the past. In comparison with modernity and its emphasis on the present, such social characteristics are deeply anti-modern.[19]

Bulgarian nihilism is a kind of passive optimism of waiting, an inexhaustible faith that the future will come only if the past will be preserved.[20] Because of this orientation to the past, it is almost as if the new future is somehow paradoxically viewed as the result of quantitative processes, not as a kind of qualitative change introduced from outside.[21]

For Nietzsche, "it is an error to consider 'social distress' or 'physiological degeneration' or, worse, corruption, as the cause of nihilism. . . . Distress, whether of the soul, body or intellect, cannot of itself give birth to nihilism (i.e., the radical repudiation of value, meaning and desirability)" (Nietzsche 1968b, 7). He later becomes more precise: "Nihilism as a psychological state will have to be reached, first, when we have sought a 'meaning' in all events that is not there: so the seeker eventually becomes discouraged. Nihilism, then, is the recognition of the long *waste* of strength, the agony of the 'in vain,' insecurity, the lack of any opportunity to recover and the regain composure - being ashamed in front of oneself, as if one had *deceived* oneself all too long" (*ibid.*, 12).[22] But since Nietzsche remains too abstract and obscure in his efforts to relieve the causes of "agony" and waste of strength, it is as if we can find in his philosophy whatever we know that we are searching for. In respect to the Nazis' mistreatment of Nietzsche's philosophy in this fashion, the key phrase in the above quotation was apparently "being ashamed in front of oneself."[23]

Nihilism, as a psychological state not only of the individual but also of groups of people, communities, or nations, is connected with feelings of shame. Nietzsche, whose moralizing upon "shame" seems to have preceded the discoveries of contemporary microsociology by a hundred years, does not see nihilism as related to the feeling of guilt. In *The Gay Science* he wrote: "*Whom do you call bad?* - Those who always want to put to shame" (Nietzsche 1982, 273); "*What do you consider most humane?* — To spare someone shame (*ibid.*, 274); "*What is the seal of attained freedom?* — No longer being ashamed in front of oneself" (*ibid.*, 275).[24]

LIFE WITHOUT MASK OR MAKE-UP: SHAME

Aristotle defines shame in *The Nicomachean Ethics* as a "quasi-virtue".[25] His interest is here directed towards the changes in "bodily conditions" produced by shame, such as blushing or turning pale. Shame then becomes identified with a type of fear, the "fear of dishonor," not much different from "the fear of death" (Aristotle 1986, 1128b 11-16). In addition, Aristotle states that although shame is a passion which "is not becoming to every age," young people should nevertheless be praised for it because they are "prone to this passion" and, living by passion, commit many errors (*ibid.*, 1128b 17-24). Shame is thus a "consequence of bad action" that older persons should not indulge because "the sense of disgrace is not even characteristic of a good man" (*ibid.*, 1128b 25-27). What is more important, Aristotle considers a bad action as not only related to passion, but also as related to deviant behavior and disobedience of the accepted rules. He notes that "if some actions are disgraceful in very truth and others only according to common opinion, this makes no difference; for neither class of actions should be done, so that no disgrace should be felt" (*ibid.*, 1128b 28-32). Aristotle later states that "it is for voluntary actions that shame is felt," and that the "good man will never do voluntary bad actions," which implies that he might be forced to do so. And the moral lesson concludes with the suggestion that while shame might be thought to be conditionally good in comparison with shamelessness, it makes no sense to be ashamed once a bad action has already been performed since "it does not make it good to be ashamed of doing such actions" (*ibid.*, 1128b 30-32).

Sociology today is ever more aware that underlying the power game of history, which selects successful and non-successful nations, lies an area of human emotions that are expressed in the complex dynamics of pride, shame, guilt and self-identity. The concepts of shame, pride and guilt have only recently begun to transcend the field of microsociology such that they indicate how it may be possible not only to overcome, but indeed to discredit the gap between micro and macro-social events.[26] The shift of attention from the macro to the micro-social world may be taken as signifying a new type of ideology in the social sciences according to which macro events are viewed as results of deep and complex processes in the micro social world.

Shame is universally recognized as a painful feeling with an external cause that is forced upon consciousness from the outside. The sense of guilt, on the other hand, is a psychological state consequent to actions of the individual that result in injury to someone else. According to Scheff's definition, the feeling of guilt is "evoked by a specific and quite delimited act or failure to act" that "involves the possibility of injuring another" (Scheff 1990, 168). Shame raises a serious question about the adequacy of the self and its basic worth, coming as it does after an injury that has been inflicted by a more powerful self (*ibid.*). Guilt, on the contrary, may even make the self stronger insofar as "guilty persons may even feel pride (the reverse of shame) that they are feeling guilt: it shows that they are basically moral persons; that is, they have intact, capable selves" (*ibid.*, 169).[27]

But the appearance of a feeling of shame has no necessary connection with having previously committed some sort of a mistake.

Shame is not necessarily the price that must be paid for guilt, and shame and guilt are not related to each other by reciprocal causality. In a hostile and aggressive social environment, for example, a child may acquire a nickname that may become a permanent source of shame irrespective of any of his actions. Shame may also be regarded as a result of the "desacralization" of the sacred, whereby something that should remain hidden from the eyes of any external observer is dragged out of the intimate and private realm of the individual into the sphere of public affairs. In addition, shame may be caused by the fact that one who is present, considers himself a person and claims a social role is ignored by others and not treated as present. A child might find it quite comfortable to remain invisible in the interaction between adults, and he may even feel embarrassment and shame if attention is directed towards him, but the contrary is certainly the case in respect to an adult whose presence remains unnoticed.[28]

Scheff agrees with Aristotle in that shame is the price that must be paid for deviant behavior, emphasizing that society is much more inclined to punish with shame that which is different rather than that which it recognizes as conforming to existing rules: "conformity to exterior norms is rewarded by deference and the feeling of pride, and non-conformity is punished by a lack of deference and the feeling of shame" (Scheff 1990, 95). Tradition thereby tends to condemn creative behavior as deviant as well, and the threat of shame, which Goffman speaks of as "loss of face," serves to preserve the convention that tolerates only conformity. Scheff maintains that while both shame and guilt result from the violation of certain laws or conventions, guilt is nevertheless a much more positive feeling than shame.[29] The latter can furthermore become ubiquitous and virtually invisible, reaching its tragic form in the case of chronic shame, i.e., a case of low self-esteem in which "one is usually not proud of one's self but ashamed" (*ibid.*, 171). Such emotional states as "feeling trapped" force an individual into a cycle of emotional reactions to previous emotional reactions, and they are capable of giving rise to panic and the inability to behave rationally. Being frightened that one is frightened or being ashamed that one is ashamed may assume such proportions "that the victim is paralysed in mind and body" (*ibid.*).

Within the context of the present discussion, shame will be

defined with a sociological reference as the feeling of those who either never had a mask, or whose mask has been removed. Stated otherwise, it is the social suffering connected with the conflict between physical presence and social absence, between the fact of being on stage and having no social role, involving the lack of access to the social medium that defines the boundary of the social system that those who are ashamed observe from without. Shame is the feeling resulting from being enchained and removed from the stage, from the only location where social action is possible.

In contrast, guilt is the feeling of a person who has a social role and, therefore, a mask. Guilt always arises as the feeling of a person on stage who experiences a particular type of distress in connection with the role he is playing, as if the force of circumstances has pressured him into doing what he did. The guilty man would like to step outside of his role, while the person who is ashamed has no role and wishes to have one. Both guilt and shame thus have a point in common in that they are expressions of the feelings of someone who does not want to be in his own social position.

Not only may a constant and overwhelming feeling of shame paralyze an individual, it may have the same effect on an entire nation. This in fact is the case that apparently corresponds to the state of Bulgarian national consciousness. Such a situation suggests that the reasons for Bulgaria's situation are not to be sought on the surface of social and political affairs or economic life. Rather, it is what may be called the "national self" that is suffering and must be cured; it is the feeling of national shame that still keeps Bulgarians unfree. But this feeling also apparently keeps them "non-modern" because not only has shame been considered not a virtue from the time of Aristotle, it has been expelled from the civilized world as a useless passion that is inappropriate for any civilized person.[30] The civilized world is the world of the guilty, not the world of those who are ashamed.

SENSELESS SUFFERING: AN INQUIRY INTO THE SPIRITUAL WORLD OF THE BULGARIAN ORTHODOX CHRISTIAN

It is not the degree of her suffering that makes the history of

Bulgaria tragic, but rather its senselessness.[31] Her suffering never acquired any meaning, and her case can hardly be understood in terms of the suffering prescribed by the ascetic ideal "placed under the perspective of guilt" that Nietzsche sought to overthrow (Nietzsche 1968a, 598). The rationale of Bulgarian suffering rather seems to contradict the idea of personal guilt, and that which can be found in the national memory is rather the image of an agent (God and other mysterious creatures) who takes something from the people for which he never pays in any form other than by causing them pain. In this sense it is God who is in debt to people.[32] In the Bulgarian consciousness there are no traces of sins committed in the past for which atonement must be paid. Their suffering is rather a "mission" whose *telos* lies in the future.

Thus, behind the seemingly disrespectful attitude of many ordinary Bulgarians toward religion, there can still be found a certain correspondence with aspects of Orthodox Christianity that reveal a quite different view of life, or a different point of observation, than that of Roman Catholicism. However, the poorly developed sociology of religion in Eastern Europe does not provide any self-analyses by virtue of which the religious differences between East and West might be clearly seen. Nor does the sociology of religion as developed in the West offer anything more than a view from the outside of Orthodox Christianity. The modern world, generally speaking, considers Eastern Orthodoxy to be an inferior spiritual "branch" of Christianity that is incapable of producing anything of cultural importance comparable to Western Christianity. It is easy to see from such an external observation position what Orthodox Christianity does not have, such as something equivalent to the Reformation, but the application of Western criteria makes it difficult to see what does comprise its actual significance and value.

Although Eastern Orthodoxy rejected the institution of Roman papacy in the Middle Ages, it did not undergo any period of Reformation and continues to place a great deal of emphasis on tradition and liturgy. For such reasons, it does not represent the same degree of interest for contemporary Western sociology of religion as does its rival Christian spirit. It might nevertheless be argued that the way in which the Eastern Orthodox Churches had to fight for survival in the face of the Muslim onslaught that began in the seventh century has been never appropriately examined and evaluated within Western Christendom.[33] As is normally the case in history, a struggle with a powerful enemy whose only positive outcome can be survival is never appropriately acknowledged or honored.

It is true that the Eastern Orthodox Church did not participate in the worldly affairs of the project of modernization because it was prevented from doing so by historical circumstances. But it suffered its unfortunate *fate* precisely because of its *faith*, whose canons prescribe inaction and social suffering rather than action, even if the latter be aimed at one's own liberation.[34]

It cannot be said that Bulgarians became atheist under the Communist regime as a result of successful Communist "conversion," as some might have expected. In fact, neither the consciousness of the Communist-atheist nor that of the Orthodox Christian significantly interfered with the well-preserved traditional and fatalistic way of thinking typical of the man from the countryside in a patriarchal society. Communist morality and beliefs might easily be seen as a kind of "modern religion" that sought to replace Christian Orthodoxy without, however, destroying the bases of the pre-Christian community morality that both of them shared.[35]

From another point of view, the Bulgarian spirit exhibits certain features that Nietzsche identified with the "atheistic spirit," even though it itself is not such a spirit (Nietzsche 1968a, 598). It manifests itself as stronger than any ideals imported from other cultures, which it constantly "Bulgarized" in order to remain true only to itself. This state of affairs relates Bulgarians to the "comedians" of such ideals, whom Nietzsche considered to be the only real enemies of the ascetic ideal, capable of raising a damaging mistrust against it. This is perhaps due to the fact that the spiritual world of Bulgarians seems to be strongly defined by a traditional wisdom that somehow always succeeds in placing itself "above" any kind of modern ideals.[36] Here, too, can be recognized the features normally attributed to the rebellious Holy Spirit of tradition and change, for whom the Eastern Orthodox Church has always had a great respect.

The particular feature of this "anti-modern" spirit is that it has clearly defined boundaries for its negating activity. "Modern" ideals hold an inexplicable fascination for Bulgarians only when these ideals "live abroad." As soon as they "cross" the border of Bulgaria and begin to "settle down," they lose their foreign halo and magical attractiveness and acquire the comic features of playful imitations.

Since ancient times Europe has been a place where schisms of different kinds replace each other without any of them being resolved. But the possibilities that they might have common roots, might well be different "hypostases" of some unresolved "primordial" problem, and that the history of European civilization is a story of incommensurable polarities that nevertheless communicate with each other, have not previously been discussed. Some of the peculiarities and differences around which European civilization obviously once originated should also be considered as responsible for differences between the "fates" of different nations, peoples, communities, strata, groups and even individuals. It can be argued, nevertheless, that the decisive advances made by the social sciences in recent decades, such as the development of powerful new theoretical schemes and methods, have finally made it possible for such important questions to be raised.

The Orthodox Christian Mystic: between East and West

Inquiring further into the causes of the unfortunate fate and suffering of certain Balkan peoples may lead to the particular features of the Orthodox Christian attitude towards the world. Weber described mysticism as being typical for the Eastern Christian Church, and it is also embedded in the Slavophile conception of the community as being tied to the concepts of ancient Christianity (Weber 1978, 550-51). One of its essential features is the conviction that all "actions in the world" are justified only when guided by the feeling of love.

Mysticism is an often noted quality of the Bulgarian spiritual world. Bulgarians often have been seen as "contemplative mystics" who have a quite different mode of behavior than the Occidental ascetics, whose meaning is neither obvious, nor intelligible, nor apparent to the senses. The true followers of a mystical way of life never apply for or perform the role of "God's instrument," but rather desire and seek to remain true to the role of "God's vessel." Thus, they do not "act in the world" but rather suffer in the world of action, trying to perform only those actions most necessary for their survival. For the Bulgarian mystics, even the effort to liberate themselves from an unbearable 500 years of servitude, when the "vessel" had already been filled with emotions, would have to be considered as a wish to become "a tool of God" and, as such, a pattern of behavior unacceptable for the true believer.

At the same time, this mysticism also differs from Eastern mysticism. It is rather a kind of mysticism that is typical for the representatives of high-land culture, who do not undertake actions to change nature in order to make it more comfortable for themselves. Rather, they adapt themselves to it and use the products of nature, changing not its substance but its organization.[37] It should also be emphasized that any advance in social organization loses its meaning under such conditions. Such a thing as slavery could never have any reason to appear among representatives of high-land culture. It might be said that the advantages of the style of life associated with high-land culture have never been appropriately discussed. In ancient times, for example, artistic activity, the invention of musical instruments, musical virtuosity, and singing were high-land cultural affairs. And this should not be surprising since only people with such a style of life could have the necessary free social time for the contemplation of nature, abstract thinking, and creation. Athenian citizens, on the contrary, enjoyed such advantages only after the establishment of the institution of slavery.

Such considerations reveal that there is another kind of mystic who is quite different from that described by Weber. This is a mystic who does not deny action in general but only particular kinds of actions, namely, those directed against nature, of which he is a part and from which he never distances himself. In order to describe this mystic adequately, we must first distinguish between internal and external activity. Thus, in contrast with both asceticism and an oriental type of contemplation, external activity is visibly minimized for this type of mystic, but not "internal activity." In some respects he can be said to be an "outer-worldly ascetic" because his close relations with nature permit him neither to harm nature nor change it in order to ensure a more "civilized" and comfortable existence for himself. His "inner world," however, is a rich emotional world produced by aesthetic appreciation. The Occidental "inner-worldly ascetic," as described by Weber, seems to have chosen the opposite path. He must suppress his feelings and emotions, distantiate himself from nature and make nature his object in order to improve the conditions for his own being in the world. In other words, we may find in this latter image of the "inner-worldly ascetic" almost everything which comprises the idea of civilization.[38]

The fact that this "other" type of mysticism is so typical for Bulgaria should not be surprising. First, it must be noted that the Thracians, who represent the substrata of the Bulgarian nation, were themselves representatives of high-land culture. As a result of processes of colonization and enslavement, as well as migration in connection with the changing centers of European civilization (Greece, Rome, Byzantium), low-land Thracian culture had practically disappeared by the time Slavs and Bulgarians came to the Balkan peninsula. Second, during the 500 year period of the Ottoman yoke, the survivors were once again those people who lived in the mountains, some of whom were never approached by the Turks. Geographical location may obviously provide a natural barrier against even the process of enslavement, and it offers remarkable advantages when it comes to social or natural survival.

If we may speak about a "world-rejecting" attitude on the part of these kinds of peoples, this involves a rejection of the social world, not the natural world, and the reasons for this are rather pre-Christian than Christian. And even when the outer world becomes extremely hostile, there always is a place of security where one may hide, namely, the inner world, which is inaccessible to any kind of colonization or enslavement.

From this point of view, the suffering of this type of mystic is also expressed in the form of spiritual tragedy. On the one hand, it is God (conceived as a metaphor for society) who makes people suffer, who paralyses their creative forces. On the other hand, the feeling of tragedy paradoxically appears to be connected with the perception of nature's beauty.[39] And as becomes clear, this is so because nature is conceived as having the same type of "social role" of passive observer of interactions in which it cannot participate.

The crying question "*Why* do I suffer?", to which the ascetic ideal gave a certain meaning (Nietzsche 1968a, 598), is still unanswered in the case exemplified by Orthodox Christians. Theirs is a silent suffering in the shadow of the grandiose stage of European history, and no justification can be found for it in the present.

In the case of Bulgarians, the question is not only "Why do I suffer?", but also "Why does this suffering have neither a beginning nor an end?", for only those things which have a beginning may also someday have an end. Why does the spirit, the very creative power of this people, still remain in chains, even after several "liberations"? One can only wonder how old are these chains and what they must be made of that they have not yet rusted to pieces.

SUFFERING AS SYMBOLIC CAPITAL

In Greek tragedy, the courageous "tragic hero," for whom suffering was inevitable and losses irretrievable, is capable of learning something through his suffering. He finally acquires the ability to understand himself, others and the general conditions of existence, as the chorus in Aeschylus's *Agamemnon* insisted. How can a tragic experience, the traces of which exist solely as feelings about past promises and opportunities that were betrayed but never completely forgotten, be considered as a decisive mode of cognition?

Meaningful suffering, as in the case of soldiers wounded in battle or ascetics who suffer for an ideal, can readily be seen as symbolic capital in Bourdieu's sense (Bourdieu 1990). But what is the ideal that Bulgarians suffer and wait for, no modern ideal being good enough for them? How can their senseless suffering, which may even remain hidden and unacknowledged, be seen as capital that may have some practical meaning?

Bulgarians have apparently learned nothing from their tragic history since they otherwise would have been able to develop a kind of pragmatic view that would help them in organizing a better life for themselves. Pragmatism insists upon the formula whereby knowledge is acquired by doing.[40] But can some cognitive advantage be found when one is not able to act, when one is a passive observer rather than a participant in the history of Europe, when one's present consists of waiting and not doing? Can suffering teach something and be a source of true knowledge?[41] Can even senseless suffering be considered "symbolic capital" that may have "cognitive value?"

Investigating such matters presupposes a reexamination of history such that the understanding of history must be obtained in a process of "decoding the past," or restoring the memories of it. It is necessary that interpretations be put forward which are recognized as what we always knew but could not express with words, as that which was sleeping in the mute unconscious and could not find its way to conscious appreciation.[42]

Suffering is connected with feelings that are typical for the subject who does not act himself. Indeed, I maintain that suffering is a feeling quite alien to the person who acts and that action is the best cure for any suffering.[43] For example, it is often said that soldiers in the heat of battle suffer much less than when they wait in the trenches, i.e., when they are deprived of action. A person who suffers from love does so through an obvious passivity and inability to act in any serious way, while a person who is in love and able to act energetically would never be recognized as a sufferer. The mythological hero Prometheus is tragic precisely because he cannot act.[44] People also suffer when they become an object of interaction in the sense of becoming a topic of discussion and witnesses of an action they can neither control nor interrupt because their presence has not even been acknowledged.

From a Freudian perspective, Aristotle's catharsis is interpreted as that effect of tragedy whereby suffering enables us to remember what has been repressed, resulting in a purging of associated emotions. In this sense, putting an end to social suffering requires a self-awareness of the observation position that is located on the very boundary between two social worlds, analogous to the position of the tragic Chorus in respect to the two interaction parties on stage. It is necessary that observation itself be acknowledged as an alternative source of human knowledge that is fully adequate for a knowledge of the social world, even if observing nature must be assisted by an "instrument" in order to be adequate. In the case of so-called "involved observation" of society, the observer himself is such an "instrument," i.e., a tool that registers all important information from the outside world.

Such considerations seem to provide a sufficient basis for acknowledging that suffering can provide a "symbolic capital" that is accumulated within the soul. Stated otherwise, social suffering is a special technology for creating that particular kind of human sensitivity whereby one is capable of taking the role of the other and understanding him. This makes social suffering the most outstanding teacher of reconciliation skills. The successful completion of humanity's struggle to eliminate social suffering would mean the total loss of any possibility to "repair" the social system when it becomes caught in an unresolvable communication schism in the course of the process of differentiation. This is because a communication conflict cannot be resolved without the creation of an appropriate communication language having the particularities and style needed for reconciliation.

Certain secrets of this style can be learned from the choruses in the ancient Greek tragedies, for whom the most important role of being the interpreter of both the main action as well as the tragic suffering was reserved. The wisdom of the Chorus was expressed in the fact that it neither took sides nor bestowed justice because every act of justice has two sides.

The Chorus did not actually belong to the system because it was not an interaction party, being rather the medium within which the system originates and develops. It is clear that the interaction language of the Chorus was quite different from that of the actors. In fact, it could be argued that its words were not as important as the ways in which they were said and the ways in which the action was symbolically interpreted.[45]

In this respect, Goffman's theatrical image of the social world suffers from the shortcoming that its modern design and "a-historical" conception does not allow any place for a Chorus. This makes it quite different from the ancient tragic theater, where the main action between two interaction parties was constantly interpreted and, therefore, finally explained. Such particular skills are not learned from a teacher but are rather acquired as a result of the persistent occupation of one and the same observation position (the Orchestra), where a "third interaction party" is always the "invisible present."

This "third party" comprises those who have been excluded from the interaction system even though they continue to be the medium from which that system emerged. From this sociological perspective, new light is cast on the peculiar structure of the ancient Choruses, who were never comprised of noble and well-to-do citizens, but rather consisted of those deprived of freedom and social action, namely, slaves.[46] Social suffering then appears to be a social construction of a different kind, a construction of a life in a world where history repeats itself and where suffering is a collective diachronic role with which not only individuals and ethnic groups, but even an entire people may be vested. In a more general sense, the role of the non-person, the socially excluded and the observer marginalized from social action observer may well be the role in which a new historical agent who does not belong to any particular race, class or sex can be seen.

Systems theory maintains that neither communications nor actions can be accumulated in the social system. What can be accumulated, however, are those actions and communications that did not receive expression.[47] In order for the capital consisting of the knowledge of social life acquired through the experience of inaction to be put to social use, feelings accumulated during the centuries of passive contemplation of the flow of European history must be expressed and articulated in concepts and words. The "culture of the soul" that has been missing from the scene of European history from ancient times must finally be recognized today as the third necessary component that is needed, in addition to the culture of the body and the culture of the mind, to transform society as a social system into a harmonious whole.

The culture of the soul expresses itself through messages, which can easily be seen as a type of "communicative actions," or as links between communications and actions. Only through messages are we able to talk about things from both sides of one and the same boundary; only in messages does the soul acquire a voice. Because of its quality as a link between present and absent people, the message is not based on individual reason but rather on wisdom or collective reason. In this sense, the "paradox of observation," according to which no social system can be objectively observed, can be resolved insofar as the "third position" is not only an imaginary construction in virtual reality, but also has an actual correlate in the "inside-outside" position of an observer located on a boundary. This is the boundary position that is responsible for the construction of a mind with a non-modern, or even post-modern, structure. The particular quality of such a mind resides in its hermeneutic skills, in the art of bridging seemingly eternal gaps and millennia-old social schisms. With the construction of this new type of mind, the social world acquired that which it was lacking, namely, a force for reconciling social conflict between two equally wrong or right reasons. It is only now that we can see that the pretensions of philosophy whereby it sought to replace poetry were completely groundless. Neither Plato nor any of his successors ever provided final proof that philosophy, the victorious Socratic reason that overpowers its enemies and always plays a game of "One against

All," ever was or can be a factor for reconciliation. Since in social life no superior individual reason can justifiably aspire to the role of Absolute Reason, sociologists always ask "Whose reason?" or "Who is the observer?"

However, there is another type of reason, namely, a collective reason that realizes itself through the accumulation of individual reason, of which it is the foundation. It is from this position that the archeology of reason can be written, from the position of the repressed collective consciousness that is the invisible medium which makes both actions and communications possible and gives them a heading. Such media in systems terms are language, money, power and truth, all products of collective labor, all of which undergo conversion-cycles in time and return to themselves.

Suffering as a result of the repression of action can be seen as responsible for the formation of a different type of social self that is always of a collective nature, the self of a member of the Chorus. Even though the theory of social selves is not yet elaborated, it is thus apparent that its main topic of discussion must be the denial of social space for expression and action. The essence of social technology in this respect resides in the repression of action and linguistic expression and their preservation in a non-linguistic form hidden from consciousness. The possibility that the "capital" consisting of the accumulated feelings generated through the repetition of such processes over many generations may be inherited had already been presumed by Freud.

Therefore, continuous suffering and the deprivation of social action accepted as a collective social role leads to the development of a particular culture of the soul that may emerge today as a third type of culture having its own particular and complex "technology." But it appears that the latter was in fact a quite ancient invention. Tragedy was the technology that was initially responsible for the construction of a particular type of social self that comprised the best "school" for cultivating the soul in a dynamic world of continually shifting boundaries. At one point this culture became almost completely extinct with the advance of settled life and the firm fixation of social boundaries. For example, in Aristophanes's newly built Kingdom of Wealth (*Plutus*), there was no place for either *Peina* (Need), nor social suffering, nor oppressors, even if they be gods. The only God who succeeded in entering the area of the new kingdom was Hermes. However, he did so not in his quality of mediator but as a reduced divinity, namely, the God of Games. It is this fact that makes it possible today to maintain that the social agent of mediation is still and always has been present within the kingdom of reason, even though the civilized world has claimed that satyrs and the ancient Chorus have long been nowhere to be seen.

Department of Sociology
Uppsala University

NOTES

1. It is perhaps in this sense that Derrida appeals not only to find "the other heading" but also "the other of the heading." The other of the heading is the lack of any heading at all, which is an attribute of the place, of the Heideggerian "Ort," where all forces will finally "join and gather" as "in the point of a spear" (Derrida 1992, 25).

2. This is the essence of the so-called "paradox of observation" in systems theory, which claims that modernity as a single world system cannot be observed because every social system is a different —between inside and outside, between system and environment, between present and past. Insofar as the difference is a two-sided form, the possibility of thematizing the union of the two sides of a single difference may be given only in the form of the "excluded third" (Luhmann 1992, 29). That is to say that insofar as the observer can apply a difference as signifying meaning or identity only to one side of a given union, and not the other, another difference is needed in order to observe the union of these two differences. This means that we have to discover a type of observation position which is located somehow between the present and the past, i.e., capable of observing not only the social system in the present as it has been differentiated, but also the social system in the past as an undifferentiated whole (*ibid.*, 219).

3. The very interesting case of *primary socialization in conflict systems* can be considered as an important addition to the rule described by Berger and Luckmann, who claim that the process of primary socialization is unproblematic in respect to identification (Berger and Luckmann 1966, 154).

4. In the Preface to *The Presentation of Self*, Goffman made one of the most important comments on the structure of the social world that, regardless of the opinion of the author himself, should not be overlooked. Goffman observes that the audience in a theater "consists a third party to the interaction - one that is essential and yet, if the stage performance were real, one that would not be there. In real life, the three parties are compressed into two; the part one individual plays is tailored to the parts played by others present, and yet these others also constitute the audience" (Goffman 1990, 9).

5. Stage design in the Greek tragic theater was meant to present precisely this three-part type of social world, i.e., a world with two interaction parties and observers who were deprived of participation in social life for some reason (gender, race, appearance, etc.). Surprisingly enough, the ancient Greek poets were more conscious of the effects of social exclusion than the modern world is accustomed to assume. And paradoxically enough, progress in the social world took place through simplifying the model of the social world by means of the deconstruction of the *orchestra* and the dissolution of the *Chorus* on the Roman stage. From this point of view, progress today may seem to be the revival of what had been lost in the shift in cultural centers in the ancient world.

6. A clear sign of the consciousness of being observed and the ubiquitous presence of the foreign master can be found in the peculiar fact that Bulgarian folk songs did not depict the image of the enemy even during the period when the Ottoman Empire was most severe and oppressive. This lack of an articulated expression of emotions, along with an unwillingness to name the power that has caused the suffering and pain, can at times produce the strange and paradoxical impression that these people lived in an unreal and even mythological world. However, this does not lessen the suffering.

7. The first history of Bulgaria was written in 1762 by the monk Paisii Hilendarski. He writes in his preface that this had been no easy task because the Turks, as they occupied the Bulgarian lands, burned down churches, monasteries and the king's palaces, causing the loss of all knowledge, including the Bulgarians' knowledge of their own history. The information Paisii used was thus collected from Greek and Latin sources, and his main motivation for writing the history of Bulgaria was in fact the painful feeling of shame that drove Bulgarians to substitute the use of Greek for their

own language. And since "shame is anger that is directed inwards," he wrote an angry and emotional book (as quoted in Karanfilov 1973, 11). It seems that Paisii discovered through his inquiry into history that the fate of Bulgaria is a product of a mysterious past that had been overwhelmed by feelings and emotions. Paisii also quoted in the preface from the Latin translation of a short Greek history of Bulgarian kings in which a certain Mavrubir wrote: "Thus say the Greeks because of their jealousy and envy towards Bulgarians." The explanation follows that the Bulgarians had defeated the Greeks many times, which perhaps could have been the source of envy. The main purpose of Paisii's book was to find in the past a "cure" capable of helping the Bulgarian spirit resist an ever-growing oppression.

8. As Paisii made clear, Bulgaria until relatively recently had a history only from the point of view of an external observer. But since this history is not sufficient for self-identification, the self is still missing.

9. Bulgaria is an example of a very strange strategy developed by people in order to gain their liberty. This was expressed in the declaration of an old oracle that liberation will come from the outside and that the Savior will be Russia. The image of the Savior was named "Grandfather Ivan," and the only thing the Bulgarian elders advised as being reasonable was to wait and watch: "Is Grandfather Ivan coming?" This is the motif of a short story well known to all Bulgarians by Ivan Vazov, the greatest Bulgarian writer, in which Grandfather Yozo spent his life watching all day long from a mountain top to see if Russia was coming. The question is why Bulgarians did not want to fight, did not trust themselves and did not think that salvation could come from within. Only the "crazy youths," as they were sympathetically called by the other villagers, did not obey the elders' advice, and they continued to make their hopeless revolutions both from abroad and from within the country.

All efforts for self-liberation ended in betrayal, failure and massacre. However, this was due neither to a lack of organization, nor to a lack of people ready to die for the liberty of their country. There were many who actually showed the almost non-human self-denial and heroism typical of people who have nothing more to lose. The "paralyzing force" was not an individual fear of death, but came rather from the community's decision that what must be preserved was not their own lives, but rather the "species" that was threatened with extinction. This psychological side of the behavior of the "sheep" has never been adequately taken into account when historians sought to explain why Bulgarians seemed to be so incapable of liberating themselves. We also need to ask how an uprising that relied on a force consisting mainly of old people, women and children could be successful at those times when the sons actually did fight on the side of the enemies (for example, as janissaries). How could these people rise in rebellion and fight against their own sons?

10. Because of the senseless way in which Bulgaria was industrialized upon the basis of a reliance on cheap natural resources imported from the Soviet Union, it is difficult today to identify a branch of industry on which her post-Communist economy may rely. Through the endless reorganizations of agriculture and the educational system, the destruction of old traditions without their replacement by more effective ones, as well as the orientation to the large and unpretentious internal market of the former Communist block, Bulgaria lost her reputation as a producer for the European market that she had enjoyed before 1944. It also should be noted that Bulgaria did not develop an industrial system capable of supporting her agriculture, as might have been expected. The fact that Bulgaria produced satellite components for the Soviet space program, and robots and electronic devices for the military, but not the machinery needed by her struggling agriculture, sufficiently reveals how Bulgaria has not been guided by "selfish" economic interests.

Bulgaria today is in last place among the East European countries in respect to the amount of direct Western investments. According to United Nations statistics, Bulgaria attracted only US$ 200 million the first five years of post-Communist reform, while US$ 6 billion were invested in only 17 percent of the enterprises in Hungary. Even Albania received more foreign investment during this period than Bulgaria, who can be compared in this respect only with certain of the former Central Asian Soviet republics ("Bulgaria Is the Last," *24 Hours*, 6 May 1994).

11. Bulgaria has seemingly never succeeded in producing an event that could place her on the front pages of authoritative European newspapers. Even the overthrow in 1989 of Todor Zhivkov, the longest serving Communist dictator, an event that

marked the beginning of the end of the Bulgarian Communist regime, did not assure her a monopoly over the sensational news of the day because, ironically enough, this event coincided with the opening of the Berlin Wall. This is only a more recent example of the constant historical misfortune that has pursued Bulgaria for centuries. From this point of view, perhaps we should discuss something other than chronological time in respect to Bulgarian history, such as time without events.

12. Ehrenberg maintains that "when people and civilizations survive it is again the spirit which plays the decisive part" (Ehrenberg 1974, 173). However, it seems that peoples who have been known for their great suffering neither survived nor were privileged because of some "tremendous power of spirit." On the contrary, they suffered because of it. This spirit demands great sacrifice on the part of peoples because its own value seems to be greater than any individual life.

13. Such considerations are in immediate relation to the fact that Bulgaria after the liberation has always sought an external authority to rule her. This apparently incomprehensible fact, which puzzles historians as well as those who explore the depths of the Bulgarian psyche, must be seen in the light of the more general rule whereby the authorities who rule any compulsory organization (total institutions) are appointed and selected from the outside.

14. The differing degrees of success with which the members of the former Communist block have adapted to market economy raises serious doubts about regarding economic freedom and reforms as a universal remedy. It becomes ever more clear that beyond the economy of the relations of production, which refers only to human physical powers, lies another type of economy, namely, the economy of the relations of production of communications. The question about what should be considered to be communication is also the question about who should be considered as capable of producing communications. This also concerns the issues of possessing a monopoly over the means of communications or over access to them.

Systems theory does not ignore the question of human actors who remain in the environment of social systems. On the contrary, it addresses this matter from a quite different point of view that opens up new perspectives for discussing the question of power.

The interaction system begins to exercise its power once it is established, an important aspect of which is the selection of those who will participate in it. This is not the matter of being free to select one or another interaction system in which to participate, even though we would prefer to think so in the supposedly true spirit of democracy.

15. A common misunderstanding is that the "other" of nationalism is "internationalism," a view which is completely misleading. The "other" of nationalism as a concept is not to be attained by a shift to some higher level of conceptualization where national attitudes would disappear as do eggs in an omelet. The "other" of nationalism is rather national nihilism, which represents the antithesis, or perfect opposite, of nationalism.

16. Paradoxically enough, such an attitude can be ascribed to the psychically healthy inmates of Goffman's total institutions, for whom there is hardly a question of solidarity or loyalty to the institution when a choice must be made between "inside" and "outside." For such people, the realm of freedom always begins beyond the boundaries of the social space in which they live.

17. There is hardly another such example of self-determination in which the love of other nations outweighs the love of freedom, the reason being that liberation had not abolished "the kingdom of necessity" and did not bring freedom. In classical Greek tragedy, the quality of *sacro altruismo* is described as being characteristic of such tragic heroines as Sophocles' Antigone and Euripides' Macaria, Iphigeneia and Alcestis, who had the common ability to "rise above every selfish thought" (Shuckburgh 1979, xxiv-xxv). But it might be said that they all took the "liberty" of sacrificing themselves precisely because they were not free. It seems that freedom is always a self-achievement. No one can make anyone else free, and freedom is not a necessary consequence of liberation.

18. The roots of either nationalism or national nihilism cannot be revealed without a retrospective reconstruction of a given people's relationships with other peoples and nations. That which can be seen in the present by students of both nationalism and national nihilism is only the tip of an iceberg whose essence cannot be grasped without diving below the surface in order to examine what makes it rise up out of the water.

19. This theme has engaged the minds of many generations of Bulgarian intellectuals, writers and poets. Classical examples of such phenomena can be found in the few early decades of capitalist development in Bulgaria that brought with them the comic characters of the new bourgeoisie, whose deficiency was seen in their efforts to modernize something that cannot be modernized. On the basis of the strong traditions that survived 500 years of Ottoman subjugation, Bulgaria could not succeed in constructing any modern present of its own. Instead, the "imported present" after being internalized began to resemble a caricature of a "misunderstood civilization."

Another example is the effort to modernize national rituals, folk music and folk dances. The gap between traditional and modern is here so great that they can exist only as completely separated from each other. The peculiar thing about this in Bulgaria is that the traditional, which survived a multitude of enforced social changes, is the more active factor. It does not become more modern in this effort, but rather dissolves the modern into itself as a caricature, such as when modern Western music is played with traditional instruments. The opposite process cannot be observed in Bulgaria. Tradition stands as something which is untranslatable and indissoluble, and the modern is helpless against tradition, whose power destroys it when provoked.

20. The strong Bulgarian belief in the coming of a "Savior" has been always expressed in the form of waiting for an external power: salvation is never expected to come from within. During the period of Ottoman domination, even the home-grown saviors had first to become emigrants in order to enter the country from abroad, or at the very least to come down from "above," i.e., from their refuge in the Balkan Mountains. Whether it be Grandfather Ivan (Russia) or the Red Army, the foreign king or the Hero of Leipzig, all are incarnations of one and the same image, namely, an alien force who liberates but never brings freedom.

21. Such a state of affairs is not inconceivable from a sociological perspective. This attitude could be compared to that of a schoolboy towards the process of education as he counts the years left until his maturity, or to the attitude of the prisoner who does not hope for amnesty and simply waits for his sentence to end. A state of waiting for the future to begin that negates the present is also well known to sailors' wives as they wait for the ship to return to

the harbor. Since the future can come for them only from where the past has disappeared, the most important thing is to keep memories of past time alive in the present, which itself is only chronological in character.

22. A contradiction often seen in *The Will to Power* is manifest in his treatment of the feeling of guilt, which, contrary to possible expectations, becomes the dominant theme of discussion instead of shame. This is perhaps because guilt comes to attract his attention in relation to Christianity, making shame, a major theme of discussion in his earlier writings, almost disappear as a topic of concern. Unfortunately, Nietzsche's shift of interests from the *Birth of Tragedy* to the *Birth of Christianity* apparently caused him to concentrate upon guilt and abandon the analysis of shame.

23. We owe the discovery of this hidden knowledge and source of power to the work of Thomas Scheff. In his renowned study, Hitler's *Mein Kampf* is seen to have "shame and rage bristling from every page," and it thus becomes exemplary in respect to the study of shame as a source of anger, which is "pointed outwards, at objects in the external world" (Scheff 1990, 171).

24. It is obvious that Nazi philosophers and practitioners read Nietzsche "as the devil reads the Bible." The whole dreadful experience of Nazism seems to have been very closely related with a deep knowledge of Nietzsche's very powerful discovery that the most easily manipulated people are the people who are ashamed, and that the ability to make people ashamed is power. As long as one is ashamed, one is not only not free, but perhaps does not even know the reason of his enslavement. Could this be the essence of the secret weapon which the Nazis discovered, surprisingly not in the natural sciences, and used to paralyze resistance forces everywhere, both in society as well as behind the walls of the concentration camps?

25. Dealing with the question whether virtue is a passion, a faculty or a state of character, Aristotle decides that the latter is the essence of virtue. "Shame should not be described as a virtue; for it is more like passion than a state of character" (Aristotle 1986, 1128 b9, 10).

26. The amount of attention given to these concepts has grown steadily since the 1950s. Examples of significant efforts in this direction include the work of G. Piers and M. Singer on guilt shame

(1953), H. Lynd's work on shame and identity (1958), H. Lewis's work on shame and guilt (1971), the work of L. Wurmser on shame (1981), the empirical work of Suzanne Retzinger on shame and emotions (1991 and 1995), and J. Braithwaite's work on shame and social integration (1989). A special place must be reserved here for the works of E. Goffman on embarrassment, face and stigma, as well as for the body of Thomas Scheff's work. These latter works are especially concerned with a broad range of human emotions that not only affect the behavior of particular individuals, but which may also serve to provide the means for setting up a new type of explanatory framework for social history.

Shame and guilt have recently come to be viewed as important for understanding such "modern" social phenomena as totalitarianism, Communism, and fascism. Agnes Heller, for example, in a joint effort to understand the nature of "real socialism" that was undertaken by scholars able to observe it from both inside and outside, introduced the quite promising notion of "shame-culture." She relates this phenomenon to patterns of behavior standardized in accordance with the morality of a single ruling party, deviations from which are punished with shame (Fehér, Heller, and Ërkus 1983, 208-213). I consider that further discussion of such phenomenon as "internalized shame," whose roots Heller saw in a world that is prior to enlightenment, leads to an important crossroads where a great variety of social theories and sciences meet, all of whose contributions and collaboration are needed for the full development of a theory of the social self.

27. A clear distinction between the concepts of shame and guilt is of great significance for the present study, but confusion between these terms even in common language can still be found in authoritative dictionaries. For example, guilt is straightforwardly defined in *Webster's Ninth New Collegiate Dictionary* as "the fact of having committed a breach of conduct esp. violating law and involving a penalty; . . . the state of one who has committed an offense esp. consciously." Shame is defined, however, as "a painful emotion caused by consciousness of guilt, shortcoming, or impropriety, . . . something that brings strong regret, censure, or reproach." This definition obviously does not serve the purpose if the point under discussion is the fine, but very important, difference between shame and guilt.

28. These issues, which refer to persons who wear "masks" and apply for social roles, not human beings in general, merit a thorough analysis in the light of systems theory. This would involve examining the relationships between the three different systems levels (interaction, organization, society) and the tension that their different criteria for the formation of boundaries obviously imposes. One and the same person within one and the same time frame may be considered as being either present or absent according to three different criteria. He may be present in all cases, or he may find himself excluded from all systems depending on the type of selection criteria utilized. It must also be noted that to become an object of discussion in an interaction system when actually present clearly means a violation of democratic interaction norms in the terms of systems theory.

29. "When one feels guilt one's self feels intact. In feeling shame, one experiences what must be the most vertiginous of all feelings, namely, the disintegration of the self or its potential disintegration. It is for this reason that guilt is infinitely more prestigious than shame. . . Shame is probably the most intensely painful of all feelings. Each person has spent what feels like an eternity of time and effort in constructing a competent, valuable self. The threat of losing that self may be more painful than the threat of losing one's life. In all cultures and historical eras, personal disgrace usually leads to extreme measures, even suicide" (Scheff 1990, 169).

30. Marcuse writes in *Eros and Civilization* that, "Freud attributed to the sense of guilt a decisive role in the development of civilization; moreover, he establishes a correlation between progress and an *increasing* guilt feeling. He states his intention 'to represent the sense of guilt as the most important problem in the evolution of culture, and to convey that the price of progress in civilization is paid in forfeiting happiness through the heightening of the sense of guilt.' Recurrently Freud emphasizes that, as civilization progresses, the guilt feeling is 'further reinforced,' 'intensified,' is 'ever-increasing.'" (Marcuse 1955, 71).

31. Nietzsche wrote in the *Genealogy of Morals* that, "What really arouses indignation against suffering is not suffering as such but the senselessness of suffering: but neither for the Christian, who has interpreted a whole mysterious machinery of salvation into suffering, nor for the naive man of more ancient times, who under-

stood all suffering in relation to the spectator of it or the cause of it, was there any such thing as *senseless* suffering" (Nietzsche 1968a, 504).

Another aspect of "senseless suffering" is revealed by studies of pain, the most private of all feelings that no external observer can ever understand. Such studies emphasize the fact that heroes injured in the heat of the battle, whose serious wounds are recognized as sources of pride, do not suffer the same level of pain that ordinary patients in hospital suffer from much more minor injuries. The difference lies in the meaning of the suffering of the wounded soldier (source of pride) and the meaningless suffering of the common patient (misfortune). In other words, a comparable level of suffering with meaning is not as painful as one without meaning.

32. This statement is supported by an analysis of Bulgarian folklore. One of the main themes in the songs performed at Christmas time concerns God as he demands ever new sacrifices from his people in order for His monasteries to be built and His work to continue. Other Christmas songs are about the *samodiva* (a mountain nymph who imposes "wildness" or "craziness" upon herself), who builds her town from human bodies. She transforms her victims into a kind of building material, but they are neither completely dead because they still have physiological needs, nor are they fully alive because they are made into the walls and windows of the building. Nothing is said about the physical sufferings imposed on this pile of bodies, who are paralyzed and cannot act. In other similar songs, the victims perform relatively enjoyable albeit senseless labor, i.e., labor that has no results. For example, one song concerns a child taken to this town who picks herbs, but he is unable to collect them in his shirt and they constantly fall to the ground.

It must also be mentioned that the victims chosen as building material are chosen because of their good human qualities (the best, the strongest, the bravest and the most beautiful people of all ages). It is obvious that the concept of guilt in no ways fits with the fact that they are the ones who have been so chosen. At the same time, the people whom God asks to cooperate with him are only of two kinds: rich men and sterile women. These two social "groups" represent the impotent, non-creative social forces from whom God did ask personal sacrifices.

Furthermore, these towns, monasteries, etc., built by different mighty forces (God, nymphs) are located neither on Earth, nor in heaven, but "inside a dark cloud." That these songs symbolically represent suffering is expressed by the strong hope that one day these buildings will be destroyed by a brave man who will liberate the people. These examples are taken from the songs collected by the Miladinovi brothers (Miladinov 1981).

33. One aspect in which the role of the Eastern Church can be seen is its activity as an interaction partner for Western Christendom, especially during periods of transition and radical change. The otherwise inexplicable interest and lengthy correspondence during the period 1573-1581 that was initiated by German Lutheran scholars in Tübingen could perhaps be viewed in this light. This correspondence is often put forward as an example of a basic lack of understanding between these two spiritual traditions that obviously proceeded from their completely different perspectives of the social world.

34. It would be difficult in a few lines to discuss the difference between Orthodox and Catholic Christianity, but it must nevertheless be emphasized that the Orthodox Christian is neither afraid of the apocalypse, nor is he permeated with a sense of guilt. He does not see Salvation in the light of a revenging justice, but rather in relation to forgiveness and the Divine overcoming of human morality and weakness. His visible passivity in the world is related to the fact that Orthodox Christianity does not focus on the First Person of the Trinity, the Father, but is rather a Christology, i.e., a doctrine of the Christ "who suffers in the flesh." It is as if the Orthodox Christian were crucified together with Christ Himself, and he waits for the Holy Spirit to come and ensure divine life in the union of believers instead of being an acting or doing Christian. The "call" that may awake him comes not from God but from the people for whom he suffers. In other words, the Orthodox Christian believer is a person of mission, not of profession.

35. As Weber pointed out, every historical instance of Communism "has either a traditional, that means, patriarchal basis or the extraordinary foundation of charismatic belief" (Weber 1978, 1119). In this sense, the ideas of Communism did not interfere with the exceptionally strong emphasis in Orthodox Christianity on tradition and charisma.

36. From many points of view, the tradition we are discussing

presents social life as shifting sands upon which nothing can be built. Another powerful metaphor could be also used, that of the Greek walnut tree, a sturdy tree that typically dies suddenly at several hundred years of age for no obvious reason. The strangest thing about this tree is expressed by the saying that "Nothing grows under the Greek walnut." And in the very place where it stood a huge diversity of plants appears, whose seeds no one suspected were there. It is supposed that this sturdy tree gives off some kind of paralyzing substance that prevents these seeds from growing, although it does not kill them.

37. Typical examples of this are flocks of domestic animals or bees, whose natures were not changed when man transformed them into collective beings for his own convenience.

38. In this context, artistic activity and aesthetic perception are arguably in contradiction with the underlying ideas of both European civilization and Protestantism. It cannot be denied that art, regardless of whatever appreciation has been shown to it by the modern world, is considered to be inferior to science and reason, the idea of which originated in, and was developed through, successful attempts to overthrow the power of art.

39. Nature always shares suffering with human beings in the Bulgarian literary and oral traditions. It is also usual for the tragic to be related to the beautiful. One such example is provided by the following line from the Bulgarian poetic arsenal: "You are beautiful, my forest, and you smell of youth, but you impose only pity and sorrow on our hearts."

40. Concerning the "primitive application" of the basic assumptions of pragmatism to modern education, Hannah Arendt writes, "The basic assumption is that you can know and understand only what you have done yourself, and its application to education is as primitive as it is obvious: to substitute, insofar as possible, doing for learning." Arendt sees this practice as ironically resulting in the "transformation of institutes for learning into vocational institutions which have been successful in teaching how to drive a car or how to use a typewriter. . . ." (Arendt 1968, 182-83).

Such a dramatic transformation can easily be seen as representing the democratic spirit of modernity. In this respect, it is legitimate to ask whether the system of education as we have known it for centuries is itself rather contradictory to democratic ideals, and whether the "teacher-student" relationship is basically the same old "father-son" relationship with which European civilization began. From this point of view, I do not think that the problem is as Arendt sees it, namely, that students are kept on the level of play and prevented from growing up, but rather that students are promoted into "fathers" and no one is left to play the roles of sons.

41. To ask such questions means to challenge the tradition, which has insisted since the time of Democritus that the "dark" knowledge provided by the senses is useless for attaining the truth.

42. In this respect, "psychohistory" offers a promising new method for historical analysis by applying the psychoanalytical approach to historical research. This initiates an examination of the "backstage" of history, i.e., the place where people have stepped out of their historical roles as actors and are presented to us as human beings with their own emotions and powerful feelings.

43. While Arendt considered principles to be something that operate from without and inspire action, there may well be certain principles that restrict and discourage action from without, even though they remain unnoticed. Perhaps the latter remain unnoticed because principles in general are observable only through action, being "manifested in the world as long as the action lasts, but no longer." Arendt also states that "men are free — as distinguished from their possessing the gift for freedom — as long as they act, neither before nor after; for to be free and to act are the same" (Arendt 1968, 152-53).

44. From this point of view, Goffman's concept of total institutions should perhaps be revised. If a total institution is something that deprives a person of freedom, then should there not also be a place within the concept for those cases of "totalitarian institutions" that deprive a person of action? The term "total institution" refers to a number of different kinds of establishments that in fact cannot be compared. The application to this particular case of the much criticized but nevertheless much used Weberian method of "ideal types" seems unable to provide the criteria necessary for distinguishing between them. Thus, according to Goffman, there are total institutions that are established "to care for persons felt to be both incapable and harmless," as well as total institutions for those who are "incapable and a threat to the community." There are also total institutions that are voluntary

"retreats from the world," as well as establishments that serve a training purpose or provide a better persuasion for some "work-like task," such as army barracks, ships and boarding schools. In these latter cases we should talk about freedom being deprived in order to assure a better concentration upon one particular kind of action, but not about the deprivation of action as such. In the first case, the inmates are incapable of taking care of themselves and performing actions. However, there are also institutions of a significantly different kind, even though Goffman includes them as the "third type of total institutions" among the five he lists as the basis for the "denotative definition of the initial definition of total institutions" (Goffman 1961, 4-5). It is for this third type, such as "jails, penitentiaries, P.O.W. camps and concentration camps" (ibid.), that I reserve the term "totalitarian institution," which designates the deprivation of action as such. It is in this quality that such institutions are related to a kind of suffering that in itself does not rely on mechanisms of physical incarceration, a kind of suffering that enables these institutions to be understood as places of painful experience where virtually "non-being" human beings can do nothing but wait.

45. The ways in which words may become such an unimportant matter in the process of interaction was best understood during the period of totalitarian regimes. From many points of view, these societies were transformed into "para-linguistic cultures" where words as such, and concepts in particular, lost their meaning and importance in interaction processes. Social linguistics preserves the term "societies with restricted codes" for such cases, in which "how things are said, when they are said, rather than what is said" is most important. These arise, according to B. Bernstein, "in prisons, combat units of the armed forces, in the peer group of children and adolescents, etc." (Bernstein 1972, 36-37). The external observer of such interaction processes, as well as of totalitarian societies, should not trust verbal explicitness since all that he would then be able to predict remains at the syntactic level. The same holds true for the Chorus, whose words were the most obscure and enigmatic part of all Greek tragedies and comedies.

46. Paradoxically enough, and quite contrary to the materialistic understanding of the use of slaves, perhaps the most important reason for the disappearance of the slavery has less to

do with a change in the mode of production than with the fact that slavery itself entered a stage of development where it actually lost its most important function, namely, that of the observer of social life. This is the role of the non-participant who loses his function when he acquires his freedom and begins to act. It can thus be claimed that neither the disappearance of the Orchestra in the Roman theater nor the appearance of today's modern type of Chorus took place by mere chance.

47. A good example of this is provided by the internal dialogue in which we at times engage with ourselves, remembering an interaction in which we did not say or do the right thing. This unbalance in social communication creates the opportunity for undischarged social interaction to be accumulated in the form of feelings. What is important for the construction of this particular new type of self is not what we did but what we did not do, having been deprived of action or expression for one reason or another. This obviously has something to do with what the ancient Greeks understood by moderation or *sophrosyne*.

REFERENCES

Arendt, H. (1968) *Between Past and Future. Eight Exercises in Political Thought*. New York: Viking Press.

Aristotle (1986) *The Nicomachean Ethics*. Oxford: Oxford University Press.

B. Bernstein (1972) "A Sociolinguistc Approach to Social Learning." In *Man, Language and Society*. The Hague and Paris: Mouton.

Berger, P. and Th. Luckmann (1991) *The Social Construction of Reality*. Hammondsworth: Penguin.

Bourdieu, P. (1990) *The Logic of Practice*. Trans. Richard Nice. Cambridge: Polity Press.

Braithwaite, J. (1989) *Crime, Shame and Reintegration*. Cambridge: Cambridge University Press.

"Bulgaria Is the Last," *24 hours*, 6 May 1994.

Derrida, J. (1992) *The Other Heading*. Bloomington: Indiana University Press.

Ehrenberg, V. (1974) *Man, State and Deity: Essays in Ancient History*. London: Methuen.

Fehér, F., A. Heller and G. MErkus (1983) *Dictatorship over Needs*. Oxford: Blackwell.

Fol, Al. (1971) "La Diaspora thrace." *Rivista storica dell'antichità* 1/2, 3-18.
_____. (1990) *Politika i Kultura v Drevna Trakiia*. Sofia: Nauka i izkustvo.
Goffman, E. (1974) *Asylums. Essays on the Social Situation of Mental Patients and Other Inmates*. Garden City, N.Y.: Anchor.
_____. (1963) *Behavior in Public Places: Notes on the Social Organization of Gatherings*. London: Free Press of Glencoe.
_____. (1961) *Encounters: Two Studies in the Sociology of Interaction*. Indianapolis: Ind.
_____. (1971) *The Presentation of Self in Everyday Life*. Hammondsworth: Penguin.
_____. (1990) *Stigma. Notes on the Management of Spoiled Identity*. Hammondsworth: Penguin.
Hilendarski (Khilendarski), Paisii (1963) *Slavjano-balgarska istorija*. Ed. P. Dinekov. Sofia: Bulgarski pisatel.
Karanfilov, E. (1973) *Balgari*. Sofia: Naroden mladezh.
Lewis, H. (1971) *Shame and Guilt in Neurosis*. New York: International Universities Press.
Luhmann, N. (1992) *Beobachtungen der Moderne*. Opladen: Westdeutscher Verlag.
Lynd, H. (1958) *Shame and the Search for Identity*. New York: Harcourt Brace.
Marcuse, H. (1955) *Eros and Civilization: A Philosophical Inquiry into Freud*. New York: Vintage Books.
Miladinov, D. and K. (1981) *Balgarski narodni pesni. Sabrani ot Bratia Miladinovi*. Sofia: Nauka i izkustvo.
Nietzsche, F. (1982) *The Gay Science*. New York: Vintage Books.
_____. (1968a) *Genealogy of Morals*. New York: Vintage Books.
_____. (1968b) *The Will to Power*, 13-14. New York: Vintage Books.
Piers, G. and M. Singer (1953) *Shame and Guilt; A Psychoanalytic and a Cultural Study*. Springfield, Ill., Thomas.
Retzinger, S. (1995) "Identifying Shame and Anger in Discourse." *American Behavioral Scientist* 38, No. 8 (August), 1104-1113.
_____. (1991) *Violent Emotions: Shame and Rage in Marital Quarrels*. Newbury Park: Sage.
Scheff, Th. (1997) *Emotions, the Social Bond, and Human Reality. Part/Whole Analysis*. Cambridge: Cambridge University Press.
_____. (1990) *Microsociology: Discourse, Emotion, and Social Structure*. Chicago: University of Chicago Press.

_____. and Suzanne M. Retzinger (1991) *Emotions and Violence: Shame and Rage in Destructive Conflicts*. Lexington, Mass.: Lexington Books, 1991.

Shuckburgh, E.S. (1979) *The "Antigone" of Sophocles*. Commentary by E.S. Shuckburgh. Cambridge: Cambridge University Press.

Webster's Ninth New Collegiate Dictionary (1996). Springfield, Mass.: Miriam Webster Publishers.

Weber, M. (1978) *Economy and Society*. Berkeley: University of California Press.

Wurmser, L. (1981) *The Mask of Shame*. Baltimore: Johns Hopkins University Press.

Philosophy Faculty
University of Sofia, Bulgaria

CHAPTER IX

BULGARIAN CULTURAL IDENTITY

ANNA KRASTEVA

Frivolous people think that human progress consists of a quantitative increase of things and ideas. Certainly not. Real progress lies in our ever more intensive perception of five or six basic mysteries.
Jose Ortega y Gasset

Liberty is one thing and liberation another. Liberation is a phenomenon of external life. Liberty is a phenomenon of internal life. True liberty starts with moral revival.
Stoyan Mikhailkovsky

To Bulgarians, democracy came as liberation from the ossification of Communist society, from the platitude of a discourse in which everything was an "announced conclusion." It was intoxicating to say and do things that previously had been taboo, such as free elections, a multi-party system, roundable debates, strikes, candlelight vigils in squares, or a fire in Communist Party headquarters. This study is not devoted to the subject of whether liberation has succeeded in evolving into liberty as civic responsibility and moral choice. It rather focuses on another dimension of the change, namely, now that passions over new themes are subsiding, intellectual discourse is increasingly centered on such perennial topics as the question of Bulgarian cultural identity.

Concerning the own/alien issue, our present reflections seem to dialogue with the pre-Communist rather than with the Communist age. For example, an anthology of interwar texts entitled *Why Are We What We Are?* was recently published. The first edition quickly sold out, indicating that the current flood of translated literature has not quenched the thirst for reflection on the "own." Current journals are also reprinting articles from the first half of the century. This purposefully constructs an intertext in which old and new texts meet in intellectual reflection as well as literally on the pages of one and the same journal, an intertext that makes it possible to trace changes in thematization and reveal both difference and similarity between former and present discourses on Bulgarian cultural identity.

Penelope asks Ulysses, who is disguised as a beggar, "Who art thou of the sons of men, and whence? Where is thy city, and where are they that begat thee?" Such questions outline a definite understanding of man in which individual and collective identity interrelate, which is why the query about the particular person is worded in the terms of ancestors, in terms of the native land. This article analyzes the conditions that orient an understanding of national identity into the terms formulated by Penelope, making other possible formulations socially irrelevant.

THE "OWN"

What do Bulgarians consider to be inherently their own, the epitome of their identity?

The Bulgarian Tongue

> Tongue of my ancestors who trod this earth,
> Tongue of great woes and age-old lamentation,
> Tongue that the woman spoke who gave us birth
> To know not joy but bitter tribulation.[1]

Language is the umbilical cord connecting us to the past, our ancestors and our forefathers. It preserves, bears and passes down memories over the centuries, and is a symbol of life passed on to us by our mother, our motherland ("tongue that the woman spoke who gave us birth"). Language bears the cross of historical suffering ("Who is there has not heaped abuse on you, / Fair tongue, or not refrained from wicked slanders?"), but it is also an expression of joy and delight in the beauty and wealth vested in it:

> ... what charm, what might
> Lies in your speech, so supple and refreshing,
> What scope in your rich tones, what splendor bright,

What swift and lively power of expression" (*ibid.*)

Language is conceived as the pivot of ethnic self-identity; language alone is capable of expressing spirituality. "If I pray in an (unknown) language, my soul prays but my mind remains barren" (*The Life of Constantine the Philosopher*). Language weaves the fibers of communication, generating a sense of understanding and community. "If I do not understand the meaning of the words, I will be a stranger to the speaker, and the speaker will be a stranger to me. . . . [I]n church I would rather say five comprehensible words so as to teach the others" (*ibid.*).

The creation of an alphabet and literature in the mother tongue is a cultural phenomenon of capital importance for all peoples. This is emphasized and elevated to an extent that demands self-sacrificial commitment. "The mediaeval biographers describe the *salvation* of native books as a fearless and sacrificial battle" (Bogdanov *et al.* 1991:169). "Immersion" in the language is a duty, a way of self-realization through merging with the community. "The language of the writer is not only his confession, but is *foremost* a device for solving major national and social tasks," and writing "a duty to the truth and to language" (Germanov 1992:13, 17). One's moral commitment to language is expressed in the way the discursive is bound to the epistemological, in the way the writer's language is bound to the duty to speak the truth. Language is for writing the truth, not merely for writing.

Eastern Orthodoxy

Eastern Orthodoxy is one's "own" through its positive presence as much as through its absence. When present, its significance has been weakened by various procedures, such as presenting it as a power intervention that failed to change the Bulgarian's intrinsically pagan *Weltanschauung*. "An ancient faith was shaken and destroyed without being adequately replaced by another. . . . Christianity [was] petrified in the formalism of a dogma incomprehensible to the masses" (Mutafchiev 1934:359).

Another way to weaken the significance of Christianity is to ascribe heresy the same, if not higher, status as the canon. The most eloquent example of this is the Bulgarian's adulation of the

Bogomils.

A third operation refers "faith" to secular subjects. "This is the god Botev worships: the god of reason, defender of slaves" (Penev 1942:155). Intellectuals and writers correlate the Bulgarian mentality with the earthly visible rather than with the transcendent eternal. Desacralization of the beyond is thus supplemented by sacralization of the earthly. "[T]he spirit of the nation is the divine principle and divine power of the people" (Yanev 1933:343).

The own/alien ambivalence is also implied by the Bulgarian's notion of the beyond. The Bulgarian does not experience the beyond as a transcendence but as a boundary which can be crossed and which divides two worlds that, while admittedly different, are not *that* different.

He has drawn the entire *heavens*, along with the Lord God [*Diado Gospod*, literally, Grandfather God], down to *earth*. And we often see this elderly gray-bearded

> "master of the heavens" . . . drop in on masters of the earth . . . or contend with some daredevil. When the Bulgarian peasant ascends the heavens, he tells how . . . the Lord God is something of a mayor, discharging his official duty quietly and kindly. *Up there* it is exactly the same as *down here* (Slaveikov 1923:58).

The drama of unattainable transcendence, the experience of faith in an ideal other who demands suffering, is not inherent in the Bulgarian. "In his yearning and ideal he never lets go, never goes beyond this world. To him the kingdom of heaven is here on earth" (Yotsov 1934:64). The ideal is assimilated by being brought "down to earth." While part of its sanctity has thereby been taken away, so has part of its alien nature.

The existential significance of Eastern Orthodoxy is proportionate to its problematic essence. The Bulgarian feels himself to be different from the Pomak not so much because s/he believes in God, but because the other worships "llah. The defenders of the faith are striking figures in folklore and literature who have left an imprint on collective memory thanks to the consistent efforts of such socializing institutions as the school. When the faith is threatened, it turns from being but one dimension of collective identity into its core. To renounce faith means to stop being part of "Us," or at least to stop being a worthy member. To lose your life, to sacrifice yourself to faith, is the surest way to remain in the community as a hero, saint or role model.[2]

The Balkan Range

In the mine/alien coordinate system, nature is neither level nor symmetrical. Bulgarians are highlanders. They feel at home on land that is high, independent, free as the wind and hard to access. "The Balkan Range was too low for me, the dark words too narrow, the sun too pale!" (Sheitanov 1925:254). Slaveikov emphasizes the "intimate" bond between the Balkan Range and the history of Bulgarians. "In the age of bondage . . . to take a breath of fresh air the Bulgarian would withdraw to the Balkan Range, seeking shelter in its barely accessible recesses. And he would leave the fertile plains to his masters" (Slaveikov 1923:50). The highlander (*Balkandzhiya*) is not a regional but a spiritual identity, designating one who is lofty in the Bulgarian spirit, not one who merely lives on high ground.

In the Bulgarian discourse on nature, we find neither the instrumental modern attitude that assimilates nature by subordinating it, nor the opposing Rousseauesque call to return to the fold of nature, both of which thematize nature within the culture/nature dichotomy. There is fusion rather than opposition, attraction rather than contrast, destiny rather than instrumentality. Nature is "a space *experienced* as destiny" (Yanev 1934:345).

Nature is assimilated through experience rather than through action, and it is not external to, but rather an organic part of, the social. These ties between nature and the social reside in the realm of the spiritual, not in the field of the material such as geography, resources or energy. "[T]he soul of a people 'rests in the native land'" (Yanev 1934:346). Theirs is not a power relationship, like use or conquest, but rather a holy relationship: "the native land is untouchable and *holy*" (*ibid.*). Love does not take its subject literally but transforms it, and this affective metamorphosis turns land into *skies*, flight and liberation. "The love of Bulgarians for the *land* is one of the best forms of love for *liberty*" (Hristov 1939:459).

The People as a Family

Land, people, kin and individual are linked together into a single "organism." These separate parts develop and blossom only if they are nourished by its life-giving fluids. "We can hope to produce something in the field of poetry only when we nurture this flower so that it too grows and develops from the *juices* of our *soil*" (Tsaneva 1992:103). The classical poet Slaveikov agrees, and present-day commentary emphasizes the same organic metaphors. "The finest flowers in Slaveikov's work grew on our native soil, nourished by the fluids of Bulgarian national culture" (Tsaneva 1992:103).

This organism is alive and viable only as long as it is intact. Not only is its dismemberment painful, so too is the mere thought and premonition of dismemberment:

> Geo Milev first uttered the secret everyone is ashamed of: we no longer have a fatherland, a motherland. We are incapable of feeling them our "own," an integral whole. Bulgaria is mother to some, but has become a stepmother to others. Each one of them knows that "The Fatherland/ Summons its sons!"/ Exquisite:/ But - what land is it?[3]
>
> This is one of the painful questions, this is ripping off live flesh (Tsaneva *et al.* 1992:236).

Problematizing the organic bond with the motherland is dramatic for both the poet and the contemporary literary critic, who borrows his vocabulary from the organic view of the ethnic idea. The motherland is "live flesh," an organic whole ("own, integral") that incorporates both those it attracts and those it alienates ("each one"). She can be good ("mother") or evil ("stepmother"), but even when questioned, the native country is there, visible and stable in her almost litany-like naming ("Fatherland," "Motherland"). The commentary is affective, the words strong and passionate ("shameful," "painful," "ripping off").

The physical body is a symbolic body to the philosopher, but philosophers are also inclined to turn the symbolic body into a physical body, such as when the Motherland becomes a mother or the Balkan

Mountains. Culture thus becomes nature, the latter having the advantages of objectivity, stability and non-arbitrariness. As an organic body sets the functions of its parts "in order," making both their relationships and their pre-coded character look natural, what is actually culture-based comes to seem unproblematic, self-evident, and "natural." "The intelligentsia is *predestined* to represent the nation (Katsarski 1992:72).

From Plato's *Symposium* (1982, vol. 2:442-445) we remember Aristophanes's myth of the Androgynes who, with indomitable force and valor, dared to challenge the very gods. Furious, Zeus punished them by splitting them in two. Yet the halves pined away for each other and longed to come together again, even if fusion at times brought death. This is one of the most eloquent "corporeal" metaphors of the idea that differentiation is inferiority, imperfection, dissatisfaction. Association is well being, and smoothing out differences and attaining integrity are harmony and achievement. Many thinkers since Plato have conceived the social within the perspective of fusion. Our understanding of "own" is within the same perspective. The well-being of the individual is inconceivable and impossible without the well-being of the community, and only the latter is conceived as having the attributes of completion and perfection.

> [T]he nation is *the fullest and most perfect community*.... [T]he well-being of each one of its members is conceivable and possible *only* as part of the well-being of the nation and *only* he who preserves its spiritual and physical *integrity* makes real progress (Mutafchiev 1940:392).

Conceiving the "own" in terms of an organic body has several important implications. For example, the links are based on "blood" rather than on contract or agreement. "Blood" is something you are born with rather than something you choose, involving predestination rather than freedom. Belonging to the "own" is determined by birth, not by self-determination.

Communal Man

In 1932, Spiridon Kazandzhiev discussed two types of relationships between the individual and collective consciousness, namely, coordination and contradiction. The archetype of the former is Collective Man, and of the latter, the Individualist. Harmony between individual and collective makes the former "complete," whereas their disrupted unity makes the latter "fragmentary and dismembered." "The first case has always been considered *normal*, and the second *morbid*" (Kazandzhiev 1932:164).

The patriarchal community is the life-world of collective man. It guarantees an objectified "animate" world consisting of domesticated animals, manmade tools, and the full labor cycle that is subordinate to the individual. This world has been assimilated by tradition and ordered through the life of the traditional community. "The worldview of the patriarchal consciousness is found in tradition; the world is constructed and *solved*" (Kazandzhiev 1932:167). Modern society distances materiality from man, mediating his relationships with it through an ever-increasing number of mechanisms, ideologies, technologies and bureaucracies. Man thereby loses not only the materiality but also the wholeness of his world, and he himself becomes relegated to its partial functions. The world becomes more and more different and "alien."

In 1994, Bogdan Bogdanov wrote about the two types of welfare, that of status and that of change. Holistic consciousness is inclined to transform and adjust every organization (company, party or foundation) to the model of the organic community. In this informal "warm, acute and non-conventional" relationships prevail, in order to lock in its own space, where time is the slow time of security.

The open mind, however, proceeds from self-reflection on "alienness," both that of others as well as one's own. The individual is not autonomous vis-à-vis one's community, but rather is inclined to regard both oneself and the community as "other." One becomes free in constructing one's identity, moving within a network of material mediators, rival ideologies and numerous communities.

For Kazandzhiev, the future man is possible only through the collective since "he cannot take spiritual values from anywhere else" (Kazandzhiev 1932:173). For Bogdanov, the solution is departure from the non-differentiated communal consciousness that does not distinguish cultural dispositions from concrete political motivations, is incapable of leaving "the slow time" of the familiar, and is not inclined to open up to the other.

Both Kazandzhiev and Bogdanov regard the community, the collective or holistic whole, as "the real own." The former views the community as a thing of the past which, although it is now absent, should be reasserted as a model of the future. The latter thinks in terms of the paradigm of multi-dimensional time, where past, present and future are intertwined and, influencing each other, weave the fabric of culture. The last half-century has problematized the value of "our own," but it has not substantially changed it. Even as the ideal of communal unification as the supreme source of meaning has begun to crack, this very process of cracking has itself begun to provide a model since it is a rift, an openness. In the one case, value is attached to what is mine, while in the other it is ascribed to mine/alien, the awareness of their difference, and their face-to-face confrontation.

I would like to go a step further in this analysis and examine why "mine" is referred to the communal in such a permanent and existentially significant way. Simmel concludes in *The Philosophical Testimony* that Europe's great discovery is objectivity.

> The East knows no objective price, but only the evaluation of two people who are bargaining; no objective right, but just the ruling of the judge; no morality that judges objectively, but "he that is without sin among you, let him first cast a stone." Plato discovers the objectivity of the spirit, Roman law the objectivity of law, Catholicism the objectivity of a religion about which Jesus knew nothing (Simmel 1990:299).

The nation is one of the "staunchest" forms of the objectivity of modernity, happily combining ontological and axiological predicates. The nation is not only objective, it is also necessary. And being both objective and necessary, it is a locus of well-being.

I would here like to put forward the hypothesis that the nation has come to replace faith. As secularization has increasingly deprived modern man of reliance on the beyond, the nation has begun to quench the thirst for transcendence, for realities that transcend the separate individual and guarantee meaning.

Paradoxically, this supreme expression of objectivity is perceived not only externally in the stability of its reality independent of the separate individual. The national is rather interiorized and experienced as the most cherished and intimate relationship. The discourse which describes it is highly emotional, amorous and even sexual, using such terms as "affection," "love," "aspiration," "devotion," "faithfulness," "flesh," "blood" and "body."

Schütz notes that the most important feature of sexual relationships is the incomparably deeper way in which the partners experience their Us as distinct from each of themselves and their partner. He writes that, "Not only is the subject experienced more or less directly, but also the very *relationship*, the targeting of the subject, the bond" (Schütz 1970:190). We develop together, mature together in this very Us - the Me/Other relationship.

This is one of the keys to understanding the sustainability of the communal as "own." It is *assimilated objectivity*. It is objective as the framework of a guaranteed world, but it is also assimilated in the relationship.

I believe that this is precisely what has escaped the analytical notice of even such profound liberal thinkers as Bogdanov. He emphasizes that the relationship between individual and community is mediated by such impersonal mediators as artifacts, technology and ideologies. However, the notion of the "own" as an Us-relationship does the very opposite in that it eliminates distance by experiencing the relationship as direct. An Us-relationship is not simply direct but also mutually beneficial, a relationship in which we "mature" together.

THE "ALIEN"

The own/alien relationship is an integral part of any reflection on selfhood, but the "own" can be unproblematically evident only in its pre-reflexive experience. The first attempt at realizing, understanding, and defining the identity of the "own" presents us with the question of its limits and its opposite, namely, the "alien." The "alien" is relevant to the "own" since the former is not merely different from the latter, but is significantly different. Eager to discern our cultural identity, we measure it not against the African or the Eskimo, but against Russia or Germany. In this sense, the "alien" has a positive content and is a specific form of interaction. As Simmel writes (1990:402), "The inhabitants of Sirius are not real strangers to us, at least not in the sociologically relevant sense; they are beyond near and far."

We differentiate various forms of the "alien," some of which we might desire and others that we would avoid. Both are relevant to ownness since they delimit its borders, that is, the line that divides ownness from *its other*, be it a negation or an ideal.

The "alien" is relevant to the "own" in another sense as well, namely, as constituting the "own." For example, Bulgarians are not devout believers, but in their relations with Turks they consider themselves Eastern Orthodox Christians. Stated otherwise, encounter with the "alien" topicalizes or even forms dimensions of identity that would otherwise remain latent or non-definitive of our own life-world.

Simmel observes that the ideal of the Frenchman is the perfect Frenchman, the ideal of the Englishman, the perfect Englishman. The ideal of the German is the perfect German, while his opposite, his other, his supplement, is the Italian (Simmel 1990). Similarly to the German, the self-reflection of the Bulgarian is inseparable from reflection on his or her opposite. Unlike that of the German, however, our own opposite is multi-faceted: Orient or Occident, Russia or Germany, Byzantium or Rome. The Bulgarian is certain neither of what he is himself nor of what exactly is his other, but his quest for the "own" is invariably and inevitably associated with reflection on the "alien." Part Two of this study deals with various hypostases of what is "alien" for the Bulgarian.

The "Own" as "Alien"

Which aspect of the "own" transforms itself into its opposite category of the "alien" in the easiest and most sustainable way? What is *alien*-ated and why?

K. Gulubov distinguishes three stages of the increasing alienation of the intelligentsia from the people. Typical of the first stage is Aleko Konstantinov, who not only has embodied in *Bai*

Ganyo the intellectual's inclination to find only shortcomings in the Bulgarian people, but also has the self-confident conviction that his vocation is to reform the people. The gap between the intellectual and the people is further widened by Pencho Slaveikov, son of the prominent national revival figure, Petko Slaveikov. He still loves his people, but he loves them "as an idea," "contemplating [them] from the high tower of his individualistic seclusion, occasionally announcing his revelations" (Gulubov 1934:229). The symbolist and individualist, Teodor Traianov, not only lives with a yet greater sense of superiority, he is even "alien" to any love for the people whatsoever.

There are two criteria for appraising the alienation of the intelligentsia, namely, (non)love of, and distance from, the popular. Invariably, the people remain significant as a point of departure:

> The leaders of the people have become "rulers" of the people. And they are guided not by the destiny of the people, but by their personal ambition, their personal selfishness. . . . All parties have by now been discredited once and for all . . . all incumbent "political activists" have nothing to do with the people (Milev 1921:183-185).

Few periods of modern Bulgarian history are inconsistent with this definition.

What is relevant to this analysis is not so much the broad sphere of validity of its pessimistic appraisal but, rather, the alternative. Geo Milev expresses his mistrust towards politicians as well as the political. If the latter mistrust was not as categorical as the former, he would have indicated how political relations themselves could be positively developed, such as new political ideas, more efficient forms for selecting political representatives, and so forth. Instead, it is proposed that formal representative political relations be replaced by direct, narrow, organic relations that substitute "sons" for "rulers." "It is time — high time! — that the people produced from its depths its pure and honest sons. They alone will bring its renewal" (Milev 1921:185).

The impersonal nature of economic ties is even less consistent with the image of an "own" that does not have the features of formal rationality. "Taxes have not been seen as a contribution to the community, but as a slavish burden" (Sheitanov 1933:272). Any mediation, whether it be institutional or political, is unilaterally interpreted as distancing, as *alien*-ating. It entails "*forgetting*," that is, a loss or rejection of knowledge of the original unity. When mediation itself becomes an irrefutable reality, organic relationships are taken over by the mediators themselves, and parties, foundations and administrations are established on the basis of nepotism, common birthplaces or "old-boy networks."

If organic relationships of kinship are so ubiquitous, that is because there are no alternatives, no other types of relationships to weld the social together. Such alternatives do exist *de jure*, but *de facto*; their efficiency is weakened by their classification as "alien" or "imported." Katsarski (1992:75), for example, speaks of the "*allochthonous* or *foreign* origin of institutions in Bulgarian society." Indeed, the very idea of the formalization and codification of social relations is assumed to be "non-ours" and, therefore, arbitrary. Foreign observers are struck particularly by the disrespect for law and the underdeveloped sense of lawfulness of both ordinary citizens and rulers. Jirecek, for example, notes that "The laws effective in the country are not a product of a centuries-old development of law but an imported commodity" (as quoted by Penev 1942:150).

The pronounced alienation of the intelligentsia and of the political class is indicative in two respects. On the one hand, the spiritual and political elite are themselves torn between the own/alien dichotomy. They have the clear possibility of being the "own" by becoming an exponent of the original identity, of ethnicity. But this position rules out both the modern perspective that speaks the "universal" language of scientific rationality, as well as the postmodern perspective with its own particular way of speaking. Yet the intellectual has no possibility of being both "own" and "other." "Other" means having not only the freedom to "express" oneself, but also the freedom to discover new horizons; not only the freedom to be loyal to one's "own" world, but also to create a world; not only the freedom to express truth and beauty, but also to err. Freedom in such a case is realized necessity *par excellence*.

On the other hand, the "own" remains unproblematic and is essentially on the side of the communal, while that which has split away from it is problematic and must be demonstrated. "The people has its own typical image, but what is the image of the intelligentsia?"

(Petkanov 1932:416). In this respect, the "own" remains somewhat hermetically sealed within its essentiality, primacy and necessity. The intelligentsia's potential to create otherness, spiritual horizons and alternatives thereby remains underestimated. So, too, does the potential of the "own" to constitute itself in interaction.

It is notable that the primacy of the communal is not seen as the totalizing homogenization and subordination of the individual, but rather as the interaction in which the individual attains a higher individual meaning through harmony with the community and unity with others.

The Deconstructed "Own"

Recent years have seen the appearance of a new figure of the "own" as "alien," a figure that results from the application of mainly two post-modern procedures that deconstruct national identity.

The first of these procedures involves the thematization of the constructed nature of national identity. It has thus been extensively argued that national identity is rooted in historical facts, having been cultivated through narratives and myths by historians, politicians, journalists, teachers, and writers. This perspective emphasizes the deformations that have resulted from the national historical narrative. These include absolutizing continuity insofar as interruptions and breaks would question the unity of the people as agent; outlining a specific "relief" where achievements stand out and periods of downfall are passed over; and appropriating whatever truth and justice are to be found in the inevitable collisions with others, who are only "occasionally allies, but in most cases enemies" (Daskalov 1994:28).

The second procedure involves a dismantling of the foundations of national pride and self-esteem that is ironic to the point of sarcasm. This begins with the anthropological peculiarities of Slavs, whom "some romantic author of textbooks, who must have preferred blondes, fell for as blue-eyed and blonde" (Daskalov 1994:29), and ends with some "bewitched and sacralized" image of the Balkans through which Bulgarians try to glorify themselves.

This post-modern critique primarily targets the narrative nature of national identity. As Daskalov has put it, "We narrate and continue narrating myths about ourselves, narrating ourselves as myth" (Daskalov 1994:44).

My own epistemological position is close to the one under consideration in that the latter ensures a productive critical distance, an opportunity to transcend "the range" of national identity, thereby turning national identity into a subject of reflection, critique and cognition. But I do not accept the absolutizing of its basic theses, namely, that concerning the construction and mythologizing of national identity and that concerning the narrative nature of national identity. The former underestimates the fact that construction is specific to all social formations, and it also ignores the achievements of historiography in the ways it shifts the emphasis from "hard" facts to historical narratives. The latter, on the other hand, has not assimilated Ricoeur's profound observation that all types of identity, and not just national identity, are narrative (Ricoeur 1990).

It should be noted that the post-modern reflection on Bulgarian national identity is still in its very early stages, far from the extremes of total deconstruction. The process of dismantling has not yet reached, nor does it aim to, the core of either the Me or the Us, nor is it meant to make us "strangers to ourselves." It rather aspires to break the fusion of the individual with the community and, widening this break, to enable the individual to approach the latter not only with the pathos of glorification but also with the irony of critique, as well as identify him/herself in ways not prescribed by the community.

"Alien" as "Own"

A quarter of a century after we Bulgarians received our alphabet, we already had a literature that none of the other "new" peoples could boast of, along with an "amazingly intensive" literary activity that made Bulgaria under Tsar Simeon as the most important center of the Eastern Orthodox Slavic world. If literate Bulgarians were few and far between immediately after the Liberation, the educated Bulgarian of only a few decades later lived with the broad spiritual interests of contemporary European civilization (Mutafchiev 1931, 1938).

What inspired these periods of meteoric rise in Bulgaria's spiritual development? Why were they always followed by a fall that was just as sudden, dramatic and irreversible? Formulating and explaining those paradoxes comprises the conceptual center of Peter Mutafchiev's philosophy of history. Not only is our historical path paradoxical, so too, at least at face value, is the explanation, namely, the influence of Byzantine and, later, West European culture. In fact, both the rise and fall have one and the same reason, that is, the assimilation of the "alien." But while adopting ready cultural models saves the effort of slow accumulation and accelerates cultural progress, imitation is not creation.

Assimilation of the "alien" is a dramatic interaction. Typically, the Bulgarian experiences this drama in two opposite ways. In the first, the "alien" subject to assimilation is a matter of choice:

> Our ship of state has had to sail through the dangerous straits of Scylla and Charybdis. Charybdis once was Catholic Rome and Scylla, Eastern Orthodox Byzantium. Then Rome was replaced by Austria and Byzantium was succeeded by Russia (Sheitanov 1925:266).

East and West are perceived not only as geopolitical realities but also as two different spiritual principles, that is, "the technical mind" of Europe and the "magic spirit" of the East (Sheitanov 1925:268). Except for the period when the Iron Curtain veiled one member of this dichotomy and made all reflection pointless, the debate has run through our entire modern history, unabated to this very day. Today the dichotomy is NATO or Russia.

In the second case, there is no choice. The "alien" seems "natural," "obvious," "normal," and is not subject to reflection: Communism before, democracy now, modernization at the turn of the century. The important point is how a definite "alien" is accepted uncritically and presented as not being subject to choice — although there is always a choice, even if only in the selective way in which the "alien" is assimilated. For example, modernity was perceived at the turn of the century as scientific and technological rationality rather than economic rationality. Poets and essayists sang praises to technology, which they saw as the "offspring of pure reason," the "power of the will," and the "ideal symbol of perfection and style" (Mutafov 1920). At the same time, it was explicitly emphasized that the Bulgarian did not seek profit, but rather cultivated the land from affection and duty, and that his attitude to it was substantial and not instrumental.

But the "alien" that has been easily assimilated can easily become alien once again — from which comes the drama. Nothing seems more "alien" than Marxism to the post-Communist intellectual who has promptly assimilated liberalism, former "universal" explanatory principles such as class theory having been totally obliterated from his intellectual memory in short order.

The debate between the supporters and opponents of a given idea is often partisan. However, it is precisely those engaged in such debate who introduce the "alien" into the dialogical field, where "alien" is plural, not singular, and does not "absorb" the "own" as "universally valid" and "necessary" but rather comprises a spectrum of possibilities. Paradoxically, a critical distance does not increase the gap between "own" and "alien" but rather enables them to approach each other in a reflexive process that makes difference a subject of choice and empathy.

"Alien" as "Other"

There are two types of "otherness" that are alien to the Bulgarian. The first indicates an "alien" which is banned from the own/alien relationship insofar as it is not only opposed to "mine" but is "alien" *per se*. Here the "alien" is not merely different from my culture, it is not considered to be culture at all. The second indicates an "alien" which has invaded "mine" to the point that it has taken over; here I become "alien" to myself.

The first case, brilliantly analyzed in Tsvetan Todorov's, *The Conquest of America* (1982), is typical of the dawn of modernity. Its chief figure is the colonizer. When the Spaniards set foot on the American continent, they discovered not cultures, but rather objects of conquest, domination and destruction. The "alien" in such a case is not "worthy" of interest, but only of ownership and subordination; it is the absolute external, and the attitude to it is instrumental. There is nothing positive in it and in a certain sense it is a "non-relation" (Simmel).

The second case, discussed by Camus (1979) and Kristeva (1991), is typical of late modernity, and its main figure is the foreigner, the wanderer, the stranger to oneself. For such a figure, the process of alienation is the only way out. As Kristeva (1991:28) asks, "How could we prevent ourselves from submerging in common sense unless we emigrate from our own country, from our language, from our sex, from our identity?" When the "alien" thus lives within us as the hidden face of our own identity, it is deontologized and has neither its own fixed space nor time. Its space is a *transition* lacking the stability and comfort of repose, which is doomed to the perpetual motion of a train or an airplane, and its time is *postponement*, which is not submersion into a flow but rather the vulnerability of a present that is "temporary" (Kristeva 1991).

But the Bulgarian sees the "alien" as a positive relationship, as *other* rather than as "alien." Indeed, the very passion and activity of the pro-Slav/pro-Western debate shows how relevant these cultural parallels are to our self-determination and how much they contribute to a number of arguments in favor of cultural interaction. The Bulgarian attitude to the other culture fluctuates between the two poles of the "alien" as model and the "alien" as antipode. The "alien" must be assimilated in the first case, while in the second it must remain beyond the limits of ownness. Either way, the other is an object of cognition and interest:

> The distant ideal would be to reconcile within ourselves German objectivity, the conscientiousness and depth of German thought, with the lively French style; to counter crude Bulgarian pragmatism with Russian moral idealism; to defeat dry dogmatism with the free forms of English creativity; to rationalize and ennoble our limited individualism with the general publicness and universal spirit of France. If we only could! (Penev 1924:143).

This thought, which is one of my favorite quotations from Boyan Penev, summarizes two opposite messages, namely, the practical unattainability of cultural synthesis and its viability as an ideal, both of which are very typical of the Bulgarian attitude toward the "alien." The "alien" is brought near by being entwined within a dialogical sphere where it is articulated, where certain of its dimensions are valued more highly than others and "distinguished" as worthy of assimilation. Cultures are here relativized to the point that they are deprived of attributes such as "absolute," "lofty," and "universal." At the same time, and this is most relevant to our attitude towards the "alien," the Bulgarian does not indulge in the degree of cultural relativism that is synonymous with indifference, where the existence of differences is merely assumed and not engaged in productive interaction.

CONCLUSION

The intellectual discourse on Bulgarian cultural identity is differentiated in regard both to the diversity of positions and to theoretical controversies. If during the first half of the century the debate centered on the opposition between traditional and modern, between race and culture, at the end of the century it centers on post-modern/modern (the traditional not being obsolete), on politics/culture. If during the interwar period there was a powerful call for the intelligentsia to be a loyal exponent of the popular, at present there is an ever greater drive to affirm the status of intellectuals and emancipate them, each of them being entitled to his or her "own" speech.

Educational discourse reacts flexibly to political changes, but it is much more resistant to the way in which the "own" is constructed. In this discourse, the "own" categorically implies the call of blood. Land, mother, and motherland are the figures which make organic metaphors "natural" and introduce the attitude that the "own" is destiny and predestination, rather than choice and reflexive empathy.

The intellectual and educational discourses not only sound different, at times they are in open contradiction. At the very time when schools sing hymns to the Balkan Range, the latter is de-mythologized by the sarcastic wit of the post-modern intellectual (Daskalov 1994).

Schools cultivate the basic patterns of interpreting the "own" and provide the main stockpile of knowledge for fleshing them out. But while the socializing effect of the school is incomparably broader than the esoteric discussions carried out at universities, the latter enrich reflection upon the "own." Discussants there play the role of "the stranger" (Schütz) who observes things "from the sideline," raises questions, and to whom the self-evidence of the community seems but a myth. But while the elements of the "own" might indeed seem to be myths from the perspective of historical facts, from the perspective of experience they are significant.

Deconstructive pathos should also be self-reflective and capable of distinguishing its subject. It is "constructive" in a positive sense when it reveals the falsification of history as a means for creating national mythology. When it starts deconstructing its very "own," however, the stakes are different, involving alienation, deprivation of the comfort of transcendence in the name of the quest, going out from oneself and one's "own," and entering into the diverse but "cold" world of numerous differences. Deconstruction can thus also be "constructive" but not in a negative sense for, when it deconstructs the myth of the "own," it lays the foundations for the myth of the "alien."

I would say that extremes provoke extremes. Over-commitment to the idea and metaphor of the "own" as an organic body triggers positions that do not simply "loosen" bonds, but present them as inconceivable. Communal unification does not lead to diversification of identities, but to their dismantling. Foucault is now one of the greatest intellectual fashions in Bulgaria, but "concern for oneself" (Foucault 1994) is yet to be thematized in the Bulgarian reflection on ownness.

Levinas distinguishes two forms of collectivity, namely, shoulder-to-shoulder and eye-to-eye collectivity. The former is a communal collectivity that says "Us," a collectivity in which the subject is eager to identify with The Other, both being submerged in the collective presentation and common ideal. The latter, an I-You collectivity, is the eye-to-eye relationship in which The Other is both proximity and distance. S/he is close enough to be conceived of and desired as a partner within a common intersubjective space, but is distant enough to prevent his/her difference from dissolving in the collectivity (Levinas 1994).

We need the "own" as locus of meaning and values that transcend us. We also need the "alien" as a stimulus for realizing and valuing difference. And we particularly need the own/alien relationship as an interaction that rules out both the indifference of cultural relativism and the aggressiveness of the instrumental "use" and subordination of the other. This is a type of interaction that does not annihilate, but rather preserves autonomy within a common dialogical field.

Institute of Philosophy
Bulgarian Academy of Sciences

NOTES

1. From Ivan Vazov, translated by Peter Tempest.
2. Toennies's distinction between "community" (*Gemeinschaft*) and "society" (*Gesellschaft*) is familiar. The careful reader will note that "community" is often used in this text, albeit in reference to modern phenomena. This is not due to the writer's conceptual imprecision but rather to the subject of study: not the specificity of Bulgarian society but the way of thematizing "the own", a way in which "society" revitalizes certain dimensions of "the community."
3. Translated by Peter Tempest.

REFERENCES

Note: The references from the anthology *Why Are We What We Are?* are quoted with the year of the initial publication and the pages from the anthology. The same approach is applied to all reprint publications.

Bogdanov, B. et al. (1991) *Literature 8*. Sofia: Prosveta (in Bulgarian).
_____. (1994) "The Two Welfares." *Lettre Internationale*, No.7, 43-57 (in Bulgarian).
Camus, A. (1979) *L'etranger*. Sofia: Narodna Kultura (in Bulgarian).
Daskalov, R. (1994). "Our National Cultural Identity: Manner of Construction. In Daskalov, R. and I. Elenkov (eds.). *Why Are We What We Are?* Sofia: Prosveta, 27-48 (in Bulgarian).
Foucault, M. (1994) *History of Sexuality*, vol. 3. (Pleven: EA (in Bulgarian).
Germanov, G. et al. (1992) *Literature 9*. Sofia: Prosveta (in Bulgarian).
Gulubov, K. (1934) "Psychology of the Bulgarian." In Daskalov, R. and I. Elenkov (eds.). *Why Are We What We Are?* Sofia: Prosveta, 1994, 213-230 (in Bulgarian).

Hristov, K. (1939) "What Is the Bulgarian?" In Daskalov, R. and I. Elenkov (eds.). *Why Are We What We Are?* Sofia: Prosveta, 1994, 454-463. (in Bulgarian).

Katsarski, I. (1992) "Towards the Biography of the Bulgarian Intelligentsia and the Bulgarian Political Elite." *Philosophski alternativi* 11-12, 72-77 (in Bulgarian).

Kazandzhiev, S. (1932) "The Collective Man." In Daskalov, R. and I. Elenkov (eds.). *Why Are We What We Are?* Sofia: Prosveta, 1994, 163-174 (in Bulgarian).

Kristeva, J. (1991) "A New Type of Intellectual. The Dissident." *Izbor* 2, 26-29 (in Bulgarian).

_____. (1991) "Toccata and Fugue to the Foreigner." *East-East* 2, 8-13 (in Bulgarian).

Levinas, E. (1994) "Time and the Other." *Philosofski alternativi* 6, 29-31 (in Bulgarian).

Milev, G. (1921) "The Bulgarian People Today." In Daskalov, R. and I. Elenkov (eds.). *Why Are We What We Are?* Sofia: Prosveta, 1994, 183-185 (in Bulgarian).

Mutafchiev P. (1934) "Pope Bogomil and Saint Ivan Rilski." In Daskalov, R. and I. Elenkov (eds.). *Why Are We What We Are?* Sofia: Prosveta, 1994, 357-369 (in Bulgarian).

_____. (1938) "A Balance." In Daskalov, R. and I. Elenkov (eds.). *Why Are We What We Are?* Sofia: Prosveta, 1994, 380-390 (in Bulgarian).

_____. (1940) "Today's Bulgaria and the Spirit of Our Renaissance." In Daskalov, R. and I. Elenkov (eds.). *Why Are We What We Are?* (Sofia: Prosveta, 1994, 391-400 (in Bulgarian).

Mutafov, T. (1920) "The Engine." In Daskalov, R. and I.Elenkov (eds.) *Why Are We What We Are?* Sofia: Prosveta, 1994, 186-188 (in Bulgarian).

Penev, B. (1942) "Introduction to Bulgarian Literature after the Liberation." In Daskalov, R. and I. Elenkov (eds.). *Why Are We What We Are?* Sofia: Prosveta, 1994, 144-162 (in Bulgarian).

_____. (1924) "Our Intelligentsia." In Daskalov, R. and I.Elenkov (eds.). *Why Are We What We Are?* Sofia: Prosveta, 1994, 131-143 (in Bulgarian).

Petkanov, K. (1932) "The Bulgarian Intelligentsia as Child and Negation of Our Village." In Daskalov, R. and I. Elenkov (eds.). *Why Are We What We Are?* Sofia: Prosveta, 1994, 412-420 (in Bulgarian).

Ricoeur, P. (1990) *Soi-meme comme un autre*. Paris: Seuil.

Plato (1982) *Dialogues*, vol. 2. Sofia: Nauka i iskustvo (in Bulgarian).

Schütz, A. (1970) *On the Phenomenology of Social Relations*. Chicago: The University of Chicago Press.

Sheitanov, N. (1925) "Bulgarian magic. The Man." In Daskalov, R. and I. Elenkov (eds.). *Why Are We What We Are?* Sofia: Prosveta, 1994, 253-262 (in Bulgarian).

_____. (1933) "The Spirit of Negation of the Bulgarian." In Daskalov, R. and I. Elenkov (eds.). *Why Are We What We Are?* Sofia: Prosveta, 1994, 270-280 (in Bulgarian).

Slaveikov, P. (1923) "The Bulgarian Folk Song." In Daskalov, R. and I. Elenkov (eds.) *Why Are We What We Are?* Sofia: Prosveta, 1994, 49-73 (in Bulgarian).

Simmel, G. (1990) *Philosophie de la modernite* II. Paris: Payot.

_____. (1964) "The Stranger." In Wolff, K (ed.). *The Sociology of Georg Simmel*. London: The Free Press of Glencoe, 402-409.

Todorov, T. (1982) *La conquete de l'Amerique*. Paris: Seuil.

Tsaneva, M. et al. (1992) *Literature 10*. Sofia: Prosveta (in Bulgarian).

Yanev, J. (1934) "Philosophy of Motherland." In Daskalov, R. and I. Elenkov (eds.). *Why Are We What We Are?* Sofia: Prosveta, 1994, 345-348 (in Bulgarian).

_____. (1933) "The Spirit of the Nation." In Daskalov, R. and I. Elenkov (eds.). *Why Are We What We Are?* Sofia: Prosveta, 1994, 342-344 (in Bulgarian).

Yotzov, B. (1933) "The Bulgarian in the Eyes of the Bulgarian Writer." *Philosofski alternativi*, 5, 62-69 (in Bulgarian).

CHAPTER X

CHRISTIAN VALUES AND MODERN BULGARIAN CULTURE

GEORGI KAPRIEV

According to a public opinion poll published in the second week of April, 1996, 19 percent of the Bulgarian population declare themselves to be Orthodox Christians. Regardless of the shortcomings of such polls, it must be admitted that this figure is more or less correct. A considerable portion of the Bulgarian population do accept positions in respect to the principles of their personal value systems that may justifiably be viewed as reflecting the Orthodox form of Christianity. Orthodox values thus enjoy a comparatively high relevance within the framework of modern Bulgarian culture. This is a phenomenon that cannot, and must not, be neglected.

However, the character of Orthodox values is a somewhat open and persistent question and the topic of much discussion today. Moreover, the image of Orthodoxy must be made specific to the present cultural situation. There are two fundamental positions in this regard. One adheres to Orthodoxy as it has been put forth in official doctrine and according to its essence, so to speak, while the other stresses the historically formed ideological presentation of Orthodoxy in Bulgaria. Both of these value structures insist on their Orthodox character, but there appears to be an insurmountable gap between them, something that could surprise only an outside observer.

In order to understand this situation, at least three thematic issues must be examined. First, it is necessary to abstract the specifics of Orthodoxy in accordance with its own canons, by virtue of which it exists in culture precisely as Orthodoxy. Second, the lot of Orthodoxy within the context of Bulgarian history must be considered. Third, and only in the light of the first two questions, the issue of the character of Orthodox values within the structure of modern Bulgarian culture must be raised.

THE NATURE OF ORTHODOXY

Viewed in its own terms, the Orthodox Church is above all a mystical fraternity in union with God, with Christ. In this sense, the Church is a spiritual reality in which the faithful are in immediate communion with the Divine Trinity. The community that is the Church understands itself as a union of sinners who, by virtue of their religious experience, are joined with the Divinity through the love, mercy, and sanctity of Christ their head. The Orthodox Christian is thus fully entitled in respect to his religious affiliation to state "I am the Church," or rather, because of his "belonging to the Church," "We are the Church." This statement has no more than a superficial resemblance to the notion of "Christians non-aligned with the Church." In other words, Orthodoxy insists not on some type of institutional structure but rather defines itself primarily through following and worshipping God in the correct way.

Pivotal for the Christian presence in the world is the mystical spirit of Orthodox existence, at the basis of which lies the firm conviction that human intelligence is unable to grasp Divine substance positively. For the believer, God can be approached only through the acts of Divine Being that flow from His substance (*ad extra*). Although these are the acts of this substance, they are not the Divine substance itself. Such an attitude is obviously unable to generate any fully articulated theological doctrine. Orthodox theology is first of all a traditionally apprehended practice, a spiritual realization, and not doctrinal instruction; however, this does not at all mean that it is irrational, illogical, chaotic, or comprised of random cases. Quite the contrary, it is sufficiently strict and orderly and possesses a very clear inner connection, but it does not claim to express itself in a normative doctrinal system. Among the Christian denominations, Orthodoxy rejects most strongly all notions of predestination and determinism regarding human beings, and it vigorously emphasizes freedom and personal responsibility. Orthodoxy does not aim at the formation of individuals as an after thought, but rather demands persons who realize themselves through their unlimited freedom, who are personally responsible for their behavior and for the intensity of their Orthodox spirituality.

This is why a uniform Orthodox institution does not exist. Not only is every local Church a manifestation of the one and only Church, it is that very Church itself. Since each of the autonomous local Orthodox Churches is in contact with all the others (there are approximately fifteen today), it is a member of the ecclesiastical body as a whole, whose head is Christ. But this is a mystical as well as a real body. For this very reason, none of the Patriarchs, including the Patriarch of Constantinople, is able to be the sole, or even primary, administrator of the ecclesiastical body. Each of the Orthodox Patriarchs runs the affairs of his own autonomous Church and is not subject to outside pressure. According to Orthodox doctrine, the head of the Church is Christ alone, Who needs no earthly proxies and places no one to act in His stead. Therefore, there can be no question of some single organizational structure for Orthodoxy, but only of its unity in identity, which is guaranteed by the Universal Cross.

In addition, Orthodoxy emphasizes the official and organizational primacy of the ecclesiastical hierarchy in an exclusively liturgical aspect and does not consider that hierarchy to be the Church itself. The "quality" of this hierarchy, which is determined by the personal characters of its various members, is not the quality of the Church as a whole and, from the viewpoint of the Church's essence, has only an indirect and non-essential influence on the latter.

For the same reason, it also follows that an Orthodox political doctrine does not exist. Orthodoxy has no need of any secular or ethnic power, nor of any coordination with similar authorities. In this sense, so-called "Caesaro-Papism" is primarily an explanatory mechanism that has been utilized in West European ecclesiastical and historical thought. It is not an Orthodox norm, but merely reflects particular historical phenomena that are aberrations from the proper canonical ordinances of the Church. As such, every use of Church or ecclesiastical authority for the purpose of any political or lay aspirations whatsoever is contrary to Orthodoxy. The well-known Byzantine "symphony" of ecclesiastical and lay hierarchies in no case implies the subordination of the Church (which would be hierarchical nonsense), but rather represents a concerted service to God on behalf of the competencies of each. Therefore, at least from the point of view of the Church, the task is not to introduce any lay norm into the Church, but, quite on the contrary, to introduce spiritual norms into the world. It is precisely for this reason that Orthodoxy recognizes any power, *granted its Christian piety*. At the same time, Orthodoxy stands in opposition to the partiality of every lay power because the Kingdom of God is not of this world. For the sake of the above mentioned symphony, Orthodox canons allotted the Christian Emperor (but not every secular ruler) the ecclesiastical order of reader, which is a lower non-priestly clerical order. But Orthodoxy emphatically insists upon both its detachment from the realm of partial, and consequently tribal or national, powers, as well as its unchanging "relatedness" to Divine eternity.

At the same time, however, the local organization of the various Orthodox Churches implies an explicit connection between the Church proper and its territorial and historical lot. The tensions induced by this state of affairs are perhaps most clearly evident in respect to the Bulgarian Orthodox Church.

ORTHODOXY IN THE BULGARIAN CONTEXT

The official establishment of Christianity in Bulgaria began with the decision of the Eighth Ecumenical Council (870 A.D.) that the Bulgarian Church should be under the jurisdiction of the Patriarch of Constantinople. The controversy concerning this affiliation had brought about the first considerable disruption in relations between Constantinople and Rome. Only a few decades later, the Bulgarian Church declared its institutional independence.

Unfortunately, this administrative establishment of Christianity resulted in a superficial Christianization and a closer commitment of the Church to the state.

After the final conquest of the Balkan peninsula by the Ottomans in the 15th century, the local Orthodox Churches lost their autonomy and became subjugated to the supremacy of the Constantinople Patriarchate. Since ethnic divisions within the Ottoman Empire were almost wholly based on religious affiliation, the determining ethnic characteristic of Bulgarians for a number of centuries was their Orthodox Christianity. This enduring entanglement between nation and religion has left its mark on the specific features of Bulgarian everyday religious awareness, particularly as it developed as a structural operator during the 19th century in respect to efforts to consolidate the Bulgarian nation.

This entanglement became a tool of the first order in the hands of the national ideologists because the operator "territory" was non-functional. This situation was conditioned not only by the fact that Bulgarians lived within the Ottoman Empire, but also by the historical vagueness of the geographical term "Bulgaria." As a consequence, language and religion were the only available factors for defining the Bulgarian nation.

The Bulgarian movement for national independence began precisely with efforts to re-establish the Bulgarian Church. These efforts were collectively a reaction to the widespread policy of assimilation of the local Greek Orthodox Church, which had been re-established in 1829 as a result of the 1821 revolution and was sanctioned by a decree of the Patriarch of Constantinople in 1850. In addition, they were also a response to efforts on the part of the Serbian Church for autonomy after 1822. After years of struggle, the Bulgarian Exarchate was finally re-established by Sultan Abdul Azis through his *ferman* of 28 February 1870.

However, this decree of the Sultan was in obvious conflict with Orthodox tradition, according to which a Church can be autonomous on a territorial or state principle, but never on an ethnic principle. In addition, the re-establishment of the Bulgarian Church was not only proclaimed by a secular authority, this authority was also of a foreign creed. For these reasons, the Council of Constantinople in 1872 denounced the newly autonomous Bulgarian Church, a situation that comprised the first schism within the bounds of Orthodoxy itself insofar as the newly established Bulgarian Church was thereby isolated within Orthodoxy for more than 70 years.

The Bulgarian Church eventually adopted the view that its chance for survival lay in closer relations with the Bulgarian state that had emerged after the Russo-Turkish War of 1877-78, and the politicians and ideologists of the Third Bulgarian Kingdom, almost without exception, fostered its consolidation. The new state did not conceal its ambitions for territorial union with all those Bulgarians who were left outside the territory of the Bulgarian Principality by the Congress of Berlin. The existence of an autonomous Church was very useful in this respect since the Church, along with language, continued to be the most powerful identifying feature of the Bulgarian nation.

Church crises closely tallied with state crises in modern

Bulgarian history, a situation that was aggravated after the imposition of the Communist regime in 1944. The Bulgarian Communists did not repeat the repression of the Church that had been carried out by their Russian comrades, but rather adopted a more flexible and, in the final analysis, more effective position. For example, the Communist government successfully interceded for the re-establishment of the Bulgarian Patriarchate in 1953. This took place, of course, not so much out of concern for the lot of Orthodoxy in Bulgaria as for the possible exclusive commitment of the Bulgarian Exarchate to the Moscow Patriarchate, which was dependent on the Kremlin.

But this "preservation" of the Bulgarian Church was achieved at too high a price. This was expressed not only by the obvious collaboration of Church officials with the government, but also by the sharp decline in ideological culture among the clergy. The price paid could also be seen in the prostrate attitude of the clergy towards the persecution of virtually every civic position that was based on Christian values. The final aim of such oppression during this period was the reduction of Christianity to a mere phenomenon of Bulgarian cultural history.

To summarize the discussion to this point, it could be said that the history of the Bulgarian Orthodox Church, especially during the last two centuries, has been the history of an on-going "deviation" from its real vocation, which, needless to say, has led to its respective deformation. In the cultural sphere, Orthodoxy has been presented not in its essence, but rather as an element of the national and ethnic character. This applies especially to the period from the 1950s to the end of the 1980s. During this period, Orthodoxy was forcibly marginalized and came to represent only the historical merit it had acquired in consolidating national identity; it thereby also served to safeguard valuable traditions of everyday life that had begun to fall into decay. In this fashion, the explicit cultural presence of the Church was reduced to a minimum, being virtually eliminated from the official ideologized culture.

ORTHODOX VALUES IN MODERN BULGARIAN CULTURE

After 1989, an obvious change occurred concerning the status of Orthodox values within the structure of Bulgarian culture. This change, however, cannot and must not be given a univocal evaluation insofar as the institution of the Church has squandered an historical opportunity to atone for its accumulated errors and reclaim its natural status of spiritual guide by means of a gesture of penance. Instead of doing so, the Church gave itself over to a pandemonious lack of unity in respect to political developments. (I insist on the term "lack of unity" instead of "schism" since the latter involves liturgical and dogmatic differences, which do not apply in this case.)

Furthermore, an obvious decline of the priesthood, an acute lack of spirituality, and an adherence to the letter at the expense of the spirit can be seen in every aspect of this situation. Regardless of what the course of development or eventual outcome of this state of confusion might be, it is reasonable to expect that neither now nor in the years to come will the institution of the Orthodox Church be capable of becoming a constructive factor in Bulgarian culture. The fact that the public debate concerning the role and meaning of Orthodoxy is now conducted exclusively by laymen provides the basis for a virtually irrefutable argument in support of this view.

The tensions within this debate are brought into focus by the fact that, in the period immediately preceding the collapse of Communism, a considerable number of Bulgarians, particularly among the intelligentsia, considered their affiliation to Christianity as a rebuff to Communist ideology. Stated otherwise, Christian values were viewed from a politically colored vantage point. While this may have had a certain positive effect, it unambiguously reinforced the instrumental embodiment of Orthodox values in the common dimensions of culture, if not elsewhere as well. The current attempt at the cultural assimilation of Orthodox values upon the platform of nationalism is widespread and aggressive, and not only by virtue of the tradition in this regard that has been discussed above. Within the Bulgarian cultural context, nationalism did not occupy a certain vacuum that arose after Communist ideology had been discredited insofar as the latter had already lost all cultural worth, even in the eyes of its own agents. Bulgarian nationalism is rooted rather in a mass complex of cultural inferiority that is intensified precisely in the circumstances of the open society, or rather semi-open society, that Bulgaria has now become. The average Bulgarian simply does not see any compelling reason to compare himself positively with his foreign contemporaries, nor would he in fact enjoy favorable odds in such an effort. Nationalism today has undertaken the task of compensating for this complex, but of course it cannot base itself on a cultural interpretation of the word "nation." Its only possible basis is the *Blut und Boden* ideology, where nation is equated with state, and both nation and state with *ethnos*.

The brief historical survey provided above should make it sufficiently evident why Orthodox values have not only become the "stock in trade" of nationalism but have also been promoted to frontline positions.

On the one hand, and as during the 18th and 19th centuries, today there are no factors more powerful for confirming Bulgarian ethnicity than religion and language. This is why Christianity is taken as the definitive Bulgarian religion and Orthodoxy as the root of national and political independence. Of great importance is the fact that Orthodox Christianity has proven to be the factor which distinguishes Bulgarians from both the European West as well as Byzantine culture by virtue of its local institution. Unfortunately, Orthodox Universalism has been completely sacrificed for the sake of this separative function.

On the other hand, it is precisely the combination of Orthodoxy and language that apparently has made it possible to overcome the illogical transition from ethnic encapsulation to Slavophile and Pan-Slav ideology. This has resulted primarily in a decline in Russian political and cultural influence.

Clerical circles have put up no resistance whatsoever to the ideological cliché whereby Orthodoxy has been bound to the "national" and the "political". In contrast, intellectual circles which took up positions in accordance with the canonical structure of Orthodoxy, not its historical context, began to take shape as early as the 1980s. These circles try to uphold Orthodox values not from the viewpoint of some ethnic or state affiliation, but upon the basis of the spiritual substance of Orthodoxy. It must be emphasized that this is the first time such intellectual programs have become valid as formative factors within the Bulgarian cultural context.

But it is nonetheless important to keep in mind that these circles, regardless of their high intellectual potential, by no means form the face of Bulgarian culture in a decisive way. Quite the contrary, Bulgarian intellectuals with grandiose ideas prefer to speak about the irrationalism of Orthodoxy, about what might be referred to as its basic cultural deficiency. Such figures thereby place Orthodoxy utterly at the disposal of the national, *Blut und Boden* ideologists. In so doing, they rely on their own ignorance of theology — which is in no way inferior to the ignorance demonstrated by these ideologists. Such ignorance is generally representative of the average and mass level of Bulgarian culture, which in its modern version tolerates only the everyday, not the elevated, forms of Orthodoxy.

In sum, certain conclusions and prognoses can be outlined upon the basis of the above discussion. First of all, it must be noted that Orthodox values are neither a decisive nor the decisive factor in modern Bulgarian culture. They have been preserved mainly at the level of political and everyday life, where they are realized not in their dogmatic constitution, but rather in an historically distorted, and distorting, context. That is why their power to shape Bulgarian culture, insofar as it can be said to exist at all, has merely an episodic and unsystematic character. However, it must be emphasized that intellectual programs which clearly state their Orthodox foundations, that is, that they have been formed explicitly upon Orthodox theological ideas, have for the first time become a fact of modern Bulgarian culture. It may be of some importance that those who comprise these circles come mostly from the young and middle-aged generations.

With regard to prognosis, it must be indicated that Christian values will not become the substantial content of Bulgarian culture for many years to come; perhaps they will never adopt such a role. This should be obvious not only from the structure of the modern cultural situation but also from the specifics of those values themselves. As has been noted, the latter demand a particular disposition of the personality and a particular spiritual power, which is why the intellectuals who now stand proxy for this value-system do not pursue its expansion and popularization. Nevertheless, these intellectual circles may eventually contribute to a change in the general formation of the Bulgarian cultural context, thereby exerting a certain influence upon its specifics provided cultural processes in Bulgaria are not forcibly interrupted but rather are left to pursue their own course of development.

CHAPTER XI

PROMOTING INTER-ETHNIC DIALOGUE IN BULGARIA

PLAMEN MAKARIEV

THE ETHNOCULTURAL SITUATION IN BULGARIA AND WESTERN POLITICAL THEORY

The population of Bulgaria is ethnically quite heterogeneous. According to the data of the latest census (1992), ethnic minorities comprise 14.3 percent of the population, the most numerous being the Turks (9.4 percent of the total number) and the Roma (3.7 percent). However, these data should not be considered as absolutely precise in that they refer to ethnic affiliation as declared by the individuals themselves. It is a well-known fact, for example, that a large number of the Roma population identified themselves as Bulgarians or Turks for various reasons. This uncertainty in respect to data has provoked ardent discussion among activists in the minority movements concerning the total number and composition of the latter. A quite special issue is the number of *Pomaks* (ethnic Bulgarians who were converted to Islam during 1394-1878, when the Bulgarian lands were controlled by the Turks). According to the census, they number about 70,000, but there are reasons to believe that their actual number is much higher (up to 200,000). The situation is even more complicated when religious affiliation is taken into account. About 60 percent of the Roma people identify themselves as Christians and 40 percent as Muslims. And not only are there Muslims who are ethnic Bulgarians, there are also Christians who are ethnic Turks (Alexandrov, 1995).

At present, the ethnocultural situation in Bulgaria can be described as being in a state of "unstable equilibrium." Even a slight disturbance can generate dynamic processes — in either a constructive or destructive direction. This instability is a consequence of the gap between, on the one hand, the various political programs for regulating ethnic relations and, on the other, prevailing socio-psychological attitudes.

The mass media and the various political party platforms in fact offer only two basic alternatives in this respect, namely, either simplistically liberal or extremely nationalistic policies on ethnic issues. Both of these are confronted, however, by such traditional qualities of the Bulgarian people as political realism and ethnic tolerance. On the one hand, overlooking the actual grounds of ethnic antagonisms is not welcomed, and claims that ethnic differences should not be a significant factor in society are not taken seriously. On the other hand, ethnic conflicts do not escalate easily. There are practically no cases of ethnic violence or persecution in the history of the independent Bulgarian state from 1878 to 1984. And all this in spite of the considerable ethnic heterogeneity, the "memories" of five centuries of Turkish dominance, and the notorious conflicts between Balkan nations that have led to a number of wars. An important example of ethnic tolerance was the mass reaction against the attempt to deport Bulgarian Jews to German concentration camps during World War II, which saved tens of thousands of lives.

Consequently, neither of the two extreme alternatives finds much support on behalf of the population. Yet the overall growth of social discontent as well as conflicts in neighboring countries could bring about a dramatic change in the situation at any moment, and this might possibly include a turn to nationalism.

The theoretical dimensions of the two political trends in question involve the well-known rival paradigms in Western political philosophy known as liberalism (various forms of which are also called individualism, universalism or social atomism) and communitarianism. The former applies universal standards of freedom and justice directly to individual cases, while the latter keeps to particular values and norms. The term "communitarianism" is a neologism. Although the school which identifies itself in this way dates only from the early 1980s, it follows an old tradition that prioritizes the communal element of social life, including German Romanticism, Hegelianism, the various socialist teachings and so forth.

We shall now briefly review the controversy arguments "pro" and "con" between these two theoretical schools to help us understand why the methods they represent are not very useful in resolving Balkan ethnic conflicts. We may thereby also uncover other prospects for conceptualizing the ethnocultural situation in

Bulgaria and finding a way to rationalize it.

First of all, discussions between liberals and communitarians address fundamental issues of social science and praxis. They concentrate, however, on the relationships between the individual and the community to which one belongs, such as state, religious congregation or family. In contrast, ethnic and national antagonisms in the Balkans originate from confrontations between different communities, each with its own cultural identity. In some cases, these communities conceive of themselves as outposts of different civilizations, competing to share a finite geopolitical and cultural space. The Bosnian Serbs, for example, have claimed in this vein that they are carrying out the historic mission of preventing the establishment of an Islamic state in the heart of Europe.

What should the attitude of the individual be towards the other community when it is "other" for him not only in the sense of "not-his-own" but also as culturally alien? This is the case when the other community confronts the individual not only as something strange and incomprehensible, but also as a threat to one's cultural identity. Furthermore, although the individual must not forget that the alien community consists of human beings who have the same universal rights as oneself, the exercise of such rights on their part is viewed as a threat.

If the basic principle of liberalism is to be applied in this case, namely, that one's rights should not contradict the rights of the others, an arbiter is needed, i.e., someone who can take an impartial, absolute stand, and judge whether or not given actions infringe upon other people's interests. Such a position is impossible, however, in a conflict between communities that have basically different value systems. The arbiter cannot belong to either of them, but the communities in question do not recognize the same outside authorities. Since the "demarcation line" between culturally different communities divides the entire world, everything that is accepted by the one is alien for the other, and vice versa.

Of course, the logic of both liberalism and communitarianism is not totally irrelevant to the realities of the ethnic and national antagonisms in the Balkans. Here, too, it is the individual who must choose between freedom and loyalty to one's own community. The specific point, however, is that when the cultural identity of the latter is threatened by external factors, the individual's loyalty to one's community becomes incompatible with certain universal values. If one would take such values as valid, one would have to "betray" one's own community. On the other hand, to ignore absolutely universal standards of behavior would mean to accept even the most disgusting forms of discrimination towards the alien individuals. How can we resolve such difficulties in applying the political strategies of liberalism and communitarianism to ethnic issues in the Balkans?

THE LIBERALISM VS COMMUNITARIANISM CONTROVERSY AND THE BALKAN CASE

In 1887, Ferdinand Toennies defined two types of social relations in his famous book *Community and Society (Gemeinschaft und Gesellschaft)*. Toennies understands "All intimate, private, and exclusive living together" as life in *Gemeinschaft* (Toennies 1957:33), while *Gesellschaft* comprises public life. There are communities of kinship, neighborhood, language, folk customs, mores and beliefs, while *Gesellschaft* exists in the realms of business, politics and the sciences. The individual lives from birth in certain communities that form one as a personality, but "one goes into *Gesellschaft* (society) as one goes into a strange country" (*ibid.*). Unity with other members of the same community is an end in itself, while the individual's associations with other agents in society is a means to achieve one's ends. The concept of *Gemeinschaft* refers to real and organic life; the concept of *Gesellschaft* refers to imaginary and mechanical structures.

Liberalism

We can draw a clear distinction between the methodologies of liberalism and communitarianism in reference to Toennies's typology. In his terms, the former theory prioritizes the relations of society, and the latter, the relations of community. Insofar as liberalism is concerned, one should bear in mind another important differentiation, namely, that between the naive liberalism of Hobbes, Locke and the French Enlightenment on the one hand, and the sophisticated theories of authors such as Kant and Rawls on the other. In the first case, the frame of reference is human nature as such and the natural rights of human beings, such as the rights to life, freedom, property, security, and freedom of speech, thought and religion. These concrete rights are valid under all circumstances for all human beings, and to deny them would mean to contradict the generally accepted view of human dignity. They are stated in such documents as the "Habeas Corpus Akte" of 1679, the "Bill of Rights" in the American Constitution of 1787, the French "Declaration des droits de l'homme et du citoyen" of 1789, and so forth.

Universalism, rationalism, individualism and egalitarianism are features common to all varieties of liberalism. Traditional forms of liberalism, however, typically base their views upon the assumption that there are certain universal and fundamental human qualities. Consequently, free action turns out to be the functioning of a mechanism (human nature), morality is interpreted in the terms of ethical naturalism, and all social relationships turn out to be *Gesellschaft* relations.

Moreover, this commitment to concrete features of human nature contradicts the basic rationalistic orientation of liberalism, which amounts to a logical inconsistency. Even though norms of behavior are declared that claim universal validity, these universal rules are nevertheless formulated with a view to a set of empirical, contingent qualities and rights, such as the "right to property," "freedom of speech," "inviolability of the home," and so forth. One could easily ask what are the criteria of selection, and why exactly these rights should be put forward and not others. Is it not possible to err and include in the list a human right that is only apparently fundamental?

This last question refers to the danger of grounding a universal norm on some particular feature of a specific cultural tradition. The given culture would *eo ipso* assume a dominant position with respect to others, who would have to adapt themselves to its particularities for the sake of humanity itself. The reality of this culture's customs would thus come to coincide with the ideal that was normatively prescribed by international agreements. In such a case, certain nations could unjustly represent themselves as a model to be followed by the rest of the world.

This is a very real possibility in respect to the influence that individualism and collectivism should have on defining universal human rights insofar as the manner in which these rights have been formulated in the most respected international documents seems to be an expression of the Western value system. If the group-oriented values that dominate societies outside the Western cultural sphere are opposed to the latter's individualism, one could justify even the chopping off of hands as a punishment for theft (Kühnhardt 1991:136). Given the relevant cultural context, such an act could pretend not only to juridical, but also to moral legitimacy insofar as respecting the inviolability of the human body could then be interpreted as giving priority to individualistic values that contradict the Islamic cultural tradition. The latter's standards attribute more importance to the common good than to the rights of the individual.

These shortcomings of traditional liberalism are overcome in the philosophy of Immanuel Kant, who introduces the idea of freedom by locating human existence outside of the empirical world. Empirical conditions determine the subject only within the field of appearance (as an "empirical character") because one exists as a thing-in-itself. "In its intelligible character this same subject must be considered to be free from all influence of sensibility and from all determination through appearances" (Kant 1987:469). In that one of these empirical circumstances is time, the intelligible character turns out to be free from all natural necessity. "No action begins in this active being itself; but we may yet quite correctly say that the active being of itself begins its effects in the sensible world" (*ibid.*). However, the subject ought to act only in conformity with the rule prescribed by his/her reason. Reformulated from Kantian language into the language of common sense, this basic moral law is equivalent to the maxim "Do unto others as you would have others do unto you."

Kant's ethics is formalistic. In order to be both universal and rational (not self-contradictory), its basic law implies no concrete moral requirements and attributes moral value to no contingent standards of human behavior. Different persons can have different notions of happiness. It might suit a given individual's ends when morality prescribes a specific orientation to activity, but this would surely contradict the ideals of others: hence, according to Kantian liberalism, the priority of the right over the good, whereby everyone should be free to decide what is good from one's own point of view. Morality should not represent any concrete requirement as a universal norm, but must rather guarantee only that individuals not stand in each other's way in the course of realizing their personal, freely chosen ends. Liberalism thus claims the priority of freedom and rights over any particular program for achieving general welfare.

Kant's ideas greatly contribute to making liberalism a consistent theory, but his transcendental philosophy seems too complicated and obscure to serve as a conceptual basis for modern liberal politics. Working in the same general tradition, John Rawls has attempted to formulate an exoteric argumentation for the priority of right. Instead of representing the subject of free will as a *Ding an sich*, he has advanced the theory of "the unencumbered self" who does not identify one with any particular personal quality nor any social role. "The unencumbered self" is rather the one to whom such qualities and roles belong. One is the agent who makes one's free choice without conforming to any momentary empirical state. No role or commitment could define the unencumbered self so completely that one could not understand oneself without it, and no project could be so essential that turning away from it would call into question the person one is (Sandel 1984:18).

The theory of the "unencumbered self" refers to self-reflexivity, which is a feature of intelligent, self-conscious behavior. In order for a person to wonder how s/he ought to act in a given situation, it is first necessary that one have already distanced oneself from one's own empirical condition. In trying to make such a choice, one juxtaposes what one feels like doing with what ought to be done, i.e., one somehow observes oneself from the outside and does not act automatically. It is this type of "observer" who can be called an "unencumbered self."

This idealization is typical for modern liberalism, and it is one of the favorite targets of communitarian criticism. First of all, no one exists as an abstract subject insofar as our personalities are formed by the communities in which we have been brought up. "The only way to understand human behavior is to refer to individuals in their social, cultural and historical contexts" (Avineri and de-Shalit 1992:2). And no one can choose one's "mother community."

However, liberalism does not claim that the autonomous subject constitutes himself *ex nihilo*. D. Gauthier admits that "it would be absurd to identify an individual with the formal process of reflection and choice in which autonomy is manifest." The liberal view of man does not refer to the causal grounds of her/his individuality since what matters instead here is self-consciousness. But even though the latter is itself a product of some type of socialization, it can assume a critical attitude towards social reality, including its own background. "In producing a self-conscious being, human society thus finds itself called into question" (Gauthier 1992:157).

The process of self-reflection and free choice requires some kind of material, certain preferences and capacities, from which to proceed. Gauthier does not see a threat to autonomy in the recognition that this frame of reference has not been itself freely chosen. He writes that, "What makes a being autonomous is his capacity to alter given preferences by a rational self-critical, reflective procedure, not a capacity to produce preferences with no prior basis" (Gauthier 1992:157).

We can assume that the very ability to reflect critically on one's own capacities and preferences is socially determined. We can even generalize that "human beings are socialized into autonomy" (Gauthier 1992:157). But the result of this socialization is not that one's personality is formed as "hardware," but rather that it is formed as a sort of "software" that can be changed and, indeed, itself can change the manner in which it is constituted (Gauthier 1992:158).

This evolution of liberalism, however, does not make it more plausible in respect to moral intuitions that concern solidarity, loyalty and unity with a finite group of people. These values give content to one's identity and designate a given place in the boundless world as the place to which one belongs. In "The Procedural Republic and the Unencumbered Self," M. Sandel questions our ability to view ourselves as autonomous such that our identity is not based on our ends and commitments. We cannot do this without sacrificing our loyalties, "whose moral force consists partly in the fact that living by them is inseparable from understanding ourselves as the particular persons we are — as members of this family or community or nation or people, as bearers of that history, as citizens of this republic" (Sandel 1984:87). Such commitments are more than values I merely happen to have, i.e., values with which I do not identify myself.

A person incapable of this type of constitutive attachments would not be an ideally free and rational agent, but rather someone without character and without moral depth. "For to have character is to know that I move in a history I neither summon nor command, which carries consequences nonetheless for my choices and conduct. It draws me closer to some and more distant from others; it makes some aims more appropriate, others less so" (Sandel 1984:87). Whenever I reflect on my history, I undoubtedly distance myself from it in some way, but this distance is always relative and the point of reflection is never outside the history itself.

In fact, the Kantian type of liberalism does not oppose the communal element in social life absolutely. The autonomy of the subject does not isolate her/him from everyone else and, from Kant's point of view, the relationships on which morality rests are relationships of community. But this is a special kind of community that does not exclude the individual in that its dimensions coincide with humankind as a whole. The position of the self-critical, rational and free subject is the position of humanity as such. This is the "material" (in Gauthier's sense) from which the subject can never distance oneself — even in the most subtle procedures of self-reflection — without losing one's human identity.

However, one could still ask why we should break the bonds with our particular communities at all. Do we not lose the meaning of life when we alienate ourselves from the needs and values of our communities? Even liberals sometimes admit that "the value or goodness of any individual citizen's life is only a reflection and function of the value of the life of the community in which he lives" (Dworkin 1992:206).

There is yet another question that sophisticated liberalism finds quite difficult to answer: How can it be possible to universalize the relations of community and speak meaningfully about loyalty to the whole of mankind? Is not the formulation "loyal to everybody" a contradiction in terms? Apparently loyalty is a necessarily asymmetric relation in which one is closer to someone at the expense of being more distant from others. From this perspective, the fundamental assumptions of liberalism contradict certain important moral intuitions.

It is another matter that the methodology of liberalism cannot be applied directly to the national and ethnic confrontations on the Balkans. The fact is that liberalism cannot help in regulating relations between communities that have different cultural identities. Liberal strategies ignore the meaning that identity has for a community confronted by an alien cultural "environment." The restrictions on the activity of individuals that the community imposes in order to defend its "physiognomy" — and they are perceived as restrictions only by aliens — are regarded as unjustifiable violations of human rights from a liberal point of view. But to demand that the community equally respect the rights of both its own members and the aliens means to demand that it give up its "defense mechanisms." Liberalism recognizes only individual rights, not collective rights, and eroding a community's cultural identity is not regarded as damaging the rights of the individuals who comprise it. It is only natural that this approach is not taken seriously in the Balkans.

Communitarianism

Communitarianism, on the other hand, justifies the discriminative treatment of aliens. From the communitarian perspective, we owe only minimal solidarity to the person who does not belong to our community. An illustration of this attitude can be found in Walzer's "Spheres of Justice." If, for example, I find an injured stranger on my way, it would be my moral duty to help him, as in the story of the Good Samaritan. But ought I to take him into my home and care for him to the end of my days? Although Walzer declares that, "My life cannot be shaped and determined by such chance encounters" (Walzer 1983:98), is it unjust to refuse to the stranger what I readily grant to my relatives and friends?

To uphold communal values and grant priority to one's own good over the rights of aliens does not attract sympathy within the Western cultural tradition. One who maintains the communal position is taken to have such narrow mental horizons that s/he is incapable of imagining more than one way of life. Consequently, such a person is judged as not taking the effort to understand the alien, to put her/himself in the latter's place.

Philosophically, communitarianism cannot justify degrading "freedom" for the sake of "the good." Even if the restrictions imposed on one's freedom are for the sake of her/his own good or for the common good, one's dignity suffers from them. This is undoubtedly the case when the restrictions come from one's own community, while the effects are certainly magnified in respect to an ethnic or national minority within an alien cultural environment.

The position of another fundamental value, rationality, is not much different. To be loyal to the community means to accept its customs uncritically, whatever they might be, but the latter are contingent forms of sociality. What if we find elements among them that are obviously unreasonable, and what if those elements are necessarily associated with the community's identity? In such a case, a true communitarian would by no means resort to a self-reflexive, self-critical procedure since to do so might initiate a series of transformations that would result in the end of community as such. Communitarianism seems to present, therefore, a quite apologetic social methodology.

As far as ethics is concerned, it has been argued that communitarianism tends towards moral relativism. If one contends that morality cannot be conceived in universal terms, that universal and absolute justice is but another illusion of individualism (Avineri and de-Shalit 1992:4), then what reasons can one give for the objective validity of moral standards? Today no one would take seriously the naive claim that only the values of a given community are absolute, all the rest being merely conventional rules of behavior. But if so, can there be any morality at all?

If all moral values and norms are relative, no room is left for ethical discussion between different communities and cultures since everyone then remains with her/his own regulations, as if those of the alien do not matter. But what could we then say about, for example, stoning to death as a legal punishment for adultery insofar as it might be an organic part of the cultural traditions of a given civilization that, practiced within its boundaries, somehow does not concern us? However, since a punishment of this type seems inhuman in the absolute meaning of the word, liberalism, with its norms that claim universal validity, would appear to be a better moral philosophy in such cases.

Moreover, the theoretical prestige of communitarianism has suffered a great deal from spontaneous "communitarian" practices in countries like Bosnia, which demonstrate the absurdity of a persistent adherence to communal values. The absolute denial of a moral commitment to the alien results here in a *bellum omnia contra omnis*, the place of individuals having been taken by ethnic communities.

THE WAY TO DIALOGUE

Our review of the controversy between liberalism and communitarianism has brought us to the conclusion that neither of these paradigms can alone serve as a basis for regulating ethnic relations in the Balkans. As mentioned above, their major conflicting values involve the rights of the individual and the good of the community, and it seems impossible to respect both of them in certain situations. It appears that when recognizing the alien's rights threatens the community's identity, then at least one of the parties must give in.

Our assertion is that dialogue may be regarded as a possible synthesis of two approaches of liberalism and communitarianism.

Let us evaluate an idealized notion of dialogue from the standpoints of both the right and the good, i.e., let us see whether the results of a successful dialogue can be considered "right," "good," or perhaps neither of these qualities. Later we shall return to the issue of the relation between an ideal dialogue and reality.

Imagine a communication community that corresponds to the ideals of discourse ethics, in which relations are regulated only by norms everyone accepts without manipulation or coercion. The process of discussing these norms can be regarded as dialogue if: 1) it is open for participation on behalf of all concerned; 2) all participants have equal rights to propose claims, ask questions and provide answers; and 3) the discussion is free from any influences and motives other than the collective pursuit of norms acceptable to all involved (Habermas 1983:65). Would the order in such a community correspond to criteria pertinent to right or rather to those of the good?

There could be no doubt about the former in that the autonomy and interests of each individual are to be guaranteed within this particular type of community. However, are not questions concerning the good life also relevant to this type of discussion?

As was stated above, the priority of right over the good means that morality should not convert any concrete requirement into a universal norm since to do so would amount to depriving the individual of choice and responsibility in determining her/his line of behavior. This would "expel" issues concerning the good from the sphere of intersubjectivity since they could then be reflected upon and resolved only within the "territory" of the self. But this would not be the case with the communication community insofar as its primary aim is precisely the discussing of those concrete norms that should legitimately regulate relations within the community. And a norm with any particular content could be adopted provided that it receives the consensual support of the participants. Stated otherwise, standards for the good life could be intersubjectively approved, which would mean that a synthesis of the basic values of liberalism and communitarianism, the right and the good, can be found in dialogical "mechanisms" for regulating intersubjective relations.

Let us illustrate this by an example in respect to the Turkish ethnic minority in Bulgaria. Prior to 1989, the dominant attitude towards Turks on the part of the authorities who represented (or rather claimed to represent) the position held by the majority of the population was one of assimilation. The rationale which they offered was that assimilation would have a positive effect on the Turks themselves because it would eliminate any grounds for discrimination and improve their career opportunities and overall economic status. It was even claimed that the majority of "Bulgarian Turks" were actually of Bulgarian descent, their distant ancestors having been moslemized centuries ago and gradually ethnically assimilated. Empirical evidence was supplied concerning the anthropological features, mores, folklore and traditional material culture of large groups of "Bulgarian Turks" that supposedly demonstrated their similarities with Bulgarians and dissimilarities with "actual Turks." The message was that these people should restore their original ethnic identity and reunite with their ethnic Bulgarian brothers and sisters. That is why the campaign to replace their Turkish names with Bulgarian ones was officially called the "Rebirth Process."

Behaving as an ethnic Bulgarian, i.e., speaking Bulgarian, wearing European-style clothing, listening to European-style music, accepting a modern type of family life and so forth, was highly valued by the authorities and rewarded in various ways. This policy constitutes a classic case of imposing upon a minority a concrete standard of the good life held by the community as a whole (the Bulgarian nation represented by state institutions), that is, to abandon one's "otherness" and absolutely join the majority.

What has happened in this respect after the democratic transition? In spite of certain inconsistencies in official policy due to changes in government, the general line has promoted the liberal priority of rights, especially the right of ethnic self-determination of the individual. As a result, ethnic Turks can now more or less freely practice their culture, and to the extent that individual behavior does not conflict with the laws and the constitution of the country, one may choose how to shape one's life. However, the actual exercise of these rights has given rise to certain tendencies that seem to endanger the integrity of society.

For example, a certain number of rural Turkish parents maintain a traditional family model and prefer their grown children to live in the same village or not far away. This minimizes the secular education of the children. Such parents are concerned that if their children pursue modern professions, they would be motivated to leave their families and move to industrial centers. Now, traditional parents are not unaware that children will be significantly isolated from social life if they attend state schools only for the compulsory minimum. They seek compensation for this through far-reaching integration into Islamic culture, such as by sending children to orthodox Islamic religious schools (Alexandrov 1995). Unfortunately, such practices increase the cleavage between modern and traditional culture in Bulgaria.

Here we have a clear contradiction between the rights of individuals and the good of the community. What could be changed in this respect by resorting to dialogue? It must be noted that the main source of conflict between right and good in the situation under discussion is the monological way in which the concrete realization of the rights is determined. Even if we take for granted the good will of individuals and assume that no one wishes to endanger the rights and interests of anyone else, their viewpoints are very limited. Each of them judges the consequences of her/his actions by looking forth, to use Bacon's metaphor, from her/his own "cave."

The elderly people in our example probably see nothing wrong in reproducing their traditional mode of family life. And they undoubtedly do not perceive the consequent movement in present conditions towards fundamentalist-Islamic cultural patterns as a threat to Bulgarian society, i.e., to the community as a whole. It is necessary that they get the message — and get it in a proper way, not through coercion or indoctrination — that there are other interests relevant to this development. Someone must present to them the present concerns about the possible expansion of Islamic fundamentalism to Bulgaria and do so in a comprehensible and plausible way. Of course, the parties of the consequent discussion should have equal conditions for articulating their claims and receiving replies to them. In addition, the discourse must be open to anyone who would like to express and defend her/his position on this matter.

Suppose that as a result of such dialogue some novel solution is reached, or at least a compromise, that wins the approval of all parties involved. This might involve, for example, changing the norms for distributing modern production units within the territory of the country so that integrating young people into modern society does not necessarily disrupt traditional family ties. We could certainly regard such a solution as both right for the individuals and good for the community. Generally speaking, when the dialogical procedure for resolving these clashes of positions is successful, it apparently pays tribute to both the right and the good.

The obstacles in realizing this type of dialogue become immediately obvious if we consider the example of an elderly peasant from a Turkish village deep in the Rhodope Mountains. It would mean adequately participating in a discussion that would be most sophisticated even if only minimal standards of discourse ethics are met. But before discussing this point, we must first clarify an issue that could lead to misunderstanding about the relation between right and good in our interpretation of dialogue. Habermas observes that discourse ethics is obviously formalistic in that it distinguishes "moral questions which, under the aspect of universalization or justice, can in principle be decided rationally, from evaluative questions... which present themselves under their most general aspect as questions of the good life, and which are accessible to a rational discussion only within the horizon of a historically concrete life form" (Habermas 1984:225). Why do we then insist on the ability of dialogue conducted according to the algorithms of discourse ethics to synthesize the rights of the individual and the good of the community?

The norms that should regulate relations among participants are the subject matter of discourse within the communication community. Discourse ethics proposes a set of rules for discussion that guarantee the legitimacy of norms accepted by the participants as a result of the rational exchange of proposals, claims and arguments. This ethical theory does not prescribe any norms prior to the discussion, nor does it deal with the justification of moral norms in general. This is the sense in which it is strictly formal in character. But it does not follow that discourse within the communication community should not deal with the issues of the good life. The only restriction in this respect is that the norms that pass the test of discussion are valid only within the given community. Since their legitimacy rests upon the consensus of the participants in the discourse, they cannot pretend to absolute validity. It is true that Habermas claims that the only justifiable norms are those which incorporate "generalizable interests" (Habermas 1983:75-77), but this means only that the norms satisfy the interests of each participant in the actual argument.

However, the most problematic issue concerning the relevance of the discourse ethics model of dialogue to relations between ethnocultural communities is clearly whether or not it can be applied in reality. Indeed, many authors consider the idealized notion of a communication community to be utopian because not only must the participants in discourse have radically abandoned all strategic attitudes towards their partners, they must also be communicatively competent. The latter is especially important in that it involves certain intellectual "skills" in addition to good will. Within this context, the validity of norms depends exclusively on consensus among the members of the communication community, but what would be the worth of such "validity" if it were based on someone's misconceptions about her/his interests or on the eloquence of a supporter of some contending norm? It is not without reason that Thomas McCarthy has introduced the issue of "the distinction between arguments and rhetoric, between convincing and persuading," into the controversies concerning discourse ethics (McCarthy 1991:194).

Furthermore, since the regulative idea of discourse within an ideal communication community refers to relationships among intelligent individuals in Western-type modern societies, is it not absurd to apply this model to the relationships between ethnocultural communities, including those belonging to traditional cultures? But however paradoxical it may sound, perhaps this model of dialogue can be made more realistic precisely by modifying its original design in an effort to make it applicable to mediation among ethnocultural communities in Balkan conditions. The community members who would be the immediate subjects of discourse would represent community interests that could be reflected upon in terms more definite than the interests of individuals. This by itself would make it much more probable that the discourse positions assumed be of a serious nature.

But, of course, a number of difficult questions remain in respect to this interpretation of dialogue as envisaged by discourse ethics. For example, how would such discourse differ from ordinary political negotiations, i.e., what would guarantee that individuals acting for the communities adequately represent the interests of the latter? Secondly, how would it be possible to ensure against repression of individuals or groups within the community such that their voices would not be heard at all? In addition, how could strategic attitudes be eliminated from relations among the parties in dialogue? Another problematic point concerns how it may be possible for traditional value systems and religious beliefs to participate in the rational exchange of arguments that is the heart of dialogue.

All of these questions are difficult, but they are not impossible to answer. Indeed, the immediate positive effect of introducing the methodology of discourse ethics and, more generally, the paradigm of dialogue into the sphere of ethnocultural relations in Bulgaria would be precisely the formulation of problems in a new way. Hopefully, this might open up prospects for escaping from at least some of the vicious circles that continue to make the theory and practice of these relations so depressing.

Philosophy Faculty
University of Sofia, Bulgaria

REFERENCES

Alexandrov, H. (1995) "Education and Minorities." *Open Education* 3.

Avineri, S. and A. de-Shalit (eds.) (1992) *Communitarianism and Individualism*. Oxford: Oxford University Press.

Dworkin, R. (1992) "Liberal Community." In S. Avineri and A. de-Shalit (eds.). *Communitarianism and Individualism*. Oxford: Oxford University Press.

Gauthier, D. (1992) "The Liberal Individual." In S. Avineri and A. de-Shalit (eds.). *Communitarianism and Individualism.* Oxford: Oxford University Press.

Habermas, J. (1983) *Moralbewusstsein und kommunikatives Handeln.* Frankfurt: Suhrkamp.

Habermas, J. (1984) "Über Moralität und Sittlichkeit — Was macht ein Lebensform "rational"? In Herbert Schnädelbach (ed.). *Rationalität.* Frankfurt: Suhrkamp.

Ivanov, M. and I. Tomova (1994) "Ethnic Groups and Interethnic Relations in Bulgaria." In V. Russanov (ed.). *Aspects of the Ethnocultural Situation in Bulgaria.* Sofia: Access.

Kant, I. (1987) *Critique of Pure Reason.* London: Macmillan.

Kühnhardt, L. (1991) *Die Universalität der Menschenrechte.* Bonn: BZPB.

McCarthy, Th. (1991) *Ideals and Illusions: on Reconstruction and Deconstruction in Contemporary Critical Theory.* Cambridge, MA: MIT Press.

Sandel, M. (1984) "The Procedural Republic and the Unencumbered Self." *Political Theory* 12.

Toennies, F. (1957) *Community and Society.* East Lansing, MI.

Walzer, M. (1983) *Spheres of Justice.* Oxford: Blackwell.

INDEX

A

Abdul Azis 233
Absolute 4, 12, 17-18, 22, 33-37, 59, 61, 74, 77-78, 108, 111, 132, 141-142, 146, 157, 186, 221-223, 239-242, 247-251, 254
Ackermann 151
Adorno 106
Aesthetics iii, 3, 9, 11-14, 42-48, 53-63, 109, 127, 180, 211
Alexandrov 239, 252, 255
Alien 6, 9, 16-17, 30, 33, 61, 76, 86-87, 91-93, 96, 101, 127, 164, 183, 193, 205-218, 220-224, 241-242, 247-250
Allen 137
Amalrik 150, 151
Åman 56, 62
Andreev 59, 62
Anthropology 13, 23, 113, 141
Antigone 192, 204
Apel 5, 7, 100, 145
Arendt 106, 199-202
Aristophanes 186, 211
Aristotle 19, 21, 81, 107, 113, 118-122, 126, 133-136, 144, 173-176, 183, 194, 202
Atomism 240
Augustinus 69, 81
Authoritarianism 108
Authority 22, 48-52, 70, 82, 122, 129, 143-146, 148, 172, 191, 231-233
Avineri 245, 249, 255-256

B

Bacon 20, 252
Balkan 5-9, 17-19, 156-169, 179, 181, 193, 209-210, 218, 223, 232, 240-242, 247-250, 255
Baumann 2
Bednář iii, 4, 9-11, 67
Berdyaev 116
Berger 160, 162, 187, 202
Bernet 60, 62
Bernstein 201-202
Bezklubenko 59, 62
Bible 132, 194
Bill of Rights 88, 93, 105, 243
Blasko i, iii, 3, 9, 11, 12, 41
Bluhm 77, 81
Bogdanov 207, 212-214, 225
Bolshevik 44, 46-47, 57, 59, 107
Borev 58, 62
Bosnia 87, 93, 101, 241, 249
Bourdieu 182, 202
Bourgeois 32, 42, 47, 193
Braithwaite 195, 202
Burma 68
Bush 85, 91, 94
Byzantine 166, 220, 231, 236

C

Cambodia 18, 94, 142
Camus 221, 225
Capitalism 33-34, 46, 149, 166, 193
Carnap 123
Carrère 150-151
Catholic 21, 99, 115-116, 145, 177, 198, 213, 220
China 36, 68, 86, 95, 142
Christian iii, 6, 14, 33, 69-73, 82, 104, 116, 126-127, 143, 146-147, 166, 171, 176-181, 194-198, 207, 215, 229-239
Christian Values iii, 6, 14, 234-237
Church 6, 13-15, 21, 99, 115-116, 145, 177-179, 188, 198, 207, 230-235
Civil society 18, 118-122
Civilization 5, 22, 30-33, 110, 113, 156-157, 161-167, 179, 181, 191-193, 196, 199-203, 219, 241, 249
Coke 69, 81
Cold War 10-11, 41-42, 45-47, 62,

67-68, 72, 81, 118
Collectivism 4, 243
Communication 48-49, 78-79, 120, 145, 160, 164, 183-186, 191, 202, 207, 250-254
Communism iii, 3, 10-14, 27-37, 41-42, 46, 72, 96, 110, 198, 220, 235
Communitarian 4, 7, 73, 80, 99, 103, 240-251, 255-256
Confucius 133
Consciousness 12, 35, 48-49, 52-55, 60-62, 104, 108-109, 112, 128, 161-166, 170, 174-178, 186, 188, 195, 212, 213, 246
Constantinople 231-233
Constitution 15, 29, 53, 77, 81, 88, 91-94, 100, 104-105, 121-124, 237, 243, 252
Corruption 1, 43, 70, 172
Crowther 60, 62
Cuba 87, 94, 95, 142
Cultural identity iii, 2, 6, 15, 19, 118, 205-206, 215, 223-225, 241, 248
Cynicism 93
Czech Republic 1, 81, 89
Czechoslovakia 27, 115, 142

D

Daskalov 218, 219, 223, 225, 226, 227
Davidov i, iii, 4, 10-13, 105
de-Shalit 245, 249, 255-256
Declaration of Independence 88, 105
Democracy iii, 2-4, 10-11, 23, 33-34, 37, 41, 55, 67-77, 80-107, 111, 119, 123, 149, 192, 205, 220
Democratization iii, 5, 7, 59, 85-87, 153
d'Entreves 81
Derrida 187, 202
Dictatorship 32-33, 107-108, 115, 202
Dilthey 102, 113

Divine 11-12, 17, 74, 114-116, 127, 143-144, 198, 208, 230, 232
Doctrine 33, 89-102, 111-112, 136, 143, 198, 230-231
Dubarle 117, 136
Dubrovin 58, 62
Dunn 81
Dworkin 100, 103, 247, 255

E

Ecumenical 232
Egypt 148
Ehrenberg 167, 191, 202
Enlightenment 23, 93, 102, 162, 198, 242
Equilibrium 17, 36-38, 136, 239
Ërkus 195
Essence 11, 21, 49-50, 61, 67, 79-80, 90, 110, 123-127, 158, 162, 186-187, 192, 194, 208, 229, 231, 234
Euripides 192

F

Fehér, 195, 202
Filmer 38
Fol 203
Foucault 102-103, 224-225
Fourier 31, 38
Fraser 103, 137
Freedom 5, 10-16, 19, 21, 31-34, 71-77, 82-83, 99, 105-109, 116-136, 167, 173, 184, 191-193, 200-202, 211, 217, 230, 240-245, 248
Freire 20
French Revolution 72, 95, 102
Freud 183, 186, 196, 203
Fukuyama 34, 38

G

Gadamer 102
Gambles 67, 81

Gandhi 134
Gasset 205
Gauthier 245-247, 256
Gerdzhikov iii, 3, 9, 13-14, 27
German Democratic Republic 142
Germanov 207, 225
Germany 55-57, 72, 85, 87, 100, 215
Giddens 170
Glasnost 59
God 17, 21, 69, 70, 74, 80, 96, 116, 123, 130-134, 143, 147, 177-181, 186-187, 197-198, 208, 211, 230-232
Goebbels 57
Goffman 162, 175, 184, 188, 192, 195, 200, 201, 203
Good 7, 9-11, 16, 19, 45, 70-71, 77, 81-82, 86, 90, 93, 98-103, 108-114, 119-135, 139, 144, 161, 173-174, 182, 197, 202, 210, 244, 247, 248-254
Governance 119-122
Gratchoff 29
Greek 22, 69, 82, 162-166, 182-189, 192, 199, 201-202, 233
Grotius 11, 74, 82
Gulf War 85, 94, 102
Gulubov 215, 216, 225

H

Habermas 5, 7, 10, 19, 88-89, 93, 98-103, 115, 145, 250, 253-256
Haiti 87, 94
Happiness 34, 96, 105, 109, 111, 119, 196, 244
Harmony 134, 212
Harmony 16, 31, 70-73, 111, 125, 128, 130, 134, 211-212, 218
Hayek 33-34, 38, 107-108, 114
Hegel iii, 4-5, 20-22, 59-62, 71, 82, 89, 100-102, 111, 117, 139, 144-145, 148, 157, 240
Heidegger 60-63, 79, 94, 102, 133, 137, 145, 187
Heineman 74, 82
Heller 195, 202
Hempel 150-151
Henry 81-82
Hilendarski 164, 188, 203
Hindu 127
Hitler 194
Hobbes 4, 11, 71, 77, 98, 124, 242
Holmes 104
Honor 56, 109, 111, 166, 171, 173, 178
Hristov 209, 226
Hugo 74
Human dignity 18, 29, 33, 77, 107-109, 111-114, 124, 147, 243, 248
Human nature 82, 88-90, 94, 97, 102, 112, 124, 126, 242-243
Human rights iii, 2-4, 10-11, 33-34, 68-77, 80-81, 86-88, 91-95, 105, 109, 125, 244, 248
Hume 123, 136
Hungary 27, 91, 115, 142, 190
Husserl 27-30, 38, 60, 62, 113

I

Identity iii, 2-7, 11, 14-19, 22, 30, 53, 59, 94, 118, 132-135, 156-157, 161-166, 170-174, 187, 195, 205-209, 212-219, 222-223, 231, 234, 241, 246-251
Ideology 2, 4, 11-12, 31, 33, 38, 44, 47, 55-59, 62, 68, 81, 90, 97, 108, 124, 145, 174, 235, 236
Individualism iii, 4, 12, 20, 94-96, 103-108, 111-116, 222, 240-249
Inter-ethnic Dialogue iii, 6, 18, 239
Iran 68
Iraq 68
Islam 127, 143, 239, 241, 244, 252, 253

J

Japan 85, 87, 93
Jefferson 41, 98
Johnson 73, 82

K

Kant 20-22, 88-89, 93-100, 110, 113,
 124-129, 132-133, 142-147, 242-247,
 256
Kapriev iii, 6, 10, 14-17, 229
Karanfilov 189, 203
Katsarski 211, 217, 226
Kazandzhiev 212, 213, 226
Kirk 73, 82
Koinonia 119
Kolalowski 56, 62
Konstantinov 58, 62, 215
Kouba 81, 82
Krasteva iii, 6, 9, 15-16, 205
Kristeva 17, 18, 221-222, 226
Kühnhardt 244, 256
Kulikova 58, 63
Kurth 67, 82
Kuwait 86
Kymlicka 104

L

Laos 68
Lask 113
Latin 101, 133, 137, 163, 166, 188-189
Leizerov 58, 63
Lévi-Strauss 141, 150-151
Levinas 17, 18, 224, 226
Lewis 195, 203
Liberal democracy iii, 4, 23, 33-34, 86-
 95, 98, 101-102, 111, 123
Liberalism iii, 4, 7, 19, 23, 68, 70-77,
 80, 86-104, 221, 240-251
Libya 68
Locke 4, 10-11, 33, 38, 69-74, 82-83,
 98, 123, 136-137, 242
Logos 3, 13-14, 31-33, 79

Lowi 74, 82
Luckmann 160, 162, 187, 202
Ludwig 80, 82
Luhmann 156, 160, 187, 203
Lynd 195, 203
Lyotard 78, 82

M

MacIntyre 102, 103, 104
Magna Charta 105
Makariev i, iii, 6-10, 18-20, 239
Marcuse 196, 203
Margolis iii, 4, 23, 85, 104
Marxism 2, 9, 13, 31-33, 42-46,
 55-58, 62, 68, 72-73, 102, 110,
 139, 142, 145, 221
Mavone 136
McCarthy 55, 254, 256
McLean i, iii, 5, 10, 22-23, 117,
 136
Merleau-Ponty 60, 63
Methexis 120
Middle Ages 126, 177
Mikhailkovsky 205
Miladinov 198, 203
Milev 210, 216, 226
Mill 98, 105
Mimesis 120
Misheva iii, 5, 155
Modernity iii, 2, 5, 9, 79, 114,
 155-157, 172, 187, 199, 213,
 220-221
Mouffe 73, 82
Multiculturalis 98-99, 100-104
Murdoch 75, 82
Muslim 177, 239
Mussolini 57
Mutafchiev 207, 211, 219, 220,
 226
Mutafov 220, 226
Mysticism 143, 179-181

N

Nature 7-11, 20-23, 31, 43-49, 57, 67-79, 88-90, 94-98, 102, 112-136, 141, 157-158, 180-186, 195, 199, 208-209, 211, 216-219, 242-243, 255
Nazism 72, 90, 194
Neumann 111
Nicaragua 95
Nietzsche 102-103, 113, 162, 171-173, 177-178, 181, 194-197, 203
Nihilism 110, 162, 169-173, 192
Norms i, iii, 2, 4, 12, 29, 47, 87-90, 96-100, 106-113, 126, 142, 175, 196, 232, 240-243, 249-254
North Korea 68, 142

O

Oligarchy 119
Ontology 12, 17, 22, 79, 98, 111-112
Openness iii, 5, 22, 117, 131-134, 213
Orthodox 6, 10, 14-15, 115-116, 143, 166, 177-181, 198, 207-208, 215, 219-220, 229-237, 252
Otherness 3, 49-54, 60-61, 78, 114, 218, 221, 251
Ottoman 164-165, 181, 188, 193, 232-233

P

Pakistan 94
Paparrigopoulos 75, 82
Patočka 75-81
Patriarchate 232, 234
Pavicevic 11
Pelican 130
Penev 208, 217, 222, 226
Perception iii, 3, 11, 22, 41, 44, 53-59, 61-62, 67-74, 77, 102, 111, 198, 218, 231
Perestroika 59
Petkanov 218, 226
Phenomenology 3, 12-14, 27-29, 63, 76-80, 106, 113-114, 126, 131-132, 137, 227
Piers 194, 203
Pinker 151
Plato 18, 21-22, 31, 38, 83, 90, 97-98, 107, 120-122, 125-130, 133, 136-139, 144, 158, 162, 185, 211, 213, 227
Poland 27, 91, 99, 115, 142
Popper 34, 38
Post-modern iii, 2, 4-6, 12, 14, 77-79, 83, 105, 110, 114-116, 185, 217-219, 223
Pride 6, 167, 174-175, 197, 218
Protestant 116, 199

R

Rajagopalachari 130
Rawls 11, 88-89, 93, 98-99, 102, 104, 124, 147, 242, 245
Realism 45, 47, 56-58, 69, 73, 104, 111, 240
Ratzinger 195, 203-204
Richardson 62-63, 137
Rickert 113
Ricoeur 219, 226
Rights of Man 88, 93-94, 105
Rockmore iii, 5, 9-10, 20-22, 139
Rogue.34 125
Romania 27, 142
Rome 14, 181, 215, 220, 232
Rorty 83, 103-104
Rousseau 4, 10-11, 71, 88, 94, 209
Rowe 91-92
Russanov 256
Russia 30, 38, 43-45, 57-58, 68, 87-89, 94, 149, 166, 189, 193, 215, 220, 222, 234, 236

S

Sandel 102-104, 245-247, 256
Santayana 46, 58, 63
Sartre 42, 61, 63

Saudi Arabia 86
Scheff 174-175, 194-196, 203
Schmitt 94
Schmitz 137
Schoepflin 107
Schütz 29-30, 39, 214, 223, 227
Self-esteem 175, 218
Seligman 117, 136
Serbian 159, 233
Sheitanov 209, 217, 220, 227
Shuckburgh 192, 204
Simmel 113, 213-215, 221, 227
Singapore 97
Singer 194, 203
Sinopoli 69, 83
Skinner 77, 83
Slaveikov 208, 209, 210, 216, 227
Social value iii, 2, 5, 20-21, 45, 139-150
Socialism 4, 27-33, 43-47, 56-58, 107, 110-115, 147, 171, 195, 240
Solidarity 95-96, 101-111, 120-122, 147, 192, 246, 248
Sophocles 192, 204
Soviet iii, 3, 9, 11, 27, 41-47, 56-59, 68, 85, 94, 96, 139, 141-142, 150-151, 190
Stalinism 90
Stranger 207, 215, 219, 221, 223, 227, 248
Strauss 104, 141, 150-151
Structuralism 140-141
Subsidiarity 120-122
Sudan 68
Sullivan 77, 83

T

Taoism 127
Taylor 77, 83, 101-104
Thracian 163-164, 170, 181
Todorov 221, 227
Toennies 225, 242, 256
Totalitarian iii, 1-4, 9-13, 28, 34, 37, 41-43, 51-52, 67-68, 72-78, 80, 96, 105-108, 110-116, 195, 200-201
Tsaneva 210, 227

U

Universalism 102, 148, 236, 240, 243

V

Values i, iii, 2-6, 11-14, 20-23, 31, 42-47, 56-58, 75, 86-89, 93-98, 100-118, 126, 129-131, 139-150, 172, 187, 235, 247-250, 254-256
Van Parijs 151
Vazov 189, 225
Vedas 132
Vietnam 68, 94, 142
Violence 1, 51, 124, 134, 206, 241
Virtue 41-49, 53-60, 69-73, 81, 98-99, 107-109, 126, 129, 139, 166, 173-177, 194, 229-230, 235-236

W

Wade 91-92
Walzer 73, 83, 102, 104, 248, 256
Weber 29, 30-34, 38-39, 104, 113, 179-180, 198, 200, 204
Westernization 107
White 18, 78, 83
Windelband 113
Wojtyla 13, 112-113
Wooten 71, 83
World War II 10, 67, 72, 85-87, 93-96, 100, 156, 240
Wurmser 195, 204

Y

Yanev 208-209, 227
Yotzov 227
Yugoslavia 27, 68, 142

COUNCIL FOR RESEARCH IN VALUES AND PHILOSOPHY MEMBERS

S. Avineri, Jerusalem
R. Balasubramaniam, Madras
M. Bednár, Prague
P. Bodunrin, Ibadan
K. Bunchua, Bangkok
V. Cauchy, Montreal
C. Pan, Singapore
M. Chatterjee, Delhi
Chen Junquan, Beijing
M. Dy, Manila
I.T. Frolov, Moscow
H.G. Gadamer, Heidelb
A. Gallo, Guatemala.
K. Gyekye, Legon
T. Imamichi, Tokyo
A. Irala Burgos, Asunçion
J. Kellerman, Budapest
M. Kente, Dar es Salaam
J. Kromkowski, Washington
J. Ladrière, Louvain

P. Laleye, Dakar
A. Lopez Quintas, Madrid
H. Nasr, Teheran/Wash.
C. Ngwey, Kinshasa
J. Nyasani, Nairobi
Paulus Gregorios, Cochin
O. Pegoraro, Rio de Jan.
T. Pichler, Bratislava
C. Ramirez, San José
P. Ricoeur, Paris
M. Sastrapatedja, Jakarta
J. Scannone, Buenos Aires
V. Shen, Taipei
W. Strozewski, Krakow
Tang Yijie, Beijing
J. Teran-Dutari, Quito
G. Tlaba, Maseru
Wang Miaoyang, Shanghai
M. Zakzouk, Cairo

BOARD OF DIRECTORS
Kenneth L. Schmitz, University of Toronto
Richard Knowles, Duquesne University
Richard T. De George, University of Kansas

SECRETARY-TREASURER
George F. McLean

ASSISTANT SECRETARIES FOR:
Research Design and Synthesis: Richard A. Graham
Moral Education: Henry Johnson
Research and Programming: Nancy Graham
Publication: Hu Yeping

THE COUNCIL FOR RESEARCH IN VALUES AND PHILOSOPHY

PURPOSE

Today there is urgent need to attend to the nature and dignity of the person, to the quality of human life, to the purpose and goal of the physical transformation of our environment, and to the relation of all this to the development of social and political life. This, in turn, requires philosophic clarification of the base upon which freedom is exercised, that is, of the values which provide stability and guidance to one's decisions.

Such studies must be able to reach deeply into the cultures of one's nation -- and of other parts of the world by which they can be strengthened and enriched -- in order to uncover the roots of the dignity of persons and of the societies built upon their relations one with another. They must be able to identify the conceptual forms in terms of which modern industrial and technological developments are structured and how these impact human self-understanding. Above all, they must be able to bring these elements together in the creative understanding essential for setting our goals and determining our modes of interaction. In the present complex circumstances this is a condition for growing together with trust and justice, honest dedication and mutual concern.

The Council for Studies in Values and Philosophy (RVP) is a group of scholars who share the above concerns and are interested in the application thereto of existing capabilities in the field of philosophy and other disciplines. Its work is to identify areas in which study is needed, the intellectual resources which can be brought to bear thereupon, and the financial resources required. In bringing these together its goal is scientific discovery and publication which contributes to the promotion of human kind in our times.

In sum, our times present both the need and the opportunity for deeper and ever more progressive understanding of the person and of the foundations of social life. The development of such understanding is the goal of the RVP.

PROJECTS

A set of related research efforts is currently in process; some were developed initially by the RVP and others now are being carried forward by it, either solely or conjointly.

1. *Cultural Heritage and Contemporary Change: Philosophical Foundations for Social Life.* Sets of focused and mutually coordinated continuing seminars in university centers, each preparing a volume as part of an integrated philosophic search for self-understanding differentiated by continent. This work focuses upon evolving a more adequate understanding of the person in society and looks to the cultural heritage of each for the resources to respond to the challenges of its own specific contemporary transformation.

2. *Seminars on Culture and Contemporary Issues.* This series of 10 week cross-cultural and inter-disciplinary seminars is being co-ordinated by the RVP in Washington.

3. *Joint-Colloquia* with Institutes of Philosophy of the National Academies of Science, university philosophy departments, and societies, which have been underway since 1976 in Eastern Europe and, since 1987 in China, concern the person in contemporary society.

4. *Foundations of Moral Education and Character Development.* A study in values and education which unites philosophers, psychologists, social scientists and scholars in education in the elaboration of ways of enriching the moral content of education and character development.

The personnel for these projects consists of established scholars willing to contribute their time and research as part of their professional commitment to life in our society. For resources to implement this work the Council, as a non-profit organization incorporated in the District of Colombia, looks to various private foundations, public programs and enterprises.

PUBLICATIONS ON CULTURAL HERITAGE AND CONTEMPORARY CHANGE

Series I.	*Culture and Values*
Series II.	*Africa*
Series IIa.	*Islam*
Series III.	*Asia*
Series IV.	*W. Europe and North America*
Series IVa.	*Central and Eastern Europe*
Series V.	*Latin America*
Series VI.	*Foundations of Moral Education*

THE COUNCIL FOR RESEARCH IN VALUES AND PHILOSOPHY

VOLUMES ON

CULTURAL HERITAGE AND CONTEMPORARY CHANGE

VALUES AND CONTEMPORARY LIFE

Series I. Culture and Values

Vol. I.1 *Research on Culture and Values: Intersection of Universities, Churches and Nations*,
George F. McLean,
ISBN 0-8191-7352-5 (cloth); ISBN 0-8191-7353-3 (paper).

Vol. I.2 *The Knowledge of Values: A Methodological Introduction to the Study of Values*,
A. Lopez Quintas,
ISBN 0-8191-7418-1 (cloth); ISBN 0-8191-7419-x (paper).

Vol. I.3 *Reading Philosophy for the XXIst Century*,
George F. McLean,
ISBN 0-8191-7414-9 (cloth); ISBN 0-8191-7415-7 9paper).

Vol. I.4 *Relations Between Cultures*,
John Kromkowski,
ISBN 1-56518-009-7 (cloth); ISBN 1-56518-008-9 (paper).

Vol. I.5 *Urbanization and Values*,
John Kromkowski,
ISBN 1-56518-011-9 (cloth); ISBN 1-56518-010-0 (paper).

Vol. I.6 *The Place of the Person in Social Life*,
Paul Peachey and John Kromkowski,
ISBN 1-56518-013-5 (cloth); ISBN 1-56518-012-7 (paper).

Vol. I.7 *Abrahamic Faiths, Ethnicity and Ethnic Conflicts*,
Paul Peachey, George F. McLean and John Kromkowski
ISBN 1-56518-104-2 (paper).

Vol. I.8 *Ancient Western Philosophy: The Hellenic Emergence*,
George F. McLean and Patrick J. Aspell
ISBN 1-56518-100-X (paper).

Vol. I.10 *The Ethical Implications of Unity and the Divine in Nicholas of Cusa*
David L. De Leonardis
ISBN 1-56518-112-3 (paper).

Vol. I.11 *Ethics at the Crossroads: Vol. 1. Normative Ethics and Objective Reason,*
George F. McLean,
ISBN 1-56518-022-4 (paper).

Vol. I.12 *Ethics at the Crossroads: Vol. 2. Personalist Ethics and Human Subjectivity,*
George F. McLean,
ISBN 1-56518-024-0 (paper).

Vol. I.13 *The Emancipative Theory of J. Jürgen Habermas and Metaphysics,*
Robert Badillo,
ISBN 1-56518-043-7 (cloth); ISBN 1-56518-042-9 (paper).

Vol. I.14 *The Deficient Cause of Moral Evil According to Thomas Aquinas,*
Edward Cook,
ISBN 1-56518-070-4 paper (paper).

Vol. I.16 *Civil Society and Social Reconstruction,*
George F. McLean,
ISBN 1-56518-086-0 (paper).

Vol.I.17 Ways to God, Personal and Social at the Turn of Millennia
The Iqbal Lecture, Lahore
George F. McLean
ISBN 1-56518-123-9 (paper).

Vol.I.18 *The Role of the Sublime in Kant's Moral Metaphysics*
John R. Goodreau
ISBN 1-56518-124-7 (pbk.)

CULTURAL HERITAGES AND THE FOUNDATIONS OF SOCIAL LIFE

Series II. Africa

Vol. II.1 *Person and Community: Ghanaian Philosophical Studies: I,*
Kwasi Wiredu and Kwame Gyeke,

ISBN 1-56518-005-4 (cloth); ISBN 1-56518-004-6 (paper).

Vol. II.2 *The Foundations of Social Life:*
Ugandan Philosophical Studies: I,
A.T. Dalfovo,
ISBN 1-56518-007-0 (cloth); ISBN 1-56518-006-2 (paper).

Vol. II.3 *Identity and Change in Nigeria:*
Nigerian Philosophical Studies, I,
Theophilus Okere,
ISBN 1-56518-068-2 (paper).

Vol. II.4 *Social Reconstruction in Africa:*
Ugandan Philosophical studies, II
E. Wamala, A.R. Byaruhanga, A.T. Dalfovo,
J.K. Kigongo, S.A. Mwanahewa and G. Tusabe
ISBN 1-56518-118-2 (paper).

Series IIA. Islam

Vol. IIA.1 *Islam and the Political Order,*
Muhammad Saïd al-Ashmawy,
ISBN 1-56518-046-1 (cloth); ISBN 1-56518-047-x (paper).

Vol. IIA.2 *Al-Ghazālī, Deliverance from Error and Mystical*
Union with the Almighty (al-Munqidh min al-Dalāl)
Arabic text established and English translation
with introduction by: Muhammad Abulaylah;
Introduction and Notes: George F. McLean
ISBN 1-56518-081-X (Arabic-English Edition)
ISBN 1-56518-082-8 (English Edition.)

Vol. IIA.3 *Philosophy in Pakistan*
Naeem Ahmad
ISBN 1-56518-108-5 (paper).

Vol. IIA.4 *The Authenticity of the Text in Hermeneutics*
Seyed Musa Dibadj
ISBN 1-56518-117-4 (paper).

Vol. IIA.5 *Interpretation and the Problem of*
the Intention of the Author: H.-G. Gadamer vs E.D. Hirsch
Burhanettin Tatar
ISBN 1-56518-121 (paper).

Vol.I.6 *Ways to God, Personal and Social at the Turn of Millennia*
The Iqbal Lecture, Lahore

George F. McLean
ISBN 1-56518-123-9 (paper).

Series III. Asia

Vol. III.1 *Man and Nature: Chinese Philosophical Studies, I,*
Tang Yi-jie, Li Zhen,
ISBN 0-8191-7412-2 (cloth); ISBN 0-8191-7413-0 (paper).

Vol. III.2 *Chinese Foundations for Moral Education and Character Development, Chinese Philosophical Studies, II.*
Tran van Doan,
ISBN 1-56518-033-x (cloth); ISBN 1-56518-032-1 (paper).

Vol. III.3 *Confucianism, Buddhism, Taoism, Christianity and Chinese Culture, Chinese Philosophical Studies, III,*
Tang Yijie,
ISBN 1-56518-035-6 (cloth); ISBN 1-56518-034-8 (paper).

Vol. III.4 *Morality, Metaphysics and Chinese Culture (Metaphysics, Culture and Morality, Vol. I)*
Vincent Shen and Tran van Doan,
ISBN 1-56518-026-7 (cloth); ISBN 1-56518-027-5 (paper).

Vol. III.5 *Tradition, Harmony and Transcendence,*
George F. McLean,
ISBN 1-56518-030-5 (cloth); ISBN 1-56518-031-3 (paper).

Vol. III.6 *Psychology, Phenomenology and Chinese Philosophy: Chinese Philosophical Studies, VI,*
Vincent Shen, Richard Knowles and Tran Van Doan,
ISBN 1-56518-044-5 (cloth); 1-56518-045-3 (paper).

Vol. III.7 *Values in Philipine Culture and Education: Philippine Philosophical Studies, I,*
Manuel B. Dy, Jr.,
ISBN 1-56518-040-2 (cloth); 1-56518-041-2 (paper).

Vol. III.7A *The Human Person and Society: Chinese Philosophical Studies, VIIA,*
Zhu Dasheng, Jin Xiping and George F. McLean
ISBN 1-56518-087-9 (library edition); 1-56518-088-7 (paper).

Vol. III.8 *The Filipino Mind: Philippine Philosophical Studies II,*
Leonardo N. Mercado
ISBN 1-56518-063-1 (cloth); ISBN 1-56518-064-X (paper).

Vol. III.9 *Philosophy of Science and Education:*

  Chinese Philosophical Studies IX,
  Vincent Shen and Tran Van Doan
  ISBN 1-56518-075-5 (cloth); 1-56518-076-3 (paper).

Vol. III.10 *Chinese Cultural Traditions and Modernization: Chinese Philosophical Studies, X,*
  Wang Miaoyang, Yu Xuanmeng and George F. McLean
  ISBN 1-56518-067-4 (library edition); 1-56518-068-2 (paper).

Vol. III.11 *The Humanization of Technology and Chinese Culture: Chinese Philosophical Studies XI,*
  Tomonobu Imamichi, Wang Miaoyang and Liu Fangtong
  ISBN 1-56518-116-6 (paper).

Vol. III.12 *Beyond Modernization: Chinese Roots of Global Awareness: Chinese Philosophical Studies, XII,*
  Wang Miaoyang, Yu Xuanmeng and George F. McLean
  ISBN 1-56518-089-5 (library edition); 1-56518-090-9 (paper).

Vol. III.13 *Philosophy and Modernization in China: Chinese Philosophical Studies XIII,*
  Liu Fangtong, Huang Songjie and George F. McLean
  ISBN 1-56518-066-6 (paper).

Vol. III.14 *Economic Ethics and Chinese Culture: Chinese Philosophical Studies, XIV,*
  Yu Xuanmeng, Lu Xiaohe, Liu Fangtong,
  Zhang Rulun and Georges Enderle
  ISBN 1-56518-091-7 (library edition); 1-56518-092-5 (paper).

Vol. III.15 *Civil Society in A Chinese Context: Chinese Philosophical Studies XV,*
  Wang Miaoyang, Yu Xuanmeng and Manuel B. Dy
  ISBN 1-56518-084-4 (paper).

Vol. III.16 *The Bases of Values in a Time of Change: Chinese and Western: Chinese Philosophical Studies, XVI*
  Kirti Bunchua, Liu Fangtong, Yu Xuanmeng, Yu Wujin
  ISBN 1-56518-114-X (paper).

Vol. IIIB.1 *Authentic Human Destiny: The Paths of Shankara and Heidegger*
  Vensus A. George
  ISBN 1-56518-119-0 (paper).

Series IV. Western Europe and North America

Vol. IV.1 *Italy in Transition: The Long Road from the First to the Second Republic: The 1997 Edmund D. Pellegrino Lecture on Contemporary Italian Politics*
Paolo Janni
ISBN 1-56518-120-4 (paper).

Vol. IV.2 Italy and The European Monetary Union: *The 1997 Edmund D. Pellegrino Lecture on Contemporary Italian Politics*
Paolo Janni
ISBN 1-56518-128-X (paper).

Series IVA. Central and Eastern Europe

Vol. IVA.1 *The Philosophy of Person: Solidarity and Cultural Creativity: Polish Philosophical Studies, I*,
A. Tischner, J.M. Zycinski,
ISBN 1-56518-048-8 (cloth); ISBN 1-56518-049-6 (paper).

Vol. IVA.2 *Public and Private Social Inventions in Modern Societies: Polish Philosophical Studies, II*,
L. Dyczewski, P. Peachey, J. Kromkowski,
ISBN 1-56518-050-x (cloth). paper ISBN 1-56518-051-8 (paper).

Vol. IVA.3 *Traditions and Present Problems of Czech Political Culture: Czechoslovak Philosophical Studies, I*,
M. Bedná, M. Vejraka
ISBN 1-56518-056-9 (cloth); ISBN 1-56518-057-7 (paper).

Vol. IVA.4 *Czech Philosophy in the XXth Century: Czech Philosophical Studies, II*,
Lubomír Nový and Jirí Gabriel,
ISBN 1-56518-028-3 (cloth); ISBN 1-56518-029-1 (paper).

Vol. IVA.5 *Language, Values and the Slovak Nation: Slovak Philosophical Studies, I*,
Tibor Pichler and Jana Gašparíková,
ISBN 1-56518-036-4 (cloth); ISBN 1-56518-037-2 (paper).

Vol. IVA.6 *Morality and Public Life in a Time of Change: Bulgarian Philosophical Studies, I*,
V. Prodanov, M. Stoyanova,
ISBN 1-56518-054-2 (cloth); ISBN 1-56518-055-0 (paper).

Vol. IVA.7 *Knowledge and Morality:*

Georgian PhilosophicalStudies, 1,
N.V. Chavchavadze, G. Nodia, P. Peachey,
ISBN 1-56518-052-6 (cloth); ISBN 1-56518-053-4 (paper).

Vol. IVA.8 *Cultural Heritage and Social Change: Lithuanian Philosophical Studies, I,*
Bronius Kuzmickas and Aleksandr Dobrynin,
ISBN 1-56518-038-0 (cloth); ISBN 1-56518-039-9 (paper).

Vol. IVA.9 *National, Cultural and Ethnic Identities: Harmony beyond Conflict: Czech Philosophical Studies, IV*
Jaroslav Hroch, David Hollan, George F. McLean
ISBN 1-56518-113-1 (paper).

Vol. IVA.10 *Models of Identities in Postcommunist Societies: Yugoslav Philosophical Studies, I*
Zagorka Golubovic and George F. McLean
ISBN 1-56518-121-1 (paper).

Vol. IVA.11 *Interests and Values: The Spirit of Venture in a Time of Change: Slovak Philosophical Studies, II*
Tibor Pichler and Jana Gasparikova
ISBN 1-56518-125-5 (paper).

Vol. IVA.12 *Creating Democratic Societies: Values and Norms; Bulgarian Philosophical Studies, II*
Plamen Makariev, Andrew M. Blasko, Asen Davidov
ISBN 1-56518-131-X (paper).

Series V. Latin America

Vol. V.1 *The Social Context and Values: Perspectives of the Americas,*
O. Pegoraro,
ISBN 0-8191-7354-1 (cloth); ISBN 0-8191-7355-x (paper).

Vol. V.2 *Culture, Human Rights and Peace in Central America,*
Raul Molina, Timothy Ready,
ISBN 0-8191-7356-8 (cloth); ISBN 0-8191-7357-6 (paper).

Vol V.3 *El Cristianismo Aymara: Inculturacion o culturizacion?,*
Luis Jolicoeur
ISBN 1-56518-104-2 (paper).

Vol. V.4 *Love as the Foundation of Moral Education and Character Development*
Luis Ugalde, Nicolas Barros, George F. McLean

ISBN 1-56518-080-1 (paper).
Vol. V.5 *Human Rights, Solidarity and Subsidiarity: Essays towards a Social Ontology*
Carlos E. A. Maldonado
ISBN 1-56518-110-7 (paper).

FOUNDATIONS OF MORAL EDUCATION AND CHARACTER DEVELOPMENT

Series VI. Foundations of Moral Education

Vol. VI.1 *Philosophical Foundations for Moral Education and Character Development: Act and Agent,*
G. McLean, F. Ellrod,
ISBN 1-56518-001-1 (cloth); ISBN 1-56518-000-3 (paper).

Vol. VI.2 *Psychological Foundations for Moral Education and Character Development: An Integrated Theory of Moral Development,*
R. Knowles,
ISBN 1-56518-003-8 (cloth); ISBN 1-56518-002-x (paper).

Vol. VI.3 *Character Development in Schools and Beyond,*
Kevin Ryan, Thomas Lickona,
ISBN 1-56518-058-5 (cloth); ISBN 1-56518-059-3 (paper).

Vol. VI.4 *The Social Context and Values: Perspectives of the Americas,*
O. Pegoraro,
ISBN 0-8191-7354-1 (cloth); ISBN 0-8191-7355-x (paper).

Vol. VI.5 *Chinese Foundations for Moral Education and Character Development,*
Tran van Doan,
ISBN 1-56518-033 (cloth), ISBN 1-56518-032-1 (paper).

The International Society for Metaphysics

Vol.1 *Person and Nature*
George F. McLean and Hugo Meynell, eds.
ISBN 0-8191-7025-9 (cloth); ISBN 0-8191-7026-7 (paper).

Vol.2 *Person and Society*
George F. McLean and Hugo Meynell, eds.

ISBN 0-8191-6924-2 (cloth); ISBN 0-8191-6925-0 (paper).
Vol.3   *Person and God*
George F. McLean and Hugo Meynell, eds.
ISBN 0-8191-6937-4 (cloth); ISBN 0-8191-6938-2 (paper).
Vol.4   *The Nature of Metaphysical Knowledge*
George F. McLean and Hugo Meynell, eds.
ISBN 0-8191-6926-9 (cloth); ISBN 0-8191-6927-7 (paper).

The series is published and distributed by: The Council for Research in Values and Philosophy, Cardinal Station, P.O. Box 261, Washington, D.C. 20064, Tel. 202/319-5636; Tel. message/Fax. 202/319-6089 and 800/659-9962; e-mail: cua-rvp@cua.edul; website: http://www.acad.cua.edu/phil/rvp.

Prices: -- Europe and North America: cloth $45.00; paper $17.50; plus shipping: surface, $3.00 first volume; $1.00 each additional; air, $7.20. -- Latin American and Afro-Asian editions: $4.00 per volume; plus shipping: sea, $1.75; air, Latin America $5.70; Afro-Asia: $9.00.